TV Transformations

The past decade has seen an explosion of lifestyle makeover TV shows. Audiences around the world are being urged to 'renovate' everything from their homes to their pets and children while lifestyle experts on TV now tell us what not to eat and what not to wear. Makeover television and makeover culture is now ubiquitous and yet, compared with reality TV shows like *Big Brother* and *Survivor*, there has been relatively little critical attention paid to this format. This exciting collection of essays written by leading media scholars from the UK, US and Australia aims to reveal the reasons for the huge popularity and influence of the makeover show. Written in a lively and accessible manner, the essays brought together here will help readers 'make sense' of makeover TV by offering a range of different approaches to understanding the emergence of this popular cultural phenomenon. Looking at a range of shows from *The Biggest Loser* to *Trinny and Susannah Undress*, essays include an analysis of how and why makeover TV shows have migrated so easily across such a range of TV cultures, the social significance of the rise of home renovation shows, the different ways in which British versus American audiences identify with makeover shows, and the growing role of lifestyle TV in the context of neo-liberalism in educating us to be 'good' citizens.

This book was published as a special issue of *Continuum: Journal of Media and Cultural Studies*.

Tania Lewis is a Senior Research Fellow in Sociology at La Trobe University. She is the author of *Smart Living: Lifestyle Media and Popular Expertise* (Peter Lang, New York: 2008). Her current research is on green lifestyles and ethical consumption, and lifestyle television in Asia.

TV Transformations

Revealing the Makeover Show

Edited by Tania Lewis

Routledge
Taylor & Francis Group
LONDON AND NEW YORK

First published 2009 by Routledge
2 Park Square, Milton Park, Abingdon, Oxfordshire OX14 4RN

Simultaneously published in the USA and Canada
by Routledge
711 Third Avenue, New York, NY 10017

First issued in paperback 2014

Routledge is an imprint of the Taylor & Francis Group, an informa business

© 2009 Edited by Tania Lewis

Typeset in Times by Value Chain, India

British Library Cataloguing in Publication Data
A catalogue record for this book is available from the British Library

ISBN 13: 978-1-138-87962-1 (pbk)
ISBN 13: 978-0-415-45148-2 (hbk)

CONTENTS

NOTES ON CONTRIBUTORS

Frances Bonner is a Reader in Television and Popular Culture and the author of *Ordinary Television: Analyzing Popular TV* (Sage, 2003) and, together with Graeme Turner and P. David Marshall, *Fame Games: The Production of Celebrity in Australia* (Cambridge UP, 2000). She is currently working on television presenters.

James Hay is Associate Professor in the Institute of Communications Research, and the Unit for Criticism and Interpretive Theory at the University of Illinois. He is co-author of *Better Living Through Reality TV: Television and Post-Welfare Citizenship* and co-editor (with Lawrence Grossberg and Ellen Wartella) of *The Audience and its Landscape*.

Alison Hearn teaches media theory and cultural studies in the Faculty of Information and Media Studies at the University of Western Ontario. She is co-author of *Outside the Lines: Issues in Interdisciplinary Research* and has published in such journals as *Topia*, the *International Journal of Media and Cultural Politics*, and *Bad Subjects*. She is currently completing a book entitled *Real Incorporated: Reality Television, Promotional Culture and the Will to Image*.

Dana Heller is Professor of English and Director of the Humanities Institute at Old Dominion University in Norfolk, Virginia. Recent publications include *The Great American Makeover: Television, History, Nation* and *Makeover Television: Realities Remodeled*. She is currently writing a book about John Water's Hairspray.

Meredith Jones teaches Media and Cultural Studies at the University of Technology, Sydney. She is the author of *Skintight: An Anatomy of Cosmetic Surgery* (Berg, 2008) and is currently working on a project about cosmetic surgery tourism.

Tania Lewis is a Senior Research Fellow in Sociology at La Trobe University. She is the author of *Smart Living: Lifestyle Media and Popular Expertise* (Peter Lang, New York: 2008). Her current research is on green lifestyles and ethical consumption, and lifestyle television in Asia.

Peter Lunt is Professor of Media and Communication at Brunel University, UK. His research interests include the mediation of public participation, media regulation and the media audience. He is the author of *Talk on Television*, with Sonia Livingstone and is currently writing a book about Stanley Milgram and working on a research project on changing forms of media regulation in the UK.

Toby Miller is the author and editor of over thirty books, and is the editor of the journals *Television & New Media* and *Social Identities*.

Albert Moran is professor in the School of Arts, Media and Culture at Griffith University. He has written or edited over 20 books, including *Copycat TV* (1998), *Television Across Asia* (2004) and *Historical Dictionary of Australian and New Zealand Cinema* (2005).

Laurie Ouellette is Associate Professor of Critical Media Studies in the Department of Communication at the University of Minnesota, Twin Cities. She is co-author of *Better Living Through Reality TV: Television and Post-Welfare Citizenship*, co-editor (with Susan Murray) of *Reality TV: Remaking Television Culture*, and author of *Viewers Like You? How Public TV Failed the People*.

Guy Redden teaches in the Department of Gender and Cultural Studies at the University of Sydney. His work focuses on the intersections between culture and economy, and he has published in the areas of alternative cultures, the Internet and consumer culture.

Buck Clifford Rosenberg has just completed his PhD in the Anthropology Program at the University of Melbourne. His thesis explored the relationship between home and lifestyle, examining concerns over home lifestyle television, DIY renovation and domestic décor. He has previously published on IKEA, the connection between home lifestyle and the risk society, and lifestyle and masculinity.

Katherine Sender is associate professor at the Annenberg School for Communication, University of Pennsylvania, and is completing the book on audiences of makeover television: *The Big Reveal: Makeover Television, Audiences, and the Promise of Transformation*.

Beverley Skeggs published *The Media* (1992, with John Mundy), *Feminist Cultural Theory* (1995), *Formations of Class and Gender* (1997), *Transformations: Thinking Through Feminism* (2000, with Sara Ahmed, Jane Kilby, Celia Lury and Maureen McNeil), *Class, Self, Culture* (2004), *Sexuality and the Politics of Violence and Safety* (2004, with Les Moran, Paul Tyrer and Karen Corteen) and *Feminism After Bourdieu* (2005, with Lisa Adkins). She is a series editor of the *Transformations: Thinking Through Feminism* book series (with Routledge). She is Professor of Sociology at Goldsmiths, University of London, previously at the University of Manchester, and before that Director of Women's Studies at the University of Lancaster. She has also taught at the Universities of Keele and York.

Margaret Sullivan received her MA in Communication from the University of Pennsylvania in 2007.

Helen Wood is Principal Lecturer in Media Studies at De Montfort University, Leicester, UK. She is author of *Talking With Television: Women, Talk Shows and Modern Self-reflexivity* (2008 in press, University of Illinois Press), and has recently co-edited working papers of the Birmingham Centre for Contemporary Cultural Studies for Routledge (2007). She has published a number of articles on television and reception in journals including *Media, Culture and Society*, the *European Journal of Cultural Studies*, *Cinema Journal* and *The Communication Review*.

INTRODUCTION

Revealing the Makeover Show

Tania Lewis

The makeover has become a ubiquitous cultural phenomenon. Once relegated to the realm of women's magazines and daytime television, over the past decade the makeover has taken up an increasingly prominent place within popular culture. As Dana Heller has observed (2007, 1–2), 'the popular idiom of reinvention' has found its way into every aspect of our social world, with calls to makeover everything from 'style-deficient infants' to the US government. The makeover television show – a mode of programming that only emerged on primetime television relatively recently with the advent of the UK's *Changing Rooms* (1996) and the US format *Extreme Makeover* (2002) – has played a pivotal role in putting the concept of the makeover to the fore of the public imagination. The past few years has seen an explosion of lifestyle makeover television shows with audiences around the world being urged to 'renovate' everything from their homes to their pets, a process that has seen the emergence of an army of lifestyle gurus on television advising us on what not to eat and what not to wear.

While blockbuster reality TV formats such as *Big Brother* and *Survivor* have to date gained the lion's share of critical academic attention (as well as popular press coverage), more recently a small but growing body of scholarship has started to focus on the 'lifestyle turn' on television and within contemporary culture more broadly (Bell and Hollows 2005; Bonner 2003; Brunsdon 2003; Lewis 2008; Miller 2007; Ouellette and Hay 2008). But why the growing academic interest in a television format whose main focus seems to be the not-so-pressing issues of shopping, home decoration and the dramatic transformation of one's personal appearance? Part of the reason lies in the fact that makeover television, concerned as it is with targeting, transforming and optimizing every aspect of ordinary people's identities and lifestyles, represents an especially rich site for understanding the shifting dynamics of selfhood and cultural value today. What models of personhood and interpersonal relations do we strive for and emulate? What sorts of lifestyles are considered desirable and what are seen as being in need of a major overhaul? And what relationship does makeover television construct between our personal lifestyle 'choices' and the well-being of the community, nation and even (in the case of, say, eco-makeover shows such as Australia's *Eco-house Challenge*) the globe? The domestic and personal concerns asked by makeover television – far from being trivial – go to the heart of a range of questions facing late modern societies.

The makeover format

In the context of makeover television, such issues are framed within the (now highly familiar) logic of the 'before and after' transformation. The classic personal makeover format, for instance, often starts with a surprise visit to the home or workplace of the unwitting participant, who has often been 'volunteered' for the role by concerned friends and family. The victim's 'deficiencies', whether in the area of health, taste and/or broader life management issues, are diagnosed by the show's resident lifestyle expert(s), with viewers (and at times the makeover recipient themselves) being shown fly-on-the-wall footage evidencing their various taste/lifestyle violations. The 'makeoveree' then undergoes a transformational new lifestyle regime under the guidance of the show's expert(s) before being shown their new self – a moment known as 'the reveal'. The visual conventions of the makeover format are thus centrally premised around the possibility of transformation and renewal.

While structured by certain distinctive narrative and aesthetic conventions, the makeover show – as an unscripted format which uses hidden cameras to capture the intimate lives of ordinary people – shares much in common with the genre of reality TV. The documentary elements of reality TV and other popular factual formats are combined in the makeover format with many of the features of melodrama, with both the transformational process and in particular 'the reveal' being highly emotional experiences for the participant, their friends and family and even the show's experts. As Lisa Taylor notes (2002, 489), while lifestyle makeover programmes (and reality formats) have to some extent displaced sit-coms and dramas from primetime television they have also borrowed the main ingredients of that programming – 'drama, conflict, emotion and stereotypes'. Where the makeover show departs both from the reality format and from drama, however, is in its focus on lifestyle advice and the provision of expertise. More than just a sub-genre of the reality oeuvre, then, makeover television has genealogical links to other forms of lifestyle advice programming on television such as daytime magazine shows, DIY and cooking shows as well as to popular advice culture more broadly.

From manners to makeovers

In my book *Smart Living: Lifestyle Media and Popular Expertise* (2008), I trace the roots of contemporary lifestyle advice and makeover television to early forms of modern advice culture, looking as far back as nineteenth-century Victorian England where the dramatic social upheavals that accompanied the industrial revolution saw the emergence of a plethora of taste, etiquette and domestic advice manuals. It might at first seem a little tenuous to link the concerns of contemporary makeover formats such as the UK's *What Not To Wear*, which targets women deemed in need of a fashion 'intervention', with the kind of domestic advice offered in say Mrs Beeton's *Book of Household Management*. Both, I would suggest, can be seen as examples of the way in which modern advice culture, since the nineteenth century, has sought to provide social, moral and personal guidelines for everyday living. From Victorian etiquette manuals to the emergence of men's lifestyle magazines in the 1980s, the rise of popular expertise has tended to be associated with times of relative uncertainty and social fluidity where people look to popular forms of advice for guidance and a sense of assurance. While the tenure of this advice has, of course, shifted over the past century and a half, it has been marked by certain persistent themes, with a particular focus on the management and presentation of the home and self as important sites of 'good' consumption, moral regulation and identity formation.

As I discuss in my essay in this collection on the history of makeover television, the contemporary reality-style makeover format departs in many ways from earlier modes of instructional and advice-based media. Nevertheless, I would suggest that much contemporary lifestyle and makeover programming continues to be centrally concerned with advising the audience in the art of everyday living; indeed, as Ouellette and Hay's essay in this collection demonstrates, today's makeover formats have, if anything, become more instructional and interventionist than previous forms of lifestyle media.

The lifestyle turn

If peaks in the ebb and flow of lifestyle advice media tend, as I have suggested here, to be linked to moments of social and cultural upheaval, what kinds of developments might we link to the emergence of the makeover show on primetime television? The success of reality and lifestyle makeover formats is often seen as a side-effect of broad economic shifts in television production (Holmes and Jermyn 2004). As relatively cheap programming that is readily franchised, the emergence of reality-lifestyle formats can be viewed as an effect of the increasing competition and deregulation of the television market. An economic analysis, however, is only one part of the story. The rise of makeover television can also be linked with a number of wider socio-cultural developments, in particular the 'lifestyling' of contemporary existence.

Today the term 'lifestyle' is used as a descriptor for everything from makeover television and magazines to New Age religious choices and sports drinks. Representing far more than just a convenient new way for the television industry to relabel popular advice programming, the concept of lifestyle has instead become one of the dominant frameworks through which we understand and organize contemporary everyday life. As David Bell and Joanne Hollows note in their book *Ordinary Lifestyles* (2005), while the term is used in a range of different contexts, from health to marketing, the notion of lifestyle is underpinned by a conception of identity that foregrounds personal choice and the malleable nature of the self. Rather than seeing selfhood as limited or constrained by one's class, race or gender, today ordinary people are held up as being able to invent (and reinvent) their own life 'biographies'. Lifestyle television, and in particular the makeover show, thus extends the DIY rubric to every aspect of one's life from home décor to selfhood.

As the chapters in this collection show, these flexible notions of 'post-traditional' selves and DIY lifestyles have become harnessed to a variety of different but often intersecting discourses within popular makeover culture, from the branding of selfhood to the growing links between personal lifestyle makeovers on television and privatized modes of good citizenship. Many of these discourses are clearly conservative and often normative – as evidenced by the 'economy of sameness' (Weber 2005) that can be seen to underpin plastic surgery makeover shows. At the same time, the emergence of popular, often feminine, concerns on primetime television around domesticity and care of the self and family can also be seen as an instance of a broader 'democratization' of television (Lewis 2008). At its most basic level this is reflected in the content of television becoming increasingly concerned with ordinary, everyday life, a shift that is marked by the sheer numbers of ordinary people who now feature on television (Bonner 2003). To some extent this process has also seen an expansion of what kinds of knowledge get valued on television and who gets to present these modes of ordinary expertise. Rachel Moseley, for instance, cites the emergence of softly masculine figures such as Jamie Oliver on primetime television as 'indicative of more general cultural shifts around gendered expertise' (Moseley 2000, 309). Also writing from a British perspective, Lisa Taylor notes that class distinctions, too, have seemingly become softened by the growing number of regional accents on UK television (figures such as Jamie Oliver again being a case in point) although, by and large, British lifestyle television and its values still tend to be resolutely middle class (2002).

Critical perspectives on the makeover show

Such debates point to the complexity of this popular phenomenon and the undesirability of attempting to 'read' the makeover show through a single critical lens. The makeover genre is highly diverse and global in its reach – from home renovation shows in Singapore to plastic surgery makeover shows in Brazil. Clearly, while such shows share some of the broad ideological characteristics and concerns discussed above, the potential meanings and significance of makeover formats are also shaped by everything from cultural context to issues of television scheduling and audience demographics.

The contributions in this collection attempt to begin the work of mapping this complex televisual genre, discussing a wide range of examples of makeover shows and drawing upon a variety of different analytic frameworks. The concern here is to understand makeover television both as a significant socio-cultural trend and as a media form, marked by distinct questions of production, textual aesthetics and reception.

Accordingly, the collection is structured as follows. Part I looks at the makeover format from the perspective of the television industry. My essay on the history of makeover television sets the primetime emergence of the genre in the context of wider economic and cultural shifts in the television industry. Discussing the influence of various pre-existing television genres, including lifestyle television and talk shows, on the development of the format, the essay compares and contrasts its development in the UK, US and Australia. Albert Moran's essay frames the burgeoning production of makeover television shows within a global economic and industry context. In particular, he locates the rise of the makeover programme within the broader development of television 'formats', standardized modes of programming that can be franchised globally and indigenized to suit local cultural concerns.

Moving on from an industry approach, the chapters in Part II – Frameworks – perform a twin task, both contextual and critical. On the one hand they each provide insights into the specific socio-cultural conditions out of which makeover television has emerged as a mainstream popular form over the past decade. At the same time they also provide theoretical tools for systematically analysing the social role of the makeover. Laurie Ouellette and James Hay, for instance, use Michel Foucault's theory of governmentality to address what they see as the changing relationship between television and social welfare. As government seeks to devolve responsibility for welfare to individuals, television, and in particular what they term 'life intervention' formats such as *Supernanny* and *Honey We're Killing the Kids*, can be seen to play an increasingly central role in inducting viewers into new neoliberal modes of self-governing citizenship. Following on from this essay, Guy Redden discusses Ulrich Beck and Anthony Giddens' theories of 'reflexive individualization', arguing that one way in which makeover television shapes viewers into self-governing consumer-citizens is through teaching audiences to adopt and value particular modes of reflexivity in their daily lives. Finally, Alison Hearn's essay locates makeover television within a broader political and economic context, arguing that the modes of reflexive selfhood promoted on makeover television can be understood as forms of branding. In the context of a post-Fordist shift away from traditional forms of labour and a growing sense of risk and insecurity in life and work, makeover television seeks to reassure people that they can 'add value' to themselves through reinvention and self-branding. The endless process of transformation played out on makeover shows, however, as Hearn argues, ironically can be seen to foreground rather than ameliorate the shifting and insecure nature of material existence.

Part III of the collection narrows its focus to a smaller scale analysis of specific types or sub-genres of makeover television, from home improvement to fitness shows. As the chapters in this section show, the makeover genre is a highly diverse one, embracing a range of concerns and marked by constant generic innovation. Opening the section, Buck Rosenberg discusses the home renovation show, a format that has led the way in the development of makeover television on primetime television. His essay touches on a range of concerns raised by lifestyle television's focus on the home, from issues of taste and distinction, and 'thrifty' approaches to consumption, to the impact of the 'risk society'.

The next two contributions focus on personal makeover shows oriented towards transforming the face and body. In Meredith Jones' essay she grapples with one of the more dramatic examples of the genre – cosmetic surgery makeover shows – drawing links between the concerns of these programmes and that of cinema, in particular horror films, with their focus on rebirth and the permeability of the skin–screen boundary. She argues, however, that despite the emphasis on radical transformation in surgical makeover shows, these programmes tend to be limited by rigid dualistic conceptions of gender and aesthetic beauty. Discussing recent developments in health and fitness programming, Dana Heller examines the Bravo series *Work Out*, a reality series based on the life of LA fitness trainer Jackie Warner. Her essay focuses in particular on the show's complex negotiation of Warner's lesbianism, her role as a fitness expert, and the show's messages about disciplining bodies, sexualities, and desires.

Moving from physical to behavioural makeovers, Peter Lunt analyses the rise of educational lifestyle shows such as *Little Angels* which aim to makeover poor parenting skills, setting his discussion of the show in the context of the growing role of 'therapy culture' in shaping popular and governmental conceptions of selfhood and citizenship. The final piece in this section, by Australian television scholar Frances Bonner, looks at one of the more recent developments in makeover programming, analysing two British and two Australian shows that offer couples two makeovers for the price of one. Like Lunt's parenting shows, the emphasis here is on renovating interpersonal relationships – with the added bonus of also making over one other aspect of the lives of the couples who appear on the show, whether it be their personal style, home décor, garden or finances.

Of central importance to the social role and meaning of makeover television are the ways in which audiences engage with these modes of programming in their everyday lives. Part IV, the final section, offers two different perspectives on audience reception of lifestyle makeover shows drawn from empirical audience studies conducted in the UK and in the US. British scholars Beverley Skeggs and Helen Wood frame the findings of their research on reality TV audiences with a discussion of the way in which the genre can be seen to deploy intimate domestic space, and its associated 'affective' relations, as a site for the rehearsal of governmental and moral concerns. Based on ethnographic research in the homes of British women from a range of class and racial backgrounds, however, they show how female, and in particular working-class, viewers do not necessarily capitulate to the normative codes of social morality enacted on makeover and reality TV but instead display a complex emotional engagement with and valuing of the forms of affective labour and moral personhood depicted in these shows. Drawing upon 1800 surveys and 140 personal interviews, Katherine Sender and Margaret Sullivan's essay discusses the ways in which US audiences responded to the depiction and treatment of obese people on two makeover shows, *The Biggest Loser* and *What Not to Wear*. Concerned with assessing claims that makeover television promotes and normalizes a governmental discourse of self-surveillance and regulation, their findings indicate that audience members were critical of a range of aspects of these shows, including their at times humiliating representations of fat people as well as the perceived limitations of the expert advice provided on the shows. At the same time, viewers tended to accept the central premise of these shows, viewing obesity and its management primarily as an issue of personal self-esteem and willpower rather than as a social structural concern – reflecting once again makeover television's privatized, therapeutic ethos and its insistence on the self as the pre-eminent site of social and moral transformation.

* * *

The generosity and support of a number of people helped this collection of essays come to fruition. Thanks to the team at *Continuum* and in particular Mark Gibson for suggesting the special issue to book route for this collection and for his support along the way. I am also grateful to the journal's reviewers who generously provided extensive critical feedback on the essays and to Joanna Kujawa for editorial support. Thanks also are due to Katherine Burton for supporting the publication of the collection under Taylor & Francis' special issue to book scheme and to Stephen Thompson for providing editorial assistance with the production of the book. Finally, I want to acknowledge the intellectual labour and commitment of the authors whose wonderful contributions have made this collection possible.

References

Bell, D., and J. Hollows, eds. 2005. *Ordinary lifestyles: Popular media, consumption and taste.* Maidenhead: Open University Press.
Bonner, F. 2003. *Ordinary television: Analyzing popular TV.* London: Sage.
Brunsdon, C. 2003. Lifestyling Britain: The 8–9 slot on British television. *International Journal of Cultural Studies* 6, no. 1: 5–23.
Heller, D. A., ed. 2007. *Makeover television: Realities remodelled.* London: I.B. Tauris.
Holmes, S., and D. Jermyn. 2004. *Understanding reality television.* London and New York: Routledge.
Lewis, T. 2008. *Smart living: Lifestyle media and popular expertise.* New York: Peter Lang.
Miller, T. 2007. *Cultural citizenship: Cosmopolitanism, consumerism and television in a neoliberal age.* Philadelphia: Temple University Press.
Moseley, R. 2000. Makeover takeover on British television. *Screen* 41, no. 3: 299–314.
Ouellette, L., and J. Hay. 2008. *Better living through television.* Oxford: Blackwell.
Taylor, L. 2002. From ways of life to lifestyle: The 'ordinari-ization' of British gardening lifestyle television. *European Journal of Communication* 17, no. 4: 479–93.
Weber, B. 2005. Beauty, desire, and anxiety: The economy of sameness in ABC's extreme makeover. *Genders* 41, http://www.genders.org/g41/g41_weber.html (accessed 21 January 2008).

Changing rooms, biggest losers and backyard blitzes: A history of makeover television in the United Kingdom, United States and Australia

Tania Lewis

Lifestyle programming – from daytime magazine formats to cooking, gardening and 'DIY' shows – has been a long-running feature of many television schedules around the world. More recently these more traditional forms of lifestyle television have been boosted by a growing number of 'lifestyle makeover' formats. The makeover represents a complex blend of television genres – combining conventions and concerns borrowed from lifestyle advice television and reality TV with a transformational 'before and after' narrative. Focusing primarily on ordinary people (although occasionally dealing with wayward celebrities), everything from homes (*House Invaders*) and pets (*It's Me or the Dog*) to parental skills (*Supernanny*) and bodies (*How to Look Good Naked*) are put under the spotlight and transformed – with the guidance of various life experts – under the gaze of the watching public.

This essay traces the development of this broad-ranging mode of programming. Locating the emergence of makeover television within the broader context of the rise of format television around the world, the essay notes the links between the lifestyle makeover show and the development of reality TV and other popular factual genres. It argues, however, that while the makeover show shares much in common with a broader turn on television towards 'real life' concerns, it is more than just a sub-genre of reality programming. In particular it emphasizes the genealogical links between the makeover show and the broader 'genre' of lifestyle advice programming on television, noting the way in which the contemporary makeover show merges the instructional concerns of lifestyle television with conventions and approaches drawn from various other genres, including talk shows and soap operas.

In tracing the generic development of the makeover format the essay frames its discussion in both transnational and national terms. Firstly, it places the rise of makeover television within the context of a broader international turn to 'the real' on television schedules before then discussing the rise of format television. It then goes on to examine the specific national contexts out of which the makeover format has emerged, focusing on its appearance first in the UK and then the US, followed by a brief discussion of Australia's engagement with the format. In a televisual era marked by the rise of globally successful formats such as *Big Brother*, *Extreme Makeover* and *Supernanny* it is increasingly difficult to talk about television cultures in purely national terms. However, the essay argues that, while the makeover format has become an international phenomenon and can be found on primetime television everywhere from Melbourne to Madrid, the historical development of the form as well as its contemporary reception has been and continues to be shaped by national cultural and televisual traditions.

From 'true life' to reality: Recent shifts in the televisual landscape

Television in the late twentieth and early twenty-first century has become increasingly enmeshed in everyday concerns and social processes. The recent rise of lifestyle makeover shows on primetime television, for instance, can be read as one symptom of a broader set of shifts in televisual culture towards a growing focus on 'the real'. As Frances Bonner points out (2003, 28), since the 1980s television has been increasingly concerned with the mundane and 'the ordinary', as reflected in its growing focus on domestic space and the lives of members of the public. Likewise, writing in the 1990s about the growing role of 'true-life-story' genres in the US, the UK and Europe, Ib Bondebjerg (1996) argues that this has occurred as part of a broader embrace of privatized modes of discourse, with the camera increasingly turning to focus on the intimacies of people's lives and relationships. The recent history of television can thus be summed up as being distinguished by a preoccupation with the 'everyday terms of living' (Corner 2004, 291).

The reasons for this turn towards the ordinary are complex and multifaceted. Reflecting not only broader socio-cultural shifts, such as the growing intrusion of public and government concerns into the private lives of citizens, it also marks economic developments within the industry itself. In particular, the shift since the 1980s towards modes of relatively cheap, 'unscripted' television focused on ordinary people can be seen as an attempt to deal with an increasingly deregulated market and a fragmented audience, with free-to-air networks now competing with pay television for viewers' attention, offering audiences an abundance of programming choices (Bonner 2003; Ellis 2000). Concomitant with these economic transitions there have been a range of shifts in the policy underpinnings and 'culture' of the industry around the world. While the nature of these developments has varied considerably in different national contexts, in general the television industry globally has been marked by a shift towards the adoption of more populist modes of address, a shift that for some reflects the 'democratization of an old public service discourse' (Bondebjerg 1996, 29) while for others suggests a growing and problematic convergence between public service and commercial concerns.

The transition over the past two to three decades to a more 'democratized' approach has been accompanied by some interesting innovations in the realm of genre. Just as news around the world has been marked by the growing prominence of 'tabloid journalism' (Hill 2005, 15) and 'info-tainment' values (Thussu 2007), the realm of entertainment television has increasingly embraced forms of 'dramatized factual television' (Bondebjerg 1996, 27), including the emergence of 'docu-soaps' such as the UK's *Airport*. In broad terms, then, there has been a growing hybridization of television genres, incorporating the fictional and the melodramatic into documentary and factual forms, and culminating in the more recent rise of purportedly 'new' formats such as 'reality TV'. While I am arguing here that makeover television has a distinct cultural genealogy, tied to developments in advice media and lifestyle culture more broadly, as a television format it shares much in common with these other popular factual genres and in particular reality TV.[1]

Rather than representing completely new genres, both reality formats such as *Big Brother* and personal makeover shows such as *Queer Eye for the Straight Guy* can be seen to borrow from a range of older televisual genres that feature ordinary people and their everyday concerns. The UK, for instance, has a strong tradition of fly-on-the-wall social observational television featuring members of the public, while on US television soaps, talk shows and to some extent quiz shows focus on everyday life concerns and ordinary people. Reality and makeover formats can be seen to borrow extensively from these pre-existing forms of programming, blending together, for instance, the competitive game show element of quiz shows with the voyeurism, melodrama and confessional dimensions of talk shows and soaps. Today's reality shows, however, bring together these older generic elements in ways that speak to distinctly contemporary concerns. As Helen Wood and Beverley Skeggs note (2004, 205), contemporary lifestyle and reality shows are distinguished by a shared focus on 'interrogations of selfhood under the pressures of particular conditions'. The reality formats that have come to dominate the last decade, then, are those that rely on increasingly contrived scenarios, from bringing together diverse people to live together in an artificial community under hothouse conditions, to encouraging people to undertake major personal lifestyle transformations under the intrusive gaze of the television camera.

The rise of format television

As noted, the reality turn on television – while linked to a range of socio-cultural issues – has also been driven partly by economic concerns. In particular, one of the reasons cited for the global success of reality and makeover television has been its ability to travel as a 'format' into a range of different television markets, as Albert Moran discusses in detail in his essay in this collection. The deregulation of the television industry around the world in the 1980s and 1990s and the emergence of a multi-channel environment has produced a situation where the pressure for product has encouraged local producers to create programmes that can potentially move across a range of markets (Moran 1998; Waisbord 2004). This situation has seen a relative challenge to US hegemony in global television traffic and trade as television formats increasingly emerge from the UK and Western Europe as well as from smaller players such as Australia and Mexico (Magder 2004; Moran and Keane 2006; Waisbord 2004).

As Waisbord comments (2004, 359), the rise and rise of format television has resulted in a situation whereby '[a]round the world, television is filled with national variations of programs designed by companies from numerous countries'. For instance, Endemol, a company that originated and continues to be based in Holland, first created the global reality TV phenomenon *Big Brother* for the Dutch market, going on to sell the format to numerous countries. Reality-lifestyle programmes offered up as format 'shells' such as the highly popular garden makeover show *Ground Force*, first aired in the UK, have been shown to have considerable transnational mobility and selling power, as they are amenable to being readily 'indigenized', even in the case of programmes emerging from non-English markets (such as the Dutch market), and are relatively risk free, having been previous tried out on an audience (Waisbord 2004).

At the same time, television formats represent sites marked by complex negotiations between globalizing forces and domestic concerns and contexts (Moran 1998). Makeover television programmes – whether sold as format shells to be localized for a domestic market or shown in their original form – do not necessarily succeed in all television markets. In part this is due to the fact that even as apparently culturally neutral format shells, television formats are shaped by and speak to certain types of cultural values and concerns. In the case of lifestyle television this is especially so. As Bonner argues (2005), the content of lifestyle television has traditionally been inward looking, reflecting everyday concerns and national beliefs and values. The makeover show on the one hand can thus be seen as a product of an increasingly globalized, format-driven television industry, drawing upon a range of transnational generic, cultural and industry influences. At the same time, the development of the lifestyle makeover format has very much reflected its ties to the 'national ordinary' while also being shaped by different nationally inflected industry histories and modes of reception or 'television makeover cultures', as Mischa Kavka (2006) has termed them. In this next section, then, I want to discuss the development of the makeover format in relation to some of these different 'makeover cultures', focusing in particular on the rise of lifestyle and makeover television in the UK and US as well as in Australia.

The 'makeover takeover' on British television

While the makeover format is often popularly associated with US television culture, industry commentators and numerous television scholars point to the UK in the 1990s as a defining moment in the emergence of the format as a major primetime player. In a frequently quoted article in the film magazine *Sight and Sound*, Andy Medhurst (1999, 103) at the end of the 1990s pronounced the decade in the UK as 'the era of lifestyle TV' while Rachel Moseley (2000) describes British television as undergoing a 'makeover takeover'.

British scholars have offered a number of reasons for the rise and popularity of the makeover format in Britain. Moseley suggests, for instance, that it marked an important shift in the gendering of the mode of address of television. Arguing that the format is 'the most visible marker' of a broader mainstreaming of feminine makeover culture, she contends that the broad-based popularity of makeover television reflects the fact that men are now engaging with a range of once feminine-coded activities associated with 'the personal, the private, the everyday' (in Brunsdon et al. 2001, 32).

While previously found primarily on daytime television where it often featured as segments on magazine shows aimed at women, the 1990s saw the makeover expand into a full-length format and move into primetime schedules. However, where daytime television makeovers often focused on issues of personal style and fashion, the first successful makeover formats were shows oriented towards investing in and improving the home rather than the self. One of the first breakthrough makeover shows on primetime UK television was the home renovation game show format *Changing Rooms* (broadcast on the BBC in 1996 and later sold into a number of international markets).[2] While this format seems at somewhat of a remove from daytime television's feminine style makeover, Moseley's argument positions it as a kind of cross-over format addressing both female and male viewers by blending 'soft' feminine interior design with the 'harder' focus associated with DIY programmes as well as with a fast-paced MTV aesthetic.

While acknowledging the importance of a gender-based analysis, Gareth Palmer (2004) has argued that the rise of lifestyle programming in the UK speaks centrally to shifts in British class culture and in particular the recent growth of an aspirational, petit bourgeoisie. Palmer reads the tips provided by the new echelon of experts that emerged on both home shows and fashion makeover formats like *What Not to Wear* (BBC 2001) as offering strongly class-inflected modes of guidance around questions of style, taste and social distinction – a focus that has remained a prominent feature of makeover programming in the UK. While many of the ordinary people featured on lifestyle television since the 1990s have been working class – reflecting in part a democratization of British television's mode of address – the rise of makeover television can also be seen as acting to police and regulate the working classes while naturalizing middle-class taste, lifestyles and values as normative. More recently, such developments can in turn be seen to dovetail more broadly with the development in the UK and elsewhere of a neoliberal surveillance culture in which personal development and the management of the self have become new sites of governmental regulation (Andrejevic 2004; Ouellette and Hay 2008; Palmer 2003).

A range of shifts in industry policy arising from an increasingly competitive, deregulated British television market also provided another important context for the 'primetiming' of the makeover format in the 1990s. The BBC, in particular, was under pressure to expand its public service broadcasting model to embrace a broader, more democratized approach to its audience (Hill 2005). Alongside growing pressures from government and the market, accusations of elitism and anti-competitive practices from other free-to-air channels saw the BBC starting to rethink its charter 'to inform, educate and entertain' along more populist lines.

In the mid-1990s a BBC strategy report emphasized the role of factual entertainment formats in responding to audience needs, and in enabling the broadcaster to 'find inventive ways to cover the leisure pursuits of our audiences' (Moseley 2003, 104), extending upon the more traditional modes of factual programming that had always been central to the BBC 'brand'. In response, the BBC introduced shows such as *Can't Cook, Won't Cook*, *Style Challenge* and *Real Rooms*, the latter two expanding upon segments that had featured in daytime magazine programming.[3] Extending its bid for ratings and a broader audience, home and garden makeover shows such as *Ground Force* and the breakthrough show *Changing Rooms* subsequently started to appear in the primetime schedules of BBC2 and then BBC1, where along with other factual entertainment formats they came to dominate the schedule (Moseley 2003, 105).

While the primetime programme-length makeover format drew directly from existing makeover segments on women's daytime magazine shows, it also could be seen as emerging out of what was a long tradition on British television of modes of leisure and advice programming aimed at both men and women. Tim O'Sullivan (2005) notes, for instance, that as far back as 1946 the BBC was broadcasting (rather blandly titled) shows such as *Television Garden* and *Cookery*, which featured male presenters and experts, while the 1950s and 1960s saw the emergence of a range of DIY and domestic advice programmes on British television from gardening to cooking and carpentry. In her essay on the 'lifestyling' of the British 8–9 p.m. slot, Charlotte Brunsdon (2003, 9) also foregrounds this long history of what she terms 'hobby or enthusiast' programming in Britain, a mode of programming aimed particularly at mothers, retirees and 'the hobbyist'.

While Brunsdon (2003, 9) sees these shows as important precursors to contemporary lifestyle television, she argues that the contemporary 'engagement with consumerism, makeovers and game shows' has seen a dramatic transformation in the form, aesthetics and mode of address of British lifestyle programming, particularly in relation to the way in which it advises its audience. Thus, while the hobbyist format was centrally concerned with instruction and with teaching the audiences 'how to' skills, the contemporary lifestyle show is distinguished by its focus on the spectacle of transformation itself. As she puts it:

> The hobby genre [. . .] addressed the amateur enthusiast. By the end of the programme, the listener would know how to do something. The new makeover programmes are different in that they offer a different balance between instruction and spectacle, which is articulated most clearly through a changing grammar of the closeup, and they most commonly address their audience as customer or consumer. (15)

As in the soap opera genre, the close-ups featured on the new makeover formats are largely of the faces of the ordinary people on the show and their emotional responses; thus, many of the pleasures offered to the audience by these new formats are those associated with melodrama (Brunsdon 2003; Moseley 2000). Such a shift again speaks to Moseley's argument that the mainstreaming of the makeover has occurred, both in the UK and elsewhere, partly in concert with a broader cultural revaluing of once feminine concerns around the private and domestic and with a growing focus on 'real life' emotions and relationships on television and in the public sphere more broadly.

As noted in the discussion of reality TV, another generic influence on the development of the makeover format is social observational television. While drawing upon a range of international influences, the genre has been particularly popular in the UK, with the BBC again playing a pivotal role in the development of fly-on-the-wall observational formats. From Paul Watson's *The Family* (BBC, 1974), which followed the daily lives and struggles of a working-class British family to Roger Graef's *Police* (BBC, 1982), these early shows displayed the public educational concerns of documentary – those of representing social diversity and difference and documenting pressing social issues. These programmes can be seen as precursors of the development of a range of popular 'docu-soaps' on UK television, from *The Driving School* to *Airport*, which, like lifestyle programming, dominated primetime scheduling in the UK in the mid- to late 1990s (Hill 2005, 29). While docu-soaps and lifestyle television in the 1990s seemed at a far remove from the original social concerns of observational television, Moseley (in Brunsdon et al. 2001) and Taylor (2002), for instance, have argued in relation to the makeover format that, in depicting ordinary people and experts from a range of social backgrounds, the format offered a relatively democratized mode of address – representing an attempt at the time to negotiate an educational public service agenda in a context of growing commercial populism.

More recently the reality makeover show in Britain (and, as Ouellette and Hay note in this collection, to a certain extent in the US) has been marked by something of a return to the educational and social concerns of the social observational form. For instance, the past couple of years have seen a variety of shows emerge out of the UK around the intersection of health, lifestyle and parenting issues, with *Supernanny* being one of the more successful and well-known of these British formats. Shows such as *Honey We're Killing the Kids*, which offers parents and in particular their children a complete lifestyle makeover, combines social observational elements and melodramatic spectacle with a strongly didactic approach to issues of diet, health and family relations. While such shows draw strongly on social documentary traditions, the educational approach here is far from sociological, tending instead to focus on the emotional dimensions of people's lives and to reduce social issues to questions of individual lifestyle choice. As Ouellette and Hay argue, this is television aimed at training a neoliberal citizenry to manage their own social welfare – with the DIY premise of early lifestyle shows here turned upon the self and the family and marked by a strong focus on self-surveillance and regulation.

US television and the personal makeover show

The emergence of the makeover format on British primetime television clearly occurred in response to a distinct combination of social, cultural and industry shifts while building upon a pre-existing tradition of leisure-oriented advice programming and social observational television. At the same time, the generic makeup of the format also owed much to the influence of other nationally inflected television traditions, particular the melodrama and spectacle of US soap operas and talk shows, and the more recent turn to reality TV formats.

Despite these shared generic traditions and the leading role played by the US in producing and promoting reality-based programming, US free-to-air networks were relatively slow to embrace the lifestyle makeover show as a primetime format. While *Changing Rooms* saw makeover television break into primetime schedules in 1996 in the UK, the breakthrough show on US network television – the surgical makeover programme *Extreme Makeover* shown on the ABC – didn't make its appearance until 2002 (Kavka 2006). Instead, US primetime television in the 1990s was preoccupied with a range of other early reality-style formats from low-budget, actuality-based television of the *COPS* variety to shows such as MTV's *The Real World* (1992), a clear precursor to the *Big Brother* format.

Any discussion of the role of lifestyle and makeover formats on American television, however, must also take the cable industry into account. Over the past couple of decades, an increasingly deregulated media environment has seen cable playing an increasingly significant role in the US market. As Toby Miller (2007) has noted, alongside the relatively diminished power of the networks, there has been a shift in the US away from traditional public service modes of factual and informational formats to a growing focus on lifestyle and consumption. Cable has been central to this process. Unlike the UK, US television has not had the same long-term tradition of lifestyle and DIY shows. The exception to this rule is the long-running popularity of PBS's home improvement show *This Old House* (first aired in 1979 and still showing today) and of figures such as celebrity cook Julia Child (Kavka 2006, 213), who starred in various series in the 1970s, 1980s and through into the 1990s, with PBS, like the BBC, being seen to bring DIY and hobbyist programming under a public service remit.[4]

Since the early 1990s, though, cable channels such as HGTV and The Learning Channel (TLC) have played an important role in popularizing lifestyle formats in the US (Everett 2004). HGTV, for instance, offers an extensive range of lifestyle and hobbyist programming themed around 'Gardening, Remodeling, Crafts, Decorating and At Home' shows, and has also created a spin-off Do It Yourself Network. TLC, meanwhile, repackaged itself in the 1990s from a primarily instructional/educational channel to a more lifestyle and consumer-oriented channel featuring shows on home improvement and arts and craft. The big success story for US cable television, however, has been the home makeover format. Two years before network television showed *Extreme Makeover*, TLC achieved high ratings (rivalling the free-to-air networks) with the first US home makeover show *Trading Spaces*, a US adaptation of the BBC's *Changing Rooms*.[5]

Despite the popularity of *Trading Spaces* and other DIY and hobbyist shows on cable television, arguably what has broadly distinguished US makeover culture and its mode of lifestyle advice from its British counterpart has been its preoccupation with personal, particularly body, makeover shows. While there has been considerable transatlantic traffic of both programme formats, ideas and personnel over the past decade,[6] Kavka (2006, 220) argues that the US focus on personal makeover programmes emerges out of and speaks to a distinct cultural context, marked by an 'unwavering belief in positive transformation'. Thus, whereas UK makeover shows often tend to be domestic in focus, playing out class- and taste-based concerns, she contends that US shows are underpinned by fantasies of individual perfectibility (Kavka 2006, 226). Melissa Crawley (2006) likewise emphasizes the centrality of surgical transformation shows to the US makeover oeuvre, noting how such shows tap into American beliefs around the power of rebirth.

While today makeover television in the US and UK shares much in common, often airing local versions of the same formats, such shows speak to very different audiences and are framed by distinctive televisual and cultural traditions. The centrality of the self-help movement to US culture is one important and distinctive cultural frame here. Biressi and Nunn (2005) argue that the rise of lifestyle television can be linked to the growing sway of a self-help-oriented 'therapeutic culture' in which broader social issues such as obesity are reduced to questions of personal transformation and self-improvement. While this self-improvement ethos has made its influence felt around the world, Dana Heller (2006) notes that such beliefs are deeply rooted in the American psyche and can be linked back to a long-term preoccupation, from the nineteenth century onwards, with the possibilities of self-transformation. Tied to a distinctly American mode of individual entrepreneurialism, the logic of the personal makeover dovetails with an 'American mythos' of upward mobility (Bratich 2007, 10), exemplified by the classic rags-to-riches scenario that recurs in Hollywood cinematic and televisual narratives.

In many ways the genealogy of US makeover television can be seen to reflect this broader cultural mythology. While British makeover formats on television emerged out of the context of a long history of DIY, cookery, fashion and hobbyist programming, contemporary US lifestyle and makeover shows can be seen to draw upon genres of programming that feature personal transformations as a central trope – types of programming often more associated with feminine-coded forms of 'trash' television than the kind of public service concerns associated, for instance, with the BBC's focus on leisure-oriented programming.

In the 1950s, for example, US daytime shows such as *Glamour Girl* – where a 'deserving' woman was chosen to be transformed over 24 hours – can be seen as clear precursors of the contemporary US makeover show (Watts 2006). *Queen for a Day* was another popular 1950s daytime show that pre-empted many of the tropes apparent in the contemporary personal makeover format. A range of ordinary women with hard-luck stories appeared on the show competing for the audience's sympathy as well as for various consumer goods that would be given to the most worthy recipient, who would be crowned (as the show advertised) as deserving 'queen' for a day. Thus the show combined 'pathos and rampant consumerism' (Watts 2006, 143) with moments of personal confession and magical transformation, as well as with the competitive edge so central to US entrepreneurialism.

Another important genre centrally concerned with self-improvement is the talk show – a televisual space where, as in lifestyle television, we see the role of lifestyle advisors and experts come to the fore and where 'ordinary' people are encouraged to confess their (often socially aberrant) lifestyles and behaviours to the public. In the 1990s, around the time when lifestyle television was starting to take off on cable, the makeover trope reappeared on women's daytime television in the US in the form of makeover segments on talk shows directed by various guest experts. While often oriented towards fashion and 'transformative glamour', Jack Bratich (2007, 7) notes that the early 1990s also saw a spate of 'makeover-themed daytime talk shows' in which, for instance, 'deviant teens' were transformed on 'boot camp'-style episodes. The US talk show thus worked to pave the way for the reality-lifestyle show, bringing together the makeover transformation – usually directed at people marked out as deviant – with the personal confession, and with a particular focus on self-surveillance in the name of community 'values'. The 1990s also saw the emergence of actuality footage-based crime, medical and accident shows on primetime television in the US, modes of programming which evolved over the 1990s into scripted reality formats often marked by competitive individualistic themes (Crawley 2006), the exemplar here being *Survivor*.

Today, elements of all these modes of programming can be seen to come together to varying degrees in the US personal makeover format. Shows such as *Queer Eye for the Straight Guy*, for instance, combine reality TV and lifestyle advice (in this case delivered by five gay men) with the consumer-driven transformations of women's daytime television shows in the 1950s and the talk show's morally charged focus on personal confession. While body makeover shows such as *The Biggest Loser* bring the 'warts and all' reality-lifestyle format together with a more competitive, boot camp approach in order both to transform and reform 'aberrant' overweight citizens into slimmer, go-getting versions of their former selves – speaking again to the centrality of entrepreneurialism, personal promotion and 'self-branding' to US makeover culture (see Alison Hearn's essay in this collection).

Australianizing the makeover

While most of the scholarship on makeover television has focused on the US and UK, another television market that has embraced the makeover format is Australia. While the British were the first to air a full-length makeover show on primetime television, Bonner's (2000, 2005) work has shown that the Australian television industry has had a long-running interest in lifestyle and info-tainment formats and has been somewhat of a pioneer in the area. Over the past couple of decades Australian primetime television has been populated by a variety of lifestyle programmes. Far from being niche programming, magazine formats such as the long-running show *Better Homes and Gardens* (produced alongside a magazine of the same name) has had a sizeable primetime audience of both male and female viewers. The lifestyle programming 'boom' took place in the 1990s in Australia, with the first low-budget lifestyle shows developed on the public service broadcaster (ABC), and subsequently picked up by the commercial channels Seven, Nine and Ten (Bonner 2000).[7] A range of innovative lifestyle formats appeared on primetime television in the 1990s, including shows such as *Sex* and *Money* which aimed to vamp up the magazine format to target a younger audience. In general, though, Australians showed a particular predilection for home and garden shows, a love affair which was given full rein with the rise of the makeover format, which took off from 2000 onwards.

As in America, the UK's *Changing Rooms* was also an important influence on the Australian industry, with the Nine Network making an Australian version which premiered in 1998. However, as Bonner (2005) points out, prior to the 1990s, Australian house and garden shows would often feature a segment where property was transformed. For instance, the popular Australian garden makeover show *Backyard Blitz* (2000) originally started out as a small segment on the pioneering Australian lifestyle show *Burke's Backyard* (1987),[8] but due to popular response was turned into a standalone 30-minute weekly show.

While Australia had a strong pre-existing tradition of lifestyle television, and in particular home renovation shows, like the US and the UK, the development of the makeover format on Australian television has been shaped by a complex exchange of international formats and ideas. Australia has aired a range of international makeover shows on primetime television (including the US version of *Queer Eye for the Straight Guy* and the US and British versions of *Supernanny*), and on pay television channels, such as the Lifestyle Channel, which features primarily imported (mainly British) lifestyle and makeover shows. The free-to-air networks have also produced Australian versions of a range of imported formats, such as the UK's *Ground Force* and the American show *The Biggest Loser*, with the Australian version of the latter format now running to a third season. At the same time, the industry has also produced its own highly successful makeover formats. For example, *The Block* (2003), in which four couples each competed to renovate a flat in the iconic beachside suburb of Bondi, was hugely popular in Australia, with the format rights also being sold to a variety of countries including Scandinavia, the UK and the US, and the Australian edition being screened around the world.

Despite this international exchange, Australia's take on the makeover has again been shaped by distinctive cultural concerns and television traditions.[9] For example, while Australian audiences have recently embraced personal makeover shows such as *The Biggest Loser*, they tend to be less comfortable with the often highly aggressive competitive individualism that is frequently central to US game show-style makeover formats. Historically, Australia has also had much less of a confessional culture than the US, although the increasing popularity of reality TV and personal makeover shows in Australia suggests a growing acceptance on the part of both audiences and the contestants on these shows of personal revelation and 'therapy speak' on television. While sharing the British obsession with home makeover shows, Australian lifestyle television has also tended to be less concerned with class issues than its UK counterparts. As Australian television executive Peter Abbott has noted in relation to translating British lifestyle formats for Australian audiences:

> a lot of the drama of UK TV is underpinned by class struggle or, for me, a disconnect between the viewer and the people on the show. There's a lot more – 'these are people you can laugh at because they're not like us'. There's a certain meanness in that to me. [...] That's why a lot of this programming doesn't translate. (Abbott 2006)

In contrast, Australian makeovers tend to be concerned less with humiliation and class conflict and more with constructing a familiar, neighbourly mode of address. Reflecting these concerns, the emphasis on the Australian version of *The Biggest Loser*, for instance, is less on US-style entrepreneurial individualism than on losing weight for one's family and the community. Likewise, the hosts and experts who feature on Australian lifestyle shows also tend to be positioned as resolutely average, often speaking with broad Australian accents. This is not to say that there are no issues of social distinction or competitive individualism at work in Australian makeover formats – aspirationalism is a key mantra in Australian lifestyle culture. The discourse of 'getting ahead', however, tends to be framed in terms of aspiring to a kind of averageness, a preoccupation which speaks to a broader cultural mythos of 'mateship' and social egalitarianism.

Conclusion: Global formats, local lifestyles

In his book *Big Brother* (2005, 40), Jonathan Bignell asks whether the transnational mobility of reality and makeover TV indicates the universalization of a Western preoccupation with 'personal confession, modification, testing and the perfectibility of the self'. Certainly the widespread uptake of these formats around the world – from Chinese-Singaporean makeover shows like *Home Décor Survivor* to the Panamanian version of *Extreme Makeover* (*Cambio Radical*) – can be seen to point to the global currency of certain types of consumerist and (neo)liberal models of selfhood and citizenship. At the same time, while the embrace of makeover culture and associated modes of lifestyle consumption might be a globalized one, as Bonner (2000, 116) has pointed out, what distinguishes lifestyle makeover television as a mode of programming is its strong connection to the local and its relative reliance on issues such as '[t]he value of local presenters and the national meanings of particular consumption patterns'.

More recently the situation has become a little less cut and dried as many foreign reality-lifestyle programmes, which feature ordinary people in their homes (such as *Queer Eye for the Straight Guy* and *Supernanny*), find themselves gaining high ratings with international audiences.[10] The increasing mobility of makeover experts and programmes across national borders suggests that lifestyle audiences are increasingly able to negotiate, and may in some cases be actively seeking out shows featuring foreign versions of ordinary everyday life. At the same time, however, there are often considerable differences between the ways in which audiences read and respond to these shows in different cultural contexts.[11] As my discussion of the development of makeover and lifestyle television in the US, UK and Australia argues – despite extensive transnational cultural and industrial flows and exchanges – at each of these sites the emergence and development of makeover television has been strongly shaped by unique cultural and televisual traditions of production and reception. British lifestyle television audiences have, for instance, been particularly partial to home renovation shows as well as 'educational' formats that draw on social observational traditions – with both styles of show in the British context often focusing on issues of class and taste. While a range of makeover formats are popular with Australian audiences, they tend to be less focused on confrontation and humiliation than their US and UK counterparts, borrowing more from the softer, neighbourly approach offered up in popular magazine formats such as *Better Homes and Gardens*. Likewise, makeover formats of all kinds have flourished in the US television market – but personal makeovers, particularly those with a competitive game show element, can be seen to exemplify a particularly American vision of contemporary selfhood. These, of course, are generalizations across complex national cultures and (particularly in the case of the US) variegated television markets and there are certainly exceptional cases that can be cited. The point to be made here, though, is that while makeover television has gone global, it has done so through a complex process of articulation with local television traditions and with local cultures and lifestyles.

Acknowledgement
The author would like to thank Frances Bonner for her critical feedback on this essay.

Notes

1. Reality TV has become a catch-all phrase used to classify a range of popular factual forms. However, as Corner (2004) points out, the term first emerged in the US context where it was initially associated with low-budget, actuality-based television of the *COPS* variety. While the term had a certain strategic edge in the US context – where it came out of the pressures of a highly competitive deregulated industry – as he notes it would have been unlikely for the term to have emerged from the UK or Europe where there was already a long tradition of 'real' modes of television in the form of social observational-style documentaries. British and European television production companies have nevertheless been highly successful at producing, marketing and selling formats internationally under the reality TV banner, with the Dutch company Endemol producing the *urtext* of reality shows *Big Brother*.

2. *Changing Rooms* was the brain child of British lifestyle television guru Peter Bazalgette, who also created groundbreaking lifestyle formats such as *Ready Steady Cook* and *Ground Force*. Bazalgette's television production company eventually became part of Endemol UK, and as chairman of the company he introduced *Big Brother* to British television audiences.

3. Again, the central role of Peter Bazalgette's production company Bazal in producing many of these formats should be noted, with Bazalgette often described in the British press as the man behind the 1990s lifestyle television 'revolution'.

4. My thanks to Frances Bonner for this point.

5. In the 1980s there was also some attempt on cable television to introduce the advice culture and transformative ethos of women's service magazines more broadly onto television via 'video magazines'. *Cosmopolitan*, *Woman's Day* and *Good Housekeeping* all produced home and lifestyle-oriented advice shows. By and large, though, these 'video magazines' were not successful as cable audiences at that time were not large enough to cover the expense of producing these shows (McCracken 1993, 293–6).

6. Indeed, Bignell (2005, 39) contends that there has been somewhat of a 'reverse colonization of US television by British programmes and producers in the Reality TV arena'.

7. Bonner (2000) notes there were a number of earlier precedents in lifestyle television, with *Burke's Backyard* (1987), a show whose focus on living in the backyard sought to bring the romantic mythology of the Australian outback to suburbia, often cited as a breakthrough lifestyle show.

8. The recent return of *Burke's Backyard* to primetime television indicates the ongoing popularity of the home and garden magazine format in the Australian market.

9. For a more in-depth examination of these issues see the chapter on the making of the Australian version of the BBC lifestyle makeover format *Honey We're Killing the Kids* in my book *Smart Living: Lifestyle Media and Popular Expertise* (Lewis 2008).

10. For instance, it is now reasonably common on Australian television for channels to purchase the format rights along with the original version of a show and to air that original version as a way of prepping audiences for the subsequent local production, as in the case of *Queer Eye for the Straight Guy*, *What Not to Wear* and *The Biggest Loser*.

11. For instance, while many popular factual and lifestyle formats travel readily across cultural borders, as Bignell (2005, 59) notes, cases like the relative disinterest in *Big Brother* in the US and *Survivor's* relatively poor ratings in Britain indicate that one should be cautious in over-generalizing the universal appeal of such formats.

References

Abbott, P. 2006. Personal interview with author. 15 May. Sydney.

Andrejevic, M. 2004. *Reality TV: The work of being watched*. Lanham, MD: Rowman & Littlefield.

Bignell, J. 2005. *Big brother: Reality TV in the twenty-first century*. Basingstoke: Palgrave Macmillan.

Biressi, A., and H. Nunn. 2005. *Reality TV: Realism and revelation*. London: Wallflower.

Bondebjerg, I. 1996. Public discourse/private fascination: Hybridization in 'true-life-story' genres. *Media, Culture & Society* 18, no. 1: 27–45.

Bonner, F. 2000. Lifestyle programs: 'No choice but to choose'. In *The Australian TV book*, eds. S. Cunningham and G. Turner, 103–16. St Leonards: Allen & Unwin.
———. 2003. *Ordinary television: Analyzing popular TV*. London: Sage.
———. 2005. Whose lifestyle is it anyway? In *Ordinary lifestyles: Popular media, consumption and taste*, eds. D. Bell and J. Hollows, 35–46. Maidenhead and New York: Open University Press.
Bratich, J.Z. 2007. Programming reality: Control societies, new subjects, and the powers of transformation. In *Makeover television: Realities remodelled*, ed. D.A. Heller, 6–22. London: I.B. Tauris.
Brunsdon, C. 2003. Lifestyling Britain: The 8–9 slot on British television. *International Journal of Cultural Studies* 6, no. 1: 5–23.
Brunsdon, C., C. Johnson, R. Moseley, and H. Wheatley. 2001. Factual entertainment on British television: The Midland's TV Research Group's '8–9 Project'. *European Journal of Cultural Studies* 4, no. 1: 29–62.
Corner, J. 2004. Afterword: Framing the new. In *Understanding reality television*, eds. S. Holmes and D. Jermyn, 290–9. London and New York: Routledge.
Crawley, M. 2006. Making over the new Adam. In *The great American makeover: Television, history, nation*, ed. D. Heller, 51–64. New York: Palgrave Macmillan.
Ellis, J. 2000. *Seeing things: Television in the age of uncertainty*. London and New York: I.B. Tauris.
Everett, A. 2004. Trading private and public spaces @ HGTV and TLC: On new genre formations in transformation TV. *Journal of Visual Culture* 3, no. 2: 157–81.
Heller, D., ed. 2006. *The great American makeover: Television, history, nation*. New York: Palgrave Macmillan.
Hill, A. 2005. *Reality TV: Audiences and popular factual television*. New York and London: Routledge.
Kavka, M. 2006. Changing properties: The makeover show crosses the Atlantic. In *The great American makeover: Television, history, nation*, ed. D. Heller, 211–29. New York: Palgrave Macmillan.
Lewis, T. 2008. *Smart living: Lifestyle media and popular expertise*. New York: Peter Lang.
Magder, T. 2004. The end of TV 101: Reality television, formats and the new business of TV. In *Reality TV: Remaking television culture*, eds. S. Murray and L. Ouellette, 137–56. New York: New York University Press.
McCracken, E. 1993. *Decoding women's magazines*. Basingstoke: Macmillan.
Medhurst, A. 1999. Day for night. *Sight and Sound* 9, no. 6: 26–7.
Miller, T. 2007. *Cultural citizenship: Cosmopolitanism, consumerism and television in a neoliberal age*. Philadelphia: Temple University Press.
Moran, A. 1998. *Copycat television: Globalisation, program formats and cultural identity*. Luton: University of Luton Press.
Moran, A., and M. Keane. 2006. Cultural power in international TV format markets. *Continuum: Journal of Media & Cultural Studies* 20, no. 1: 71–86.
Moseley, R. 2000. Makeover takeover on British television. *Screen* 41, no. 3: 299–314.
———. 2003. The 1990s: Quality or dumbing down? In *The television history book*, ed. M. Hilmes, 103–6. London: British Film Institute.
O'Sullivan, T. 2005. From television lifestyle to lifestyle television. In *Ordinary lifestyles: Popular media, consumption and taste*, eds. D. Bell and J. Hollows, 21–34. Maidenhead and New York: Open University Press.
Ouellette, L., and J. Hay. 2008. *Better living through television*. Oxford: Blackwell.
Palmer, G. 2003. *Discipline and liberty: Television and governance*. Manchester and New York: Manchester University Press.
———. 2004. 'The new you': Class and transformation in lifestyle television. In *Understanding reality television*, eds. S. Holmes and D. Jermyn, 173–90. London and New York: Routledge.
Taylor, L. 2002. From ways of life to lifestyle: The 'ordinari-ization' of British gardening lifestyle television. *European Journal of Communication* 17, no. 4: 479–93.
Thussu, D.K. 2007. *News as entertainment: The rise of global infotainment*. London: Sage.
Waisbord, S. 2004. McTV: Understanding the global popularity of television formats. *Television & New Media* 5, no. 4: 359–83.
Watts, A. 2006. Queen for a day: Remaking consumer culture, one woman at a time. In *The great American makeover: Television, history, nation*, 141–57. New York: Palgrave Macmillan.
Wood, H., and B. Skeggs. 2004. Notes on ethical scenarios of self on British reality TV. *Feminist Media Studies* 4, no. 2: 205–8.

Makeover on the move: Global television and programme formats

Albert Moran

Introduction

In 2006 Freehand TV produced the local version of the BBC lifestyle programme *Honey We're Killing the Kids* for Network Ten in a format deal with BBC Worldwide Australasia. In 2004 the Seven Network had already previously made an Australian version of the BBC's personal makeover series *What Not to Wear* which was unsuccessful with local audiences and ended up being relegated to the lifestyle channel of cable television. Of course, there has been a long history of the Australian broadcasting and reworking of British programmes derived both from the BBC and from the other UK network broadcasters. Once the Australian public broadcaster, the ABC was inevitably involved in adapting BBC programmes for local audiences. What makes the recent revamping arrangements significant is the fact that the BBC now finds a ready market with the Australian advertiser-supported networks such as Channels Seven and Nine. By dint of its joint involvement in producing or overseeing local versions of its formats, BBC Worldwide derives a production as well as a licence fee from the Australian commissioning that is returned to corporate funds. This case, where the BBC bypasses its traditional sister organization in Australia in favour of a more commercial marketplace and is now actively involved in the Australian television production sector, is by no means unique. BBC Worldwide has fixed on a plan to expand its television format programme business across the globe. As part of this move, it will initially focus on four television markets: Australia, Canada, India, and the United States. It has identified these as format adaptation target-territories where it will be involved in various joint-venture arrangements in the production and marketing of programmes first devised for broadcast by BBC Television in the UK market (ABC 2007).

As such an example suggests, contemporary international television is involved in the complex task of transformation, not only at the level of the makeover genre discussed in these pages and elsewhere (Heller 2006, 2007) but also at other levels. Hence the remarkable international success of the Columbian telenovela *Yo soy Betty, la fea* (*Ugly Betty*) (Schmitt, Bisson, and Fey 2005). *Yo soy Betty* does not belong to the domain of factual infotainment television – as do *What Not to Wear* and *Honey We're Killing the Kids* – where the genre of makeover has mostly appeared to reside. The show is scripted, with on-screen roles played by professional actors. After the astonishing worldwide popular success of reality television programme formats over much of the past decade – especially *Survivor* and *Big Brother* – *Yo soy Betty* is a breakthrough programme that challenges conventional television forms of fiction and drama. It is not makeover television in a generic sense, although in part its plot contains a reworking of one of the most famous of makeover fairy stories, that of Cinderella. *Yo soy Betty*'s success presents the possibility of an international transformation of the form of scripted drama in the mode of the Latin American telenovela (LaPastina 2004).

Even more significantly, the franchising of this telenovela into at least 12 national territories (as well as several unauthorized remakes elsewhere), like much of makeover television and even reality television, turns on industrial practices of adaptation. Hence this essay is concerned with understanding the institutional framework of global television, which offers broad homologies of makeover that anticipate and contextualize subjects and themes occurring at more micro levels in specific programmes.

Aim

How does format-remake television work as a worldwide institution? Answering such a question involves locating this kind of television adaptation within the broader context of shifts in the global television industry. This analysis of television format exchange is split into four stages. First, the most significant features of a global television business are identified. The second part of the analysis concentrates on the rise of format television. The third section of our discussion sketches the historical background to this kind of television transformation. These latter two parts discuss the dynamics of trade in television programme formats that led to their revamping in national and regional industries across the world. In the last part of the essay, I discuss attempts to conceptualize levels of programme adaptation in order to further clarify this kind of programme transformation.

The global television industry

Since the late 1980s, television in many parts of the world has found itself in a new era (cf. Moran 2005). This is brought about by a unique intersection of modern technologies of transmission and reception, innovative forms of financing, fresh ways of imagining the audience, novel forms of content, and new constructions of the television commodity. Technological convergence has become a dominant notion with new players entering the distribution arena, including companies based in the telecommunications and computer sectors. Alongside the move to privatize many television broadcasting services, there has been a parallel shift towards the use of independent production companies. Hollywood is no longer the sole centre for the global production of popular television. The emergence of format programming has enabled other capitals such as London, Amsterdam and Berlin to rise to prominence. Television genres which once were marginal such as game shows, talent contests, self- and home improvement programmes, and hidden-camera 'documentary', have now become centralized forms of programming output. These programme forms highlight the capacity of the 'ordinary' person to go on television and are part of a neoliberal zeitgeist. The multi-channel abundance of services offered by technology shares the same outlook. These are complementary to the information and entertainment provisions of broadcasters and are increasingly more interactive than the older services. Finally, new forms of finance are also important. Not only do these include the incidental commercial services available through domestic technologies of telephone and computer but, especially, have to do with Intellectual Property (IP) rights.

These developments have not just occurred in the West but have also been apparent elsewhere. Many scholars see this increasing uniformity as evidence of an evolving global order in television (Waisborn 2004; Chalaby 2005; Tunstall 2008). In any case, though, it is worth recalling that an older term, 'world television', is an equally appropriate label for such a configuration (Parks and Kumar 2003, 14). Chalaby identifies four interconnected components of a planetary system that are complexly interrelated and changing (Chalaby 2005). First, there is the media industry component, itself constituted by seven giant transnational corporations supplemented by other multinational organizations with strong regional sales or those with global reach specializing in niche markets. Clearly, BBC Worldwide is such a player even if it belongs to this second tier rather than to the first. Second, there is a technological infrastructure in the shape of worldwide communication networks that include cable, satellite, and the Internet; this facilitates and maintains the operation of these organizations. Additionally, there is the news and entertainment content and associated data and services that circulate through the system. Finally, there is the global regulatory regime that includes various international bodies, technical and trade agreements, and legal decisions and ordinances. Such a scheme is rudimentary, and various other interconnected sectors might and should be added. One such domain, for example, is the vital matter of television and media labour with associated issues such as employment, worker association, new technology, skill and craft in constant flux and contestation, etc. (Miller et al. 2001; Wasko and Erickson 2008).

Chalaby's own particular focus of interest has to do with transnational satellite television as it operates in five different geolinguistic world regions: Europe, Latin America, Greater China, India, and the Middle Eastern Arab world. This development was contingent on the emergence of a new technology that considerably outstripped the geographical reach of cable landlines. First developed for military purposes, satellite has facilitated the increased spread of television channels across national boundaries to other geolinguistic territories in the same region over the past 20 years. Transnational satellite television is certainly an important component of the complex evolving jigsaw of world television, but so too are other developments. One of these – the development of formatted programming – is especially important for this study. It can be approached in terms of the content and related services that Chalaby identifies as the third of his four interrelated components of the global television industry.

Format programmes

Canned, or finished, television programmes had previously been the form in which television shows travelled around the world. Since the 1950s, the technology was available to record programmes as they were broadcast on air. In turn, industries such as those of the United States, Japan, Russia and Egypt could then license the re-broadcast of these programmes in other territories, with or without subtitling or dubbing. However, a more recent form of television programme content has emerged. It goes by the name of television format. The latter is a kind of recipe or guide to the remaking of a programme adaptation in another territory. The format programme is devised, developed and broadcast in one television market. Once this has occurred, there is an opportunity to license a re-broadcast of the programme in other parts of the world. However, what is put to air is a new programme produced in this other territory and using the format of the original as a kind of template that will help to direct the remaking of the adaptation.

Local and national audiences invariably prefer to see a programme that looks and sounds like one of their own. They ask that on-screen figures act and sound like them, that situations and places shown feel familiar and recognizable, and that stories told on screen have to do with their world. In short, they would prefer a programme that is tuned to their sense of who they are. The idea of the television programme format has been evolved with this situation in mind. Licensing the re-broadcast of a finished or canned programme allows for very little cultural adaptation in a particular market. However, with a television format, what the trade seeks to export is the successful commercial knowledge and know-how bound up in a programme that will help ensure its adaptation and remaking in another territory. The format package is a kind of recipe that comes complete with accessories and tips for the programme's reproduction elsewhere. Or it makes available a kind of mould that controls and shapes the efforts of production teams in other markets in making their own version of a programme.

Hence, for example, the format for the Australian-devised series *The Block* (Channel Nine), involving four teams engaged in home renovation, carried extensive information and advice for would-be producers elsewhere. This advice concerned many elements that went well beyond a rudimentary script or shooting order. Financial data were particularly important, so the format package contained guidelines concerning the costs of buying the properties for makeover, advice regarding financing the cost of materials and additional labour, how and when to sell the properties back to the public, and guidelines for commercial involvement by home viewers, including telephone voting.

Of course, the elements contained in a format package may vary considerably from one programme to another, from one genre to another and even from one time to another. For instance, although *Ground Force* and *Extreme Makeover* belong to the same genre in the shape of the makeover programme, there are quite different and specific social, ethical, cultural and even personal matters raised by their particular dramatic premises. A full-format 'bible' or rule book will address and advise on all of these matters.

The core notion involving a television format is far from new. The premise is that a good creative idea in one place can be successfully established elsewhere, especially if suitable care is taken with the adaptation. Michael Storper (qtd in Moran, with Malbon 2006, 14) has usefully explained 'knowledge exchange' as 'the transfer of economically useful practices, routines and conventions, which are complex and coherent assemblages of different kinds of information'. Adopting such a framework, one might suggest that a television format is a multifaceted, unified package of industry knowledge that is licensed to facilitate the remaking of a programme in another television market. With canned or finished programmes, the processes of devising, development, and production will typically occur in one television setting even if subtitling or dubbing assists a programme's broadcast in another (Hasranpour 2004). On the other hand, with the format programme, the devising and development of the programme can occur in one location before a body of know-how is assembled so that the programme can be made over in another territory for an audience that may be linguistically, ethnically, historically, geographically, and culturally different from that of the programme's original broadcast audience (Moran 1998). Clearly, the exchange of television format programmes is not dependent on physical technologies in the way that canned programme exchange is. Instead, format knowledge comes in the shape of a set of services designed to help in the remaking of the programme elsewhere.

Up to 20 individual elements or services can be identified in a format package. There is no invariable ingredient but it is the case that depending on a format's longevity and success in different territories then the more extensive the format package is likely to be. For example, Endemol's *Big Brother* package of materials would far outstrip the BBC's *Top Gear* format bundle. Among written forms frequently provided are scripts, running-order sheets, studio floor plans and set designs, accumulated schedule and ratings data, marketing and promotion information, and sample press releases and programme synopses. Software is another important form of the know-how to be licensed. It can include DVDs of the programme broadcast in other territories. Other digitalized resources might consist of programme titles, music, special effects, programme logos, graphics, and promos. Two other services may far outweigh these in importance. One of these is the consultative production service offered to a format licensee to help the latter execute a successful local adaptation of the format. The last element may be even more important, although less tangible. This is the calculation that past success of the format is likely to be repeated through a new remake. In the uncertain world of television programming, a broadcaster in another territory seeks the commercial likelihood of programme success by licensing a format.

A television programme format, then, refers to that set of industry know-how and resources that allows the development and production of a television programme in another place and time. What is marketed and distributed is not a completed programme but rather a body of knowledge and accompanying resources that will help in the remaking of a programme. The format, then, is a complex, comprehensive body of materials which can guide and assist in the makeover of an earlier version of a programme to produce a later version that may be more suitable for a particular television industry and its local audiences somewhere else in the world.

Various other details of this kind of arrangement are worth adding by way of amplifying the kind of transformation taking place. First, the fact is that the programme idea or nucleus may by no means be a magic bullet in the process. Instead, other knowledge or services may be vital and more important to the franchising arrangement, including: details of tie-ins between television programme, the Internet, and telephony services; confidential information regarding audience ratings and scheduling in other territories; and consultative production services. A striking instance of this concerns the *Pop Idol* format devised by British entertainment impresario Simon Fuller, and co-produced with FremantleMedia (Moran forthcoming). This is a talent show and there is nothing especially original or striking in the programme idea as such. However, the franchise's value lies in the numerous commercial opportunities that it provides in the pop music industry, including those to do with management, CD sales, endorsements, tours, marketing and promotion, and so on.

Licence fees are not especially lucrative in their own right, so a franchiser's licensors usually seek to derive additional fees from helping to produce a local version of their format in another territory. The recent activity of BBC Worldwide in the Australian television production market discussed above underlines this point, with BBC executives often travelling to Australia to advise on one of their formats, such as *Top Gear*.

Another reason for taking on an active advisory role in the production of one's format is the fact that there is a good deal of plagiarism and piracy across the industry. Format devisors attempt to protect their properties both by elaborating the range of elements that constitute a programme format package and by recourse to the law; however, often these measures fail to stop others profiting from their efforts. For example, legal action was taken against Channel Nine, the maker of the Australian garden makeover show *Backyard Blitz*, by the rival Seven Network, which at the time was set to debut an Australian version of the UK format *Ground Force* and argued that *Backyard Blitz* was an imitation of the UK format.

It must be pointed out, though, that the sanctioned as well as the unsanctioned circulation of the makeover television programme format is by no means a recent phenomenon. An examination of the development of this kind of industry practice underlines such a point.

Historical background

The emergence of a format-based television programme trade came about in three stages. The first phase of international programme exchange occurred in radio and started at least as early as the late 1930s. Radio industry connections between the United States, the United Kingdom and Western Europe allowed the flow of radio formats (Camporesi 2000; Hilmes 2003; Rudin 2003). By the early 1940s, for example, Australian commercial radio had its own versions of several popular US radio network series, including the anthology drama series *Lux Radio Theatre* which began in 1939, and a large number of soap opera drama serials beginning in 1942 with *Big Sister* (Moran and Keating 2007).

A new element was added as early as 1951. That year saw two separate nationally based organizations enter into a licensing agreement concerning a radio format. The BBC paid a fee to Goodson–Todman, US devisors and owners of the panel show *What's My Line?*, permitting its reconfiguration for BBC Radio, and later BBC Television (Brunt 1985; McDermott 2004). In the 1960s and 1970s there was also a series of licensed remakes of UK television comedy series in the United States, the most notable being the adaptation of *Steptoe and Son* (as *Sanford and Son*) and *Till Death Us Do Part* (as *All in the Family*) (Miller 2000; Alley 2004).

Despite these developments, this kind of adaptation was mostly sporadic in occurrence and instigated from the overseas market rather than deliberately orchestrated and planned by the owner or creator of the original programme. There was generally little thought given to increasing either the adaptability of an original programme or its accessibility as far as foreign radio and television producers were concerned. The appearance of the US daytime children's television programme *Romper Room* (Hyatt 1987, 364) marked the advent of a new business arrangement as far as programme trade was concerned. It also prefigured a second stage in the development of broadcast makeover programme distribution. *Romper Room* first appeared on a local television station in Baltimore in 1953. The year was an auspicious one as a US small business organization was beginning to undergo a transformation with the emergence of a new kind of franchising operation (Dicke 1982). Hitherto, franchising had been organized around the circulation of material goods but it was now expanding to include the distribution of services and know-how. One of the most spectacular examples of this latter kind of distribution arrangement had to do with new fast food restaurant franchising arrangements, including those associated with Burger King, Kentucky Fried Chicken, and McDonald's (Dicke 1982).

Instead of selling the *Romper Room* rights to a network, its owners, Bert and Nancy Claster, licensed the format to a string of local television stations across the country (Hyatt 1987, 364). Those that signed up to produce their own version of the programme received the rights to select and employ their own hostess and to obtain merchandise and materials representing the programme. As part of the franchise remaking arrangement, Nancy Claster, who had been the original on-air Baltimore hostess, ran week-long courses for college graduate hostesses who would front the programme in the new markets (364). By 1957, 22 stations were licensing the format. Six years later, 119 US stations had their own *Romper Room*, each led by a college graduate hostess. By then, the format was being distributed internationally, and included several adapted versions in Australia and Japan (Hyatt 1987, 364; Moran and Keating 2007, 325–6).

Despite the *Romper Room* example, programme devisors and owners mostly continued to ignore the fees that might be garnered in other territories. As late as 1980, overseas producers from such territories as South America, Western Europe, and Australia were still visiting the United States to tape programmes in hotel rooms; they would then remake these in home territories without paying permission fees (van Manen 1994; Moran 1998). Circulation of knowledge and skills that would aid format adaptation remained haphazard and underdeveloped. The only exception to such a situation was that to do with the circulation of game show and other 'live' talk-based formats (Cooper-Chen 1994; Moran 1998). With these genres – not least because of the emergence of the syndication market in US television from the late 1960s onwards (Fletcher 2004) – television game show devisors such as Goodson–Todman, Merv Griffin, and Ralph Edwards were increasingly involved in licensing the remaking of their quiz and talk shows (McDermott 2004; Timberg 2004). By the late 1970s, international exchanges of programme formats, sanctioned by the shows' owners, were beginning to take place in many markets, although they were still limited by the then relative scarcity of broadcasting channels.

Another phase of the television format business runs from 1990 to the present. Branding practices had grown significantly in the 1980s so that there was an increasing awareness of the commercial value not only of programme titles but also of their ingredients (Bellamy and Trott 2000). Brands could be sub-licensed for different territories, so why not apply the same principle to the franchising of programme brands elsewhere? Television programme producers began moving towards a more careful and systematic distribution of the knowledge, skills, and resources involved in reworking programme formulas for different audiences and markets. By 1995 there was a growing abundance of channels thanks to the already discussed elements of deregulation, new technologies, and privatization producing a situation whereby the industry required an increased amount of relatively cheap programming to fill up air time. Several large European licence owners had developed out of this context, including the BBC, Endemol, and Pearson Television (later FremantleMedia) (Moran, with Malbon 2006). By the early 1990s, various sub-genres of the makeover programme had emerged. These included the self-rehabilitation programme in the form of *Love Letters*, *Forgive Me* and *All You Need is Love* and the home renovation programme in the form of *Ground Force* and *Changing Rooms*. By 2000, Moseley could refer to the makeover takeover of UK television (Moseley 2000). Meanwhile, the watershed year of 1998/1999 saw the appearance of three reality formats – *Who Wants to Be a Millionaire?*, *Survivor* and *Big Brother* – that were enormous successes in key markets including the United States, the United Kingdom and Western Europe (Bazalgette 2005). The main genres of the new television era had arrived with a vengeance. So too had television programme remaking, which is now a principal driver in global television.

Since then the television programme makeover trade has rapidly coalesced and formalized. Developers and owners now attempt to ensure the simultaneous remaking of their formats on a world scale. In the new television landscape, other more expensive forms of content such as drama and current affairs have been (temporarily at least) displaced in favour of less expensive forms whose economies are, at least in part, based on the local remaking of global formats. Format trading has become serious business at the international round of television trade fairs (Moran, with Malbon 2006). In 2000, many companies came together and established an industry body, the Format Recognition and Protection Association (FRAPA). Several legal battles have been fought, the collective outcome of which has been the beginning of legal recognition of television programme formats (Moran, with Malbon 2006; Alvarado 2006). Training courses have come into being and format handbooks or 'bibles' have begun to appear. In short, international format exchange is now one of the pillars of the modern global system of television, with makeover programmes representing one particularly successful example of format mobility.

Modelling programme remaking

In his work on cultural transmission of literary texts, Yuri Lotman (1990) has developed a semiotic model of exchange in which he outlines five stages of the adaptation of cultural imports, stages which are potentially useful in conceptualizing the cultural processes involved in format remaking on television (see Table 1). The first phase of Lotman's dialogic process is one described as involving a retention of 'strangeness'. In this kind of remaking, the imported texts or formats 'hold a high position in the scale of values, and are considered to be true, beautiful, of divine origin' (Lotman 1990, 146). Given this kind of allocated value, there is little attempt to alter or transform any of the elements of the predecessor, which are coveted for their own sake. In turn, Lotman's second stage can be labelled as one of 'indigenization'. At this point, the 'imported texts and the home culture restructure each other' (147). Lotman believes that, in this phase, 'translations, imitations and adaptations multiply' and 'the codes imported along with the texts become part of the meta lingual structure' of the importing culture (150). Commenting on this stage in terms of Australian cinema, O'Regan (1996) has claimed a particular synthesis between the local and the imported: 'This second stage gives rise to a relatively strict division

Table 1.   Categorical stages of adaptation.

Makeover	Lotman
Minimal	1. Strangeness
	2. Indigenization
	3. National-internationalism
	4. (In between)
Maximum	5. Commendation

Source: Lotman (1990).

of labour: the Australian is the content, the flavour, the accent and the social text, while the international provides the underlying form, values, narrative resolutions, etc.' (218).

The third stage of Lotman's model might be termed national-internationalism. There is a mutual accommodation between the 'imported' text and the 'home' culture wherein the two reorganize one another (Lotman 1990, 151). This new system is not seen as a domination by imported codes, but rather as an adjusted internationalism. The fourth stage is one that is least articulated and developed by Lotman. Noting this scarcity of attention, O'Regan finds it necessary to offer his own designation. He describes this phase as the 'in between stage' (1996, 220). In practice, it seems to be an intensification of the previous stage. As Lotman puts it:

> the imported texts are entirely dissolved in the receiving culture; the culture itself changes to a state of activity and begins rapidly to produce new texts; these new texts are based on cultural codes which in the distant past were stimulated by invasions from outside, but which now have been wholly transformed ... through the many asymmetrical transformations into a new and original structural model. (Lotman 1990, 147)

Similarly, perhaps pointing to the same incompleteness of the designation or its similarity with earlier stages, O'Regan also detects an overlap with the second stage (1996, 221). Finally, Lotman's fifth stage is one in which exemplary texts are produced by the receiving culture. The process might be labelled commendation. The latter culture 'becomes ... a transmitting culture and issues forth a flood of texts directed to other, peripheral areas' (Lotman 1990, 150).

Up to a point at least, Lotman's categories are clear and relatively easy to apply. For instance, the importation and broadcast on Australian television of the BBC programme *Top Gear* as shown in the United Kingdom constitutes the first stage of Lotman's typology. In turn, a remake by SBS TV for Australian viewers of the *Top Gear* format would belong to a second level of translation. In the third and fourth stages, however, the translation is more radical. When no licence fees have been paid, there are frequently accusations of plagiarism. Hence, for example, Fox's *Trading Spouses* appeared to be a clone of RDF's *Wife Swap* while Granada's *Nanny 911* seemed to have a lot in common with Channel 4's *Supernanny*.

However, this is not to deny the blurring that occurs between any format type and its neighbours. In addition, such analysis indicates that the different types of adaptation may be in operation simultaneously and that, in practice, the stages are not sequential or progressive. In effect, the process of absorption and indigenization may be more dialectic than this kind of model is capable of suggesting. Bakhtin's (1986) notion of dialogue as a complex, multidimensional environment without discernible or predictable boundaries and limits suggests new means of grasping some of the very different ways in which a 'localized' television format might circulate inside a specific industry and culture on the periphery of the television world system that has been outlined. It also helps anticipate the very different meanings, examples, practices, understandings, and so on that they might embody for different kinds of subjects, including broadcasters, regulators, producers, viewers and critics. In turn, Bakhtin suggestively summarizes the play of repetition and difference at work in the utterance:

> The unique speech experience of each individual is shaped and developed in continuous interaction with others' individual utterances. This experience can be characterized to some degree as the process of assimilation – more or less creative – of others' words (and not the words of a language). Our speech, that is, all our utterances, (including creative works), is filled with others' words, varying degrees of otherness or varying degrees of 'our-own-ness', varying degrees of awareness and detachment. (1986, 88)

This proposition is very resonant for the matter in hand, the process whereby a television format is actioned at the local level in an operation wherein it becomes a television programme that has an enduring, material existence. The process of cultural adaptation is a complex one that involves many elements negotiated between a visiting consultant and a local production team.

Some parts of such a process seem to lend themselves to understanding under the categorical model of exchange, while others are more usefully seen in the light of this relational model of transfer. In effect, both schemas are useful tools in coming to grips with the activity of television programme format makeover.

Conclusion

In sum, the international television format trade is an important component of the global television industry. Doing television in this way helps to reconfigure and reconfirm various televisual genres. These include not only the makeover genre but also quiz and game shows, reality programmes, talent shows, children's programmes, and even drama series. This essay has outlined the principal features of this form of distribution, stressing the malleability for cultural exchange that is generally built into the television programme format. Invariably, canned programmes have less audience appeal in other television markets. By contrast, the format programme has the capacity to be customized or indigenized to help meet local tastes and expectation. The format programme is chameleon-like in its capacity for this kind of transformation. Television programme imitation is by no means a new feature of the international mediascape. However, as the historical analysis has stressed, it has only been with the emergence of new business practices to do with franchising and IT protection that a worldwide trade in this kind of makeover television has come about.

Stressing the multiplicity of commercial elements involved in a television programme, format franchise licensing underlines the point that this kind of format exchange is never a one-dimensional process. Instead, remaking is usually multifaceted and complex. As Lotman's model of the process emphasizes, transformation can run the gamut from the minimal to the extreme, pointing to the fluid and dynamic nature of format translation.

Many elements touched upon deserve further consideration than has been possible in this essay. Two such subjects can be mentioned to indicate the wide range of avenues of approach to this form of the television format trade. One area has to do with the comparative study of format remaking in particular television markets and cultures, and the institutional and cultural factors that may be at work in such adaptations. Transnational comparative analysis of format remaking exists around quiz shows and reality programmes (Cooper-Chen 1994; Andrejevic 2003; Brenton and Cohen 2003; Holmes and Jermyn 2004; Murray and Ouellette 2004; Mathijs and Jones 2004). Such work has also recently been extending to the makeover genre itself (Kavka 2006; Bonner 2005; Lewis 2008; Heller 2006, 2007). A second line of analysis might concern itself with a more historically and socially informed view of generic television remaking along the lines pioneered by Miller's (2000) study of British television programme adaptation in US television in the 1960s and Heller's (2003) discussion of US sitcom remakes in Russia in the 1980s and 1990s.

Economically and culturally, the worldwide trade in television makeover programmes binds more and more broadcasting and production components of hitherto local, national, and regional television industries into a more transnational business. If this is television globalization, then it is globalization with a local look and sound. Yet such terms as 'global' and 'local' (as well as many contingent labels such as 'national') remain tantalizingly unclear and paradoxical. Above all, they call for ongoing reflection and interrogation.

References

ABC. 2007. The British are coming. *Media Report*, 22 November.

Alley, Robert S. 2004. Lear, Norman (1922–). In *Encyclopedia of television*, ed. H. Newcomb, 1335–7. Chicago: Fitzroy Dearborn.

Alvarado, Manuel. 2006. Interview with Jonathan Coad. London.

Andrejevic, Marc. 2003. *Reality television: The work of being watched*. New York: Rowman & Littlefield.

Bakhtin, Mikhail. 1982. Discourse in the novel. In *The dialogic imagination: Four essays*, 259–422. Austin: University of Texas Press.

———. 1986. The problem of speech genres. In *Speech genres and other late essays*, 60–102. Austin: University of Texas Press.

Bazalgette, Peter. 2005. *Billion dollar game: How three men risked it all and changed the face of TV*. London and New York: Time Warner.

Bellamy, Robert V., and Paul L. Trott. 2000. Television branding as promotion. In *Research in media promotion*, ed. S. Eastman, 127–59. Mahwah, NJ: Lawrence Erlbaum.

Bonner, F. 2005. Whose lifestyle is it anyway? In *Ordinary lifestyles: Popular media, consumption and taste*, ed. D. Bell and J. Hollows, 35–46. Maidenhead and New York: Open University Press.

Brenton, Sam, and Reuben Cohen. 2003. *Shooting people: Adventures in reality TV*. London: Verso.

Brunt, Rosalind. 1985. What's My Line? In *Television mythologies*, ed. L. Masterman, 21–8. London: Comedia.

Camporesi, V. 2000. *Mass culture and national traditions: The BBC and American Broadcasting, 1922–1954*. Fucecchio: European Press Academic Publishing.

Chalaby, Jean K. 2005. *Transnational television worldwide: Towards a new media order*. London and New York: I.B. Tauris.

Cooper-Chen, Anne. 1994. *Games in the global village: A 50-nation study*. Bowling Green, OH: Bowling Green University Popular Press.

Dicke, Thomas S. 1982. *Franchising in America, 1840–1980: The development of a business method*. Chapel Hill: University of North Carolina Press.

Fletcher, James E. 2004. Syndication. In *Encyclopedia of television*, ed. H. Newcomb, 2247–8. Chicago: Fitzroy Dearborn.

Hasranpour, Amir. 2004. Dubbing. In *Encyclopedia of television*, ed. H. Newcomb, 764–5. Chicago: Fitzroy Dearborn.

Heller, Dana. 2003. Russian 'sitcom' adaptation: The Pushkin effect. *Journal of Popular Film and Television* 31, no. 2: 60–86.

Heller, Dana, ed. 2006. *The great American makeover: Television, history, nation*. New York: Palgrave Macmillan.

———, ed. 2007. *Reading makeover television: Realities remodelled*. New York: I.B. Tauris.

Hilmes, Michele. 2003. British quality, American chaos, historical dualisms and what they leave out. *Radio Journal: International Studies in Broadcasting and Audio Media* 1, no. 1: 13–27.

Holmes, Su, and Deborah Jermyn, eds. 2004. *Understanding reality TV*. London: Routledge.

Hyatt, Wesley. 1987. *Encyclopedia of daytime television*. New York: Billboard.

Kavka, M. 2006. Changing properties: The makeover show crosses the Atlantic. In *The great American makeover: Television, history, nation*, ed. D. Heller. London: Palgrave Macmillan.

LaPastina, Antonio C. 2004. Telenovela. In *Encyclopedia of television*, ed. H. Newcomb, 2292–4. Chicago: Fitzroy Dearborn.

Lewis, T. 2008. *Smart living: Lifestyle media and expertise*. New York: Peter Lang.

Lotman, Yuri. 1990. *Universe of the mind: A semiotic theory of culture*. London: I.B. Tauris.

Mathijs, Ernest, and Janet Jones, eds. 2004. *Big Brother international: Formats, critics and publics*. London: Wallflower.

McDermott, Mark C. 2004. Goodson, Mark (1915–1992) and Bill Todman (1918–1978). In *Encyclopedia of television*, ed. H. Newcomb, 1013–6. Chicago: Fitzroy Dearborn.

Miller, Jeffrey. 2000. *Something completely different: British television and American culture*. Minneapolis: University of Minnesota Press.

Miller, T., G. Govil, J. McMurria, and R. Maxwell. 2001. *Global Hollywood*. London: British Film Institute.

Moran, Albert. 1998. *Copycat TV, globalization, program formats and cultural identity*. Luton: University of Luton Press.

———. 2005. Configurations of the new television landscape. In *A companion to television*, ed. J. Wasko, 291–307. Malden, MA: Blackwell Publishing.

———. Forthcoming. In *New flows in global TV*. Bristol and Portland: Intellect.

Moran, Albert, and Chris Keating. 2007. *Historical dictionary of Australian radio and television*. Lanham, MD: Scarecrow.

Moran, Albert, with Justin Malbon. 2006. *Understanding the global TV format*. Bristol: Intellect.

Moseley, Rachel. 2000. Makeover takeover on British television. *Screen* 41, no. 3: 299–314.

Murray, Susan, and Laurie Ouellette, eds. 2004. *Reality TV: Remaking television culture*. New York: New York University Press.

O'Regan, Tom. 1996. *Australian national cinema*. London and New York: Routledge.

Parks, Lisa, and Shanti Kumar, eds. 2003. *Planet TV: A global television reader*. New York: New York University Press.

Rudin, Richard. 2003. United States influence on British radio: Commercial thinking and public service systems. In *Museum of Broadcast Communication encyclopedia of radio*, ed. C. Sterling, 1434–7. Chicago: Fitzroy Dearborn.

Schmitt, D., G. Bisson, and C. Fey. 2005. *The global trade in television formats*. London: Screen Digest.

Timberg, Bernard M. 2004. Griffin, Merv (1925–). In *Encyclopedia of television*, ed. H. Newcomb, 1034–7. Chicago: Fitzroy Dearborn.

Tunstall, Jeremy. 2008. *The media were American: US mass media in decline*. New York: Oxford University Press.

van Manen, J.M. 1994. *Televisiefor mats: en-iden nar Nederlands recht*. Amsterdam: Otto Cranwinckle Uitgever.

Waisborn, Silvio. 2004. McTV: Understanding the global popularity of television formats. *Television and New Media* 5, no. 4: 359–88.

Wasko, Janet, and Mary Erickson, eds. 2008. *Cross-border cultural production: Economic runaway or globalization?* Youngston, NY: Comedia.

Makeover television, governmentality and the good citizen

Laurie Ouellette and James Hay

In June 2006, ABC TV encouraged families to 'get healthy' in conjunction with its new reality series, *Shaq's Big Challenge*. Each week, NBA champion Shaquille O'Neal worked with a 'dream team' of nutritionists, coaches, medical experts and physical trainers to improve the bodies – and the lives – of six overweight middle school children while the cameras rolled. As the kids endured the physical and emotional challenges of Shaq's transformational 'boot camp', the basketball star consulted with local school districts and government officials to develop a suggested 'wellness program' for the State of Florida, where the series was filmed. Television viewers were encouraged to implement their own lifestyle makeovers in partnership with the *Big Challenge* website, where they could generate customized health report cards, replay material from the television broadcast and download resources for getting themselves and their children into shape. While *Shaq's Big Challenge* was packaged as reality entertainment, it was also promoted as an effort to transform the way 'we approach the health of a nation – one child, one community, one state at a time, until we truly are a happier, healthier, fitter America'. In this paper, we analyse the changing relationship between television and social welfare implied by this mission statement, and show how the impulse to remake television viewers into active and healthy citizens speaks to the 'reinvention' of government in neoliberal capitalist democracies such as the United States.

Practical instruction by experts in the care and improvement of the self, the family, and home – the basic elements of makeover television – is hardly new. In the early twentieth century, progressive social workers sought to disseminate the 'science of right living' to working-class and immigrant populations, believing that positive changes of habit and conduct would improve the quality of life for these groups, and stabilize society as a whole.[1] With the growth of the culture industries – movies, magazines, radio and eventually television – pedagogies of self and lifestyle transformation were situated within the cultural economy of serial entertainment and advertising.[2] What has changed is the 'political rationality' of the makeover as a resource for achieving the changing demands of citizenship: Today, we contend, the impetus to facilitate, improve and makeover people's health, happiness and success through television programming is tied to distinctly 'neoliberal' reasoning about governance and social welfare.

The spirit of personal reinvention endemic to the current spate of makeover television has gained visibility and social currency as part of the reinvention of government as a decentralized network of entrepreneurial ventures on the one hand, and the diffusion of personal responsibility and self-enterprise as ethics of 'good' citizenship on the other.[3] 'Reinventing government' is a technical term used by policy analysts and advocates since the late 1980s to refer to the re-conception of the public sector as the primary administrator of social assistance (Osbourne and Gaebler 1992).[4] As the liberal capitalist state is reconfigured into a network of public–private partnerships, and social services from education to medical care are outsourced to commercial firms, citizens are also called upon to play an active role in caring for and governing themselves through a burgeoning culture of entrepreneurship.[5] Within this context, cultural technologies such as television, which have always played an important role in the formation of idealized citizen subjects, become instrumental as resources of self-achievement in different and politically significant ways.

Reality television, which has proliferated in the context of deregulation, welfare reform and other attempts to reinvent government, has become the quintessential technology of citizenship of our age. Our book *Better Living through Reality TV*: *Television and Post-welfare Citizenship* (2008) analyses this development in the United States, showing how reality-based entertainment enacts experiments in governance and 'civic laboratories' for testing, refining and sharpening people's abilities to conduct themselves in accordance with the new demands being placed on them.[6] As Anna McCarthy demonstrates in her seminal study of *Candid Camera* (2004), television's capacity to govern through entertaining 'real-life' human experiments was mobilized as early as the 1950s, but only now are social and political conditions ripe to position television as a resource for achieving 'post-welfare' citizenship. Not only does reality television provide an experimental training ground for the government of the enterprising self, it has also adopted an active and visible role in coordinating non-state resources (money, expertise, outreach) for achieving the ethic of self-sufficient citizenship promoted by neoliberal regimes. In this sense, reality television is being inserted into the reinvention of government in complex, everyday, constitutive ways.

Reality television governs less through the dissemination of ideology than through the enactment of participatory games and lifestyle tutorials that guide, test and supposedly enhance subjects' capacity to play an active role in shaping uncertain outcomes – to govern themselves through freedom, not control, in the language of political philosophy. As an early adopter of what scholars now call convergence culture, much reality television extends the experimentalism and participatory flair of its programming to viewers at home, so that the 'programme' in the old sense of broadcast media becomes the entry point into a broader menu of customizable entertainment and self-fashioning opportunities and requirements. Contrary to the stereotypical equation of television watching with passivity, the contemporary viewer – like the contemporary citizen – is increasingly expected to purposefully navigate the array of multimedia resources that television coordinates.

Makeover television has achieved a visible role in the new circuitry of citizenship formation afforded by reality entertainment. Utilizing techniques from behavioural experiments and self-tests to lifestyle instruction and role modelling, programmes such as *Shaq's Big Challenge* diffuse and amplify the government of everyday life, utilizing the cultural power of television (and its convergence with new media) to evaluate and guide the behaviours and routines of ordinary people, and, more importantly, to teach us how to perform these techniques on ourselves. Makeover programmes enact the promised freedoms as well as the apparent burdens of enterprising citizenship on screen, utilizing coaches, lifestyle experts and motivators to transform floundering individuals into successful self-managers. At the same time, makeover programmes challenge a wide range of citizens organized by lifestyle clusters to expand their capacities, work harder on themselves, and exploit the resources of self-care made available to them. We are all called upon by the governing logic of our times to play the makeover game, and television – through the regularity of its programming as well as its interactivity – has played a powerful role in inserting the imperative to make and remake ourselves as citizens into the fabric of everyday life.

Television and the 'state of welfare'

Before elaborating on makeover television, a discussion of our terminology and theoretical orientation will be helpful. Our work applies critical theories of governmentality to media culture, particularly reality television. The term governmentality, as developed by philosopher Michel Foucault and his followers, refers to the processes through which individuals shape and guide their own conduct – and that of others – with certain aims and objectives in mind (Foucault 1991; Gordon 1991; Burchell 1996; Rose 1996; Cruikshank 1999; Dean 1999). Scholars of governmentality look beyond the formal institutions of official government to also emphasize the proliferation and diffusion of the everyday techniques through which individuals and populations are expected to reflect upon, work on and organize their lives and themselves as an implicit condition of their citizenship. These techniques do not emanate directly from the state, nor can they be traced to any singular power centre. Rather, techniques of governmentality are circulated in a highly dispersed fashion by social and cultural intermediaries and the institutions (schools, social work, the medical establishment) that authorize their expertise. Television, along with other popular media, are an important – if much less examined – part of this mix in that they too have operated as technologies called upon to assist and shape citizens 'who do not need to be governed by others, but will govern themselves, master themselves, care for themselves' (Rose 1996, 45).[7]

Because governmental practices and rationalities are never stable, attempts to map and analyse them must be contextual, geographic and historical. Our focus is on the neoliberal present, by which we mean the bipartisan effort to 'reinvent' government (particularly in the United States) and to remodel the welfare state through dispersed networks of privatization and self-responsibilization. While we are charting television's crucial contribution to this remodelling, we are not implying that welfare no longer exists, nor are we pitting neoliberal strategies of governing at a distance against a romanticized view of the state as public welfare administer. We use the term 'post-welfare' citizenship to indicate the re-privatized arrangements, political reasoning, and individualized responsibilities demanded by the reinvention of government in the United States, but we also understand welfare in a broader sense, as a mutating but nonetheless integral component of liberal rule. Reality television, for better or worse, has come to play an important role in the transformation of welfare by helping to reconstitute the way it is conceptualized and practised in the United States.

Foucault's chronicle of the birth of the liberal state showed how its ability to govern relied on nascent social and cultural technologies for cultivating the perceived health and wellness – i.e. the welfare – of the citizenry (Rabinow 1997; Faubion 2000). The dispersion of technologies of governance, as a matter of guiding and shaping habits and behaviours through expertise, provided the initial basis for state power as well as the origins of modern welfare as a dispersed strategy of governing populations outside state apparatuses through religious institutions, charities, clinics and asylums.[8] What Nikolas Rose (1996) calls a 'state of welfare' emerged in the twentieth century to provide publicly coordinated and administered public services, including education, health care, public assistance, social work and mental hygiene. Technologies of governing through welfare that had developed privately were brought more squarely under the control of state bureaucracies, partly as a means of 'civilizing' the industrial working classes, notes Rose. Yet this move also represented a progressive move towards social democracy to the extent that the autonomous individual of liberal rule was recast as a 'citizen with rights to social protection and social education in return for duties of social obligation and social responsibility' (Rose 1996, 49).

Since the 1980s, the social contract implied by the 'state of welfare' has been the target of vigorous attempts to reinvent the public sector – in part because state involvement in welfare is seen as a breech of liberalism's emphasis on governing at a distance. Particularly in the United States, public-sector welfare programmes are claimed to have bred passive and dependent citizens who do not respond to market incentives.[9] The 'reinvented' state is still concerned to ensure the health and wellness of the population as the basis of its capacity to rule, however. As Wendy Brown (2003) points out, it now relies on a combination of overt and indirect strategies to produce citizens who are self-sufficient as well as self-governing.[10] Harsh penal policies (i.e. 'Three Strikes You're Out') and welfare-to-work schemes exemplify the former; the Bush Administration's 'Compassion Agenda' and Get Fit Campaign illustrate the latter. Today, however, the state relies primarily on the private sector rather than public bureaucracies to produce 'good' citizens. Acting more as a supporter and less as an 'overseer', the United States has offloaded much of the responsibility of governing onto public–private partnerships and depends more than ever before on cultural technologies such as television to translate what Rose calls the 'goals of authorities' into guidelines for enterprising living (Rose 1996, 58). Reality television's experiments, tests, challenges, and instructions have flourished within this context.

Reality television does more than evaluate and advise the conduct of citizens: increasingly, it also plays a visible role in stitching public service into privatized networks of self-care. This is especially evident in the United States, where commercial television networks have partnered with private and non-governmental entities to provide charity and social services (*Extreme Makeover: Home Edition*, *Three Wishes*) to cultivate volunteerism (*American Idol Gives Back*) and to coordinate an array of privatized self-help resources. Television is thus quite literally helping to produce a privatized system of welfare, one that is significantly more aligned with a market logic than was the case in the 'state of welfare' and the earlier stage of welfare that preceded it. Under neoliberalism, civic well-being is increasingly both commodified (produced for profit) and tied to entrepreneurial imperatives, while 'lifestyle maximization' (Rose 1996, 57–9) is joined to (and often supersedes) the nation and electoral politics as the domain through citizenship is tested and achieved. Within this context, expertise becomes authorized by corporate and business sectors, with coaches, motivational speakers, corporate sponsors, and celebrities taking over the dispersed governmental work once performed by social workers, educators and other professionals.

The reinvention of government also provides the necessary context for understanding television's own changing ethic of public service. Whether operated as a public service or regulated in the public interest, this ethic has become increasingly controversial due to its affiliation with the old 'state of welfare'. The state's role in overseeing the provision and diversity of broadcasting in the name of public enlightenment and citizenship training was authorized by the discourse of 'social rights and responsibilities' discussed by Rose. The ideal citizen cultivated by broadcasting was expected to serve the goals of the nation (and earn her/his enfranchisement). In the United States, this approach to public service reached its zenith in the 1960s, when the Public Broadcasting System was created to operate as a technology of public education and citizenship (Ouellette 2002). Since the 1980s, deregulation and market competition have largely freed commercial broadcasters from the unprofitable, and (particularly in the United States) unrealized expectations of serving the 'public good' so defined; these same forces have forced public broadcasters in Europe to accommodate a wider range of consumer choices and lifestyles.

While these developments have not eliminated education as the basis of citizenship formation through television, they have reconfigured and repurposed institutions and technologies of education: Today, televised instruction is more apt to be articulated to lifestyle governance and everyday regimes of self-care facilitated through interactive reality entertainment. The skills, problem-solving techniques, step-by-step demonstrations, intimate feedback, motivational support mechanisms and suggestions for everyday application offered by the makeover genre, as one dimension of this shift, are more useful to current strategies of governing than is the residual public service ethic. The new curriculum is also more profitable than earlier incarnations of citizenship education by television – not only because it renders learning more inclusive and pleasurable, but because in a climate that demands enterprising skills and dispositions of all citizens, the civic training it provides has become a desirable commodity.

Television has also linked public education to new models of social service provision. While the earlier public service ethic emphasized the transmission of 'enlightenment' and civility through well-conceived programmes, today's reality entertainment is increasingly inserted into privatized social networks and resources of citizenship that transcend television viewing. Makeover television's civic engagement lies in its ability to bind work on the self to the reinvention of government; its role as a facilitator for customizing programmes of self-care makes it an attractive partner for a policy agenda that seeks to deputize private administrators of welfare.

The makeover as life intervention

The political rationalities we are describing can be glimpsed across makeover sub-genres, from style transformation programmes to home and gardening television. For example, Katherine Sender (2006) shows how the lifestyle and fashion training provided by *Queer Eye for the Straight Guy* also encourages citizens to take personal responsibility for the unstable job market. However, they are particularly acute in the *life intervention*, the term we use to describe helping ventures that mobilize resources to help ordinary people overcome problems in relation to children (*Supernanny*), pets (*Dog Whisperer*), sexuality (*Sex Inspectors*), unemployment (*Starting Over*), addiction (*Intervention*), hygiene (*How Clean is Your House?*), health and fitness (*Honey We're Killing the Kids*), safety (*It Takes a Thief*), and finance (*Suze Orman*). Life interventions address risks, problems and challenges, guiding and shaping citizens within television's cultural economy. As commercial ventures, the governing capacities of reality television's life interventions are realized (particularly within the United States) within a market logic that values entrepreneurialism, mass customization and profit accumulation. Similar to the reinvented state, the format relies on a range of partners (corporate sponsors, advertisers, clinics, professional associations and non-profit agencies) to enact its helping missions. As social service, life interventions operate within networks of support, offering serialized entertainment and popular instruction, often tailored to specific demographics and lifestyle clusters. While television as a social institution carries out its work independently of official government, the state plays a supportive role in this new strand of programming by activating the spirit of public–private cooperation in which the life intervention has thrived.

Because television in the United States is now a largely unregulated enterprise, life interventions pursue civic and public service goals within the logic of cultural commerce and its allegiance to ratings, advertising, product placement revenue, format licensing and merchandising tie-ins. In this sense, they are perfectly compatible with the logic of entrepreneurial government. The programmes deploy a continuum of governing strategies, from detainment in a private facility to self-help strategies that liken running one's life to managing a business. Their aims run the gamut from instilling good behaviour in children to improving health and longevity to avoiding toxic relationships to achieving self-esteem as a path to professional growth. What unites the life intervention as a politically significant strand of makeover television is a concern to facilitate care of the self as a strategy of freedom and empowerment. No matter how controlling some of the techniques used can appear (i.e. hidden-camera surveillance, public humiliation, detainment), the impetus is not really to display cruelty and punishment as a means of deterring misbehaviour, as Foucault hypothesized of the pre-modern spectacle of torture in public. The political rationality of the life intervention is to enact the reasoning that people who are floundering can and must be taught to develop and maximize their capacities for normalcy, happiness, material stability, and success rather than rely on a public 'safety net'.

Life interventions circulate techniques for a government of the self that complement the value now being placed on choice, personal accountability and self-empowerment as ethics of neoliberal citizenship. In an era when the state has offloaded much of the responsibility of facilitating the welfare of the citizenry to individuals and the private sector, reality television's efforts to help people improve their 'quality of life' plays another governing role as well. As Brown points out, the 'withdrawal of the state from certain domains, and privatization of certain state functions does not amount to a dismantling of government, but is a technique of governing – rational economic action suffused throughout society replaces express state rule or provision' (2003, n.p.). As neoliberal regimes shift the 'regulatory competence of the state onto responsible, rational individuals' with the aim of encouraging them to 'give their lives a specific entrepreneurial form', the scope and strategies of citizenship training change. The capacity to make enterprising lifestyle choices in matters of health, security, consumption, family and household takes on more urgency in a political climate where individuals are expected to maximize their interests as a condition of self-rule.

Central to the enterprising 'government of the self' enacted by television's life interventions is the convergence between television and the Web. Convergence allows television viewers to acquire, customize, and personalize the helping resources offered through the cultural economy of television, and to participate in the lifestyle clusters served by makeover programming and its websites. Interactivity provides a framework for enacting entrepreneurial citizenship in both senses. While the reinvention of the self is performed with the help of motivators and guides who administer the rules and techniques, it is performed on the self in the name of personal empowerment and can provide an entry point into group membership based on similar lifestyle challenges. While television provides the everyday framework for supervising the development of personal regimens, viewers are encouraged to take matters into their own hands, using the interactive resources available to them (or not).

Motivating healthy citizens

Life interventions geared to changing people's diet, exercise regimens and nutrition habits have proliferated on cable channels such as Discovery, The Learning Channel and Fit TV, a network entirely devoted to teaching consumers how to develop a lifestyle based on home exercise, rational grocery shopping and healthy eating. The major commercial broadcast networks have also developed how-to health and fitness makeover programmes such as *The Biggest Loser* and *Shaq's Big Challenge* that insert television into a circuit of resources for caring for oneself and improving one's lifestyle. This development has occurred at a time when the US government is concerned about obesity and other costly health 'problems' allegedly caused by improper lifestyles, but is unwilling to intervene in ways that might compromise a deregulatory ethos and reliance on privatized networks of welfare administration. Unlike the Progressive Era, when social workers promoted national legislative reforms as well as education and individual compliance, today's helping culture is focused mainly on maximizing personal responsibility (doing it yourself) as a path to self-regulation and empowerment. When public interest organizations do push for policy action, they are cast as proponents of a nanny state that seeks to regulate freedom of choice. During the 2004 House Government Reform Committee's hearings on 'The Supersizing of America', for example, Marshall Manson of the conservative Center for Individual Freedom criticized the Center for Science in the Public Interest for pushing 'extreme' measures such as regulating the food sold in schools and 'mandated labeling of restaurants with detailed nutrition information'. Linking such regulatory possibilities to the curtailing of market incentive and 'free choice', Manson told the committee:

> Our democracy is founded on the idea that individuals have basic freedoms. Among these, certainly, is the right to choose what we put on our plates and in our goblets ... anti-food extremists like CSPI would gladly take away that freedom and mandate our diet in order to save us from ourselves. It is time for these zealous advocates to understand that it is not the federal government's job to save us from ourselves by making our choices for us. (2004)

For Mason, the state's role is not to oversee but to support 'responsible decision-making' in consumers who are not only free to manage their own health but are also expected to do so. George W. Bush's Steps to a Healthier US, a programme designed to encourage 'simple improvements in physical activity, diet and behavior' as a means of controlling chronic disease, is an example of how the new approach reconstitutes welfare. Steps to a Healthier US is sponsored by the Presidential Program on Physical Fitness and Sport, which dates to the Kennedy administration but is now administered through more than 600 'partnerships' with corporations, non-profits and local governments. Similarly, the President's Fitness Challenge was created in 2002 as a network of corporate, non-profit and regional/municipal partners, including major sports and athletic businesses, food companies (Burger King, Coca-Cola, General Mills) and television networks (including ESPN and the Cartoon Network). These partnerships between government, corporations, and non-profits are how the state currently supports health as a dimension of welfare – not as a publicly administered 'entitlement' but as a personal responsibility to be achieved through individualized networks of support.[11]

Like other initiatives promoted by the Bush administration, including the Citizen Corp., the Faith-based and Community Initiative, and the short-lived campaign for privatizing Social Security, the Fitness Challenge is about reinventing government and enabling citizens to manage their personal welfare. The Steps to a Healthier US similarly seeks to makeover the mission of the Department of Health, Education, and Welfare (HEW): instead of breeding passive and dependent citizens, HEW's new role is to mobilize private providers and supporters with a stake in personal fitness. Inserting HEW within the culture of entrepreneurialism, the Challenge's injunction to 'Get Fit' cast the network of corporate partners as coaches motivating their subjects to succeed by taking advantage of their resources. As a mantra for empowering citizens to take control of their own welfare, the expression 'You're It; Get Fit' cast the private sector and individual citizens as the primary line of defence against unhealthy behaviours that might lead to physical illness and a life of dependency. This programme and similar efforts to embed social welfare in privatized networks of personal responsibility have changed the economic and political value of the makeover as a technology of citizenship.

At a jogging event inaugurating his Fitness Challenge, Bush claimed that it is part of a larger initiative ' ... to help Americans live longer, better, and healthier lives. And the good news is this: when it comes to your health, even little steps can make a big difference.' These steps may have referred to the joggers surrounding him at the event, but they also referred to the everyday measures through which each citizen is now expected to work on herself, and to the various non-state institutions – including corporate sponsors – who administer resources to them. The website for the President's Challenge differentiates between non-profit 'advocates' and corporate providers, including Dasani Water, Starbucks and a long list of brands (Pepsi, Coke, Burger King, Kellogg, and General Mills) whose association with the network rearticulates their social value away from unhealthy consumption and towards a new-and-improved regime of personal makeover. The website also distinguishes between different lifestyles – kids, teens, adults and seniors – and assigns to each a different set of fitness resources and techniques. Here, as with television's life interventions, the achievement of health through the marketing and education of lifestyle clusters is a process open to consumer customization through television and Web resources.

Bush's recruitment of television networks to the Challenge is also significant in light of television's perceived association with passivity and a sedentary lifestyle. In recent years, a number of high-profile programmes have challenged that association by enlisting television as a resource in helping people get healthy and lose weight. In 2005, NBC broadcast *The Biggest Loser*, providing the services of nutritionists and personal trainers to people who agreed to slim down on television, and offering a cash prize to the person who shed the most body fat. Cameras documented the contestants as they carried out intense physical exercise regimes, learned about nutrition and developed balanced and 'disciplined' eating habits. Evoking Foucault's discussion of the care of the self in ancient Greece (1986) where the feast was one of many rituals for testing one's capacity for self-control, the cast was regularly tempted with vast displays of decadent foods to test their determination and willpower. At the end of each episode, the 'outcome' of these physical and mental activities was measured live on television in a dramatic weighing ceremony.

Television viewers were invited to stage their own lifestyle intervention by slimming down and 'getting healthy'. NBC constructed an interactive website complete with nutritional guides, dieting tips, sample recipes and menus, customizable exercise regimes and weight loss tools, including a body mass index calculator. Tie-in merchandise – including workbooks and the *Biggest Loser* exercise DVD – was available for purchase, and participants were urged to join the *Biggest Loser* email club and sign up for informative podcasts. Finally, for people on the go there was also the much-promoted *Biggest Loser* wireless service. For only $2.99 per month, anyone with a mobile phone could sign up to receive a daily health tip, an exercise pointer or inspirational message. In extending these body and health management resources and techniques to individuals, the network fused popular entertainment (weight loss as competitive game) and self-shaping activities with current dynamics of governing and the demand for citizens to make use of privatized networks of support and accept accountability for the consequences of their lifestyle choices.

On *Honey We're Killing the Kids*, which originated on the BBC and was shown in the United States on The Learning Channel, a nutritionist shows how 'everyday choices can have long-term impacts on children, and offers both the motivation and the know-how to help turn families lives around'. Armed with scientific research and a team of advisors, she aims to change the 'bad habits' of a family in a period of just three weeks. The parents, who are often scolded for smoking and overeating, are shocked into a lifestyle regime change by the accusation they're 'killing their kids' by letting them eat too much junk food and watch video games and watch television instead of exercising. Digitally aged images of the children at 40 show the ill effects of their current habits, and the parents are told their children are 'at risk' of developing obesity and other health problems. In teaching care of the self, the programme objectifies the child-subject, turning him/her into an undesirable stranger. Not surprisingly, the parents usually agree to cooperate with the new 'rules, guidelines and techniques' for improving their children's health and lifestyle.

The programme follows the generic template of many television life interventions. The diagnostician arrives at the home, observes the family, diagnoses their nutritional problems and introduces a new lifestyle regimen. Cameras capture some initial resistance as well as the eventual mastering of the healthy lifestyle that the subjects come to desire as their own. At the end of each episode, the objective 'outcome' of the regimen is demonstrated by new digitalized photographs that show the children ageing in a healthier manner and the parents promise to enforce the new diet and exercise programme once the diagnostician has moved on to assist other needy families.[12]

Repetition and redundancy do not diminish the importance of *Honey We're Killing the Kids* as a form of citizenship training. In fact, repetition is crucial to the creation of a personal 'programme' as a technical everyday regimen of self-care. This programme teaches personal responsibility, risk-avoidance and choice by diagnosing and rehabilitating cases of 'ignorance' and self-neglect, and allowing the television viewer at home to identify as normal in comparison. At the same time, the programme coordinates resources for the health-conscious: television viewers are invited to seek out and master the skills required to create a healthy lifestyle on the programme's website, which includes interactive resources, games and merchandising tie-ins.

Honey We're Killing the Kids operates as a technology of citizenship, helping to solve the crisis of obesity by issuing a 'critical wake-up call for parents'. Reformers like Manson have no problem with television programmes adopting this role, because their authority to administer new forms of welfare is sanctioned not by the state but by the commercial logic of supply and demand and its ability to capitalize on welfare as outreach and instruction. The programme exemplifies television's contemporary utility for ensuring the health outcomes of the population, illustrating Rose's argument that while healthy bodies are still a 'public value and political objective' of the state, we no longer need public bureaucracies to 'enjoin healthy habits of eating ... with compulsory inspection, subsidized incentives to eat or drink correctly and so forth'. In the new context of public–private cooperation and personally regulated consumption, 'individuals will want to be healthy, experts will instruct them on how to be so, and entrepreneurs will exploit and enhance this market for health. Health will be ensured through a combination of the market, expertise, and a regulated autonomy' (Rose 1998, 162).

Like many television interventions, *Honey We're Killing the Kids* puts the impetus to succeed in health and in life on individuals, offering a regimen for personal change but overlooking inequalities related to the price of healthy food, lack of low-cost health care, and a sharpening class system that makes fast food an attractive option for many people. *Shaq's Big Challenge* also emphasizes the transformation of extreme behaviours to teach healthy living to a wide range of citizens. More explicitly than *Honey We're Killing the Kids*, this programme also stitches welfare into private–public partnerships of support that include not only television but also local school districts and professional sports. *Shaq*'s intervention is, in this sense, more specifically tied to the reinvention of government in the United States. However, it allows a broader range of governmental tactics and outcomes (such as private citizens and celebrities calling on public schools to remove fast food) than does Manson's free-market approach to personal responsibilization, thus demonstrating the contingency – and the stakes of political engagement – *within* neoliberalism as a governing rationality.

The first episode reintroduces the audience to one of the National Basketball Association's most recognizable and beloved players. Shaquille O'Neal has agreed to help seven children overcome obesity, a 'big problem' he ascribes to a combination of poor diet, inactivity, and lack of motivation. Some of the children are also depicted as immersed in unregulated television-watching, video game playing and Web surfing, and these activities are also targeted as 'causes' of an unhealthy lifestyle. Shaq's role as motivator and welfare facilitator is to break the children's presumed dependency on unhealthy food as well as entertainment regimens, moving the kids out of their sedentary lifestyles and onto the playing field valorized by professional sports. Over the course of the first season, he emerges as a paragon of tough love who combines gentleness and discipline to help children whose futures appear bleak if they fail to learn how to take steps towards fitness and self-care.

Shaq has relied on his own entrepreneurial instincts to locate and assemble a 'dream team' of professional coaches, motivators, doctors and lifestyle specialists to assist with the boot camp. Like other television diagnosticians (Dr. Phil, finance advisor, Suze Orman, *Queer Eye*'s Carson Kressley, or Cesar Milan, the 'dog whisperer'), these experts facilitate and monitor the children's gradual progress out of obesity; they also operate as agents of surveillance on Shaq's behalf, recording slip-ups such as a 'lack of discipline' during workouts. While much of the action hinges on the ultra-disciplinary boot camp, the team also educates the parents to become 'coaches' at home and works with local school officials and neighbours to create an extended 'support network' for the children.

While *Shaq's Big Challenge* is not formally affiliated with the White House, the programme repeatedly invokes the President's Physical Fitness Test as the standard against which to measure the children's progress. The programme combines the conventions of the contest and the civic laboratory to verify who is an active, motivated and entrepreneurial citizen and to affirm the current rationality of 'challenging' citizens to help themselves through television. The interactivity afforded by the Web is crucial to this affirmation, not only in the sense of extending the logic of the boot camp to the customizable menu made available through the Web but also in guiding television viewers towards presumably 'healthy' forms of media engagement.[13] Not unlike Shaq's regimen for moving sedentary kids into physical activity, the life intervention is about moving passive television viewers into the role of resourceful, enterprising and active citizens.

ABC's role in enacting an alternative to the 'state of welfare' was stressed throughout the series. In the first episode, Shaq discusses the problem of childhood obesity with Jeb Bush, the governor of Florida. In this climate of outsourcing welfare and emphasizing personal responsibility, O'Neal must justify to the governor the rationality of a venture (the Fitness Challenge) already sponsored by the President, the governor's brother. This provides the basis for differentiating television's helping ventures from stigmatized state regulations and welfare programmes. To combat the extent to which many public schools – including those in Florida – have cut mandatory physical education and allowed fast food companies to set up shop in cafeterias, the basketball star and his team also consult with school officials to create a 'suggested' wellness regimen, exemplifying the spirit of public–private partnership. This spirit is also extended through media convergence, in that ABC positions *Shaq's Biggest Challenge* as both entertainment and community outreach on its website, while the site created by the programme's producers links the programme to the website for Bush's fitness initiatives. Both sites operate as self-described 'download centers' that facilitate the regulation of obesity and other health risks through the management of individual choice, providing, for example, scorecards of 'daily drills', membership information, personal pledge cards, and tips for combating everyday 'snack attacks' (a play on sportscasters' idiom for stopping a 'Shaq attack' on the basketball court). In this way, they make membership in Shaq's programme tantamount to a form of healthy citizenship in a nation where a citizenship test is a President's Challenge.

Conclusion

Reality television, as we have shown, has instrumentalized the personal makeover as a technology of citizenship in new ways. No longer outside the logic of public service, these popular non-scripted entertainment formats have become the domains through which television contributes to the reinvention of government, the reconstitution of welfare and the production of a self-sufficient citizenry. Critical questions remain: how do we evaluate television's efforts to insert itself into diffuse, privatized networks of self-fashioning and care? How do the generic conventions of makeover television intersect with new ways of delivering and administering social welfare? How might citizens hold television accountable as a form of social service? What does it mean when celebrities, television executives and casting agents take over the role of public officials or social workers? And, how might critical media and cultural studies intervene in this process?

Because our analysis considers television as operating within changing programmes and networks of government, rather than merely as an 'ideological apparatus', we want to emphasize that television does not represent or distort welfare as much as it produces new formations of welfare by providing citizens with the resources that currently valorize their freedom and empowerment. In this context, we might reasonably ask from television the practical questions asked of other 'customer-oriented' social service providers: how are the subjects treated? Is the application process reasonable and fair? What are the outcomes of the interventions? This approach can only get us so far, however. We are still left with the contradictions and potentially devastating consequences of relegating public service, including social welfare, to private networks of support. Who provides for people who don't have access to privatized welfare networks, including the technologies of instruction, customization and self-fashioning facilitated through television and convergence culture? If television aims to make citizens/consumers more productive of their own welfare, how has this process also contributed to the growing class of people who, lacking access to resources, eventually are deemed unproductive or 'disabled' and thus a new problem for a healthy economy?

Michael Moore's documentary *Sicko* (2007) foregrounds this latter contradiction, documenting widespread instances when privatized health care in the United States has been unwilling to provide for citizens who lack the financial resources to participate in that system. The film's title refers ironically to the regime of truth that has 'rationalized' the current governmental arrangement between the state, the insurance industry, and private health care providers, and to an increasing population whose health is put at risk by this arrangement. Moore chronicles the disparity between the US health care system (whose emphasis on financial profit has left citizens without medical care) and socialist democratic strategies of health care provision in Canada and Western Europe. In some respects, the premise of the television makeover – particularly the life interventions we are examining – are simply other instances of the tendency in the United States that Moore's film represents. Yet reality television's impetus to help produce 'healthy' citizens also complicates Moore's approach to activism in several ways.

One is that the countries valorized by *Sicko* have also increasingly reinvented television (as public service) around makeovers and interventions similar to those shown in the United States. Some of these formats originated in European countries with national health care systems, indicating an impetus to create healthy citizens in new ways across the different cultural economies of national broadcasting systems. While the transnationalism of makeover television may indicate the global turn towards neoliberal strategies of governing at a distance, socialized medicine and public health care are, as Moore points out, still operational outside the United States – at least for now. Public services and a governing rationality that values self-enterprise and personal responsibility co-exist outside the United States, complicating any causal understanding of market privatization as a causal factor in the transformation of welfare and demonstrating the geographic complexities of the dynamics charted here.

While Moore's film draws attention to a growing portion of US citizens who lack health care, his political economic critique neglects the productive valence of the new system of welfare implemented in the United States since the 1990s. Television's life interventions promote health and wellness through privatized and entrepreneurialized networks of support, calling on each individual to achieve citizenship as an obligation to him/herself. This system has lethal effects, as Moore documents, but it also allows politicians to claim that 'something is being done' – and conversely to blame unmotivated citizens when the system fails. It comes as no surprise that the US Congress, while downscaling and outsourcing virtually every other welfare programme, has authorized the public subsidy of digital converters so that television remains technically available to all (Labaton 2005). Television has become one of the cultural instruments through which healthy citizenship – for better or worse – is accomplished. Likewise, the object of political intervention for those seeking an *alternative* to neoliberalism can include both the political economic failures of the current rationality of government (as Moore documents) and the cultural technologies such as television through which 'resources' of self-empowerment and care are made available to citizens. We have taken the latter approach by documenting how reality television's interventionist forms of civic and personal instruction simultaneously speak to the broader reinvention of government and complicate any conclusion that there is *no* welfare in the United States. By taking these ventures seriously, and attending to their nuances and specificities, we might better understand the remodelling of welfare and the remaking of citizens.

Acknowledgements

The authors would like to thank Mark Andrejevic, Gareth Palmer, Anna McCarthy and an anonymous reviewer for helpful comments on some of the arguments developed in this essay.

Notes

1. For the history of social work in the United States see Ehrenreich (1985); for a study of professional expertise as a related technology of governing see Ehrenreich and English (1978).
2. For the role of magazines in demonstrating self and lifestyle pedagogies within the cultural economy of consumerism see Ohmann (1998) and Lears (1983). For early US television's engagement in self and lifestyle instruction see Leibman (1995), Watts (2006) and Cassidy (2005).
3. See Osbourne and Gaebler's influential *Reinventing Government: How the Entrepreneurial Spirit is Transforming the Public Sector* (1992) for the changing rationalities of governing that we are describing here. President Bill Clinton endorsed the book, claiming it 'should be read by every elected official in America. Those of us who want to revitalize government ... have to reinvent it. This book gives us a blueprint.'
4. We elaborate in more detail how this term is useful for thinking about contemporary television in *Better Living through Reality TV* (2008).
5. For a useful summary of the move to make social services (as a dimension of the public sector) accountable to an entrepreneurial ethic see Rom (1999). Several critics have also observed reality television's parallel encouragement of a self-governing culture of entrepreneurialism. Gareth Palmer (2004), for example, has noted similarities between makeover television and the 'personal development movement', showing how both resonate with notions of entrepreneurial citizenship.
6. Our use of the term 'civic laboratories' is indebted to Tony Bennett's (2005) use of the term to describe the civic training provided by museum culture.
7. Rose (1998, 1999) has traced the dispersion of technologies of governance in a number of important studies. For an influential discussion of the role of culture in governing see also Bennett (1998).
8. Foucault discusses the relation between 'welfare states', governmentality, and the biopolitical in 'Security, Territory, Population' (1997b, 67–71). He discusses the relation between liberalism and neoliberalism in 'The Birth of Biopolitics' (1997a, 72–9). Foucault analyses early programmes for 'social health' in 'The Politics of Health in the Eighteenth Century' (2000b, 90–105). He discusses the state's role in administering 'social medicine' in 'The Birth of Social Medicine' (2000a, 134–56). The 'right to health' in contemporary France is discussed in 'The Risks of Security' (2000c, 365–81).
9. The 'genealogy' of welfare dependency as a regime of truth, and the gendering of the dependent welfare citizen, is charted in Fraser and Gordon (1997). The racialization of the female welfare subject is charted in Gilens (2000).
10. For an excellent analysis of the changing 'state of welfare' see also Clarke (2004).
11. We draw from material found on the 'Healthy US' website, the remarks of George Bush at his Fitness Challenge, the President's Challenge website 'You're It, Get Fit', and the website for the President's Council on Physical Fitness, with links to the Department of Health and Human Services.
12. Our discussion of *Honey We're Killing the Kids* is elaborated in *Better Living through Reality TV*.
13. For more on interactivity as viewer labour see Andrejevic (2004).

References

Andrejevic, Mark. 2004. *Reality TV: The work of being watched*. New York and Oxford: Rowman & Littlefield.

Bennett, Tony. 1998. *Culture: A reformer's science*. London: Sage.

———. 2005. Civic laboratories: Museums, culture objecthood, and the governance of the social. *Cultural Studies* 19, no. 5: 521–47.

Brown, Wendy. 2003. Neoliberalism and the end of liberal democracy. *Theory & Event* 7, no. 1. http://muse.jhu.edu/journals/theory_and_event/v007/7.1brown.html

Burchell, Graham. 1996. Liberal government and techniques of the self. In *Foucault and political reason: Liberalism, neo-liberalism and rationalities of government*, ed. A. Barry, T. Osborne, and N. Rose, 19–36. Chicago: University of Chicago Press.

Bush, George W. 2002. Remarks by the President at Fitness Challenge. The White House. http://www.whitehouse.gov/news/releases/2002/06/20020622-2.html

Cassidy, Marsha. 2005. *What women watched: Daytime television in the 1950s*. Austin: University of Texas Press.

Clarke, John. 2004. *Changing welfare, changing states: New directions in social policy*. London: Sage.

Cruikshank, Barbara. 1999. *The will to empower: Democratic citizens and other subjects*. Ithaca, NY: Cornell University Press.

Dean, Mitchell. 1999. *Governmentality: Power and rule in modern society*. London: Sage.

Ehrenreich, John. 1985. *The altruistic imagination: A history of social work and social policy in the United States*. Ithaca, NY: Cornell University Press.

Ehrenreich, Barbara, and Deirdre English. 1978. *For her own good: 150 years of the experts' advice to women*. New York: Doubleday.

Faubion, James, ed. 2000. *Power*. New York: New Press.

Foucault, Michel. 1986. *The care of the self: The history of sexuality volume 3*. New York: Vintage.

———. 1991. Governmentality. In *The Foucault effect: Studies in governmentality*, ed. G. Burchell, C. Gordon, and P. Miller, 87–104. Chicago: University of Chicago Press.

———. 1997a. The birth of biopolitics. In *Ethics: Subjectivity & truth*, ed. P. Rabinow, 72–9. New York: New Press.

———. 1997b. Security, Territory, Population. In *Ethics: Subjectivity & truth*, ed. P. Rabinow, 67–71. New York: New Press.

———. 2000a. The birth of social medicine. In *Power*, ed. J. Faubion, 134–56. New York: New Press.

———. 2000b. The politics of health in the eighteenth century. In *Power*, ed. J. Faubion, 90–105. New York: New Press.

———. 2000c. The risks of security. In *Power*, ed. J. Faubion, 365–81. New York: New Press.

Fraser, Nancy, and Linda Gordon. 1997. A genealogy of 'dependency': Tracing a keyword of the US welfare state. In *Justice interruptus: Critical reflections on the 'postsocialist' condition*, ed. N. Fraser, 121–50. New York: Routledge.

Gilens, Martin. 2000. *Why Americans hate welfare: Race, media, and the politics of antipoverty policy*. Chicago: University of Chicago Press.

Gordon, Colin. 1991. Governmental rationality: An introduction. In *The Foucault effect*, ed. G. Burchell, C. Gordon, and P. Miller, 1–54. Chicago: University of Chicago Press.

Labaton, Stephen. 2005. Transition to digital gets closer. *New York Times*, 20 December. http://www.nytimes.com/2005/12/20/technology/20digital.html

Lears, Jackson. 1983. From salvation to self-realization: Advertising and the therapeutic roots of the consumer culture 1880–1930. In *The culture of consumption*, ed. R. Wrightman Fox and J. Lears, 1–38. New York: Pantheon.

Leibman, Nina C. 1995. *Living room lectures: The fifties family in film and television*. Austin: University of Texas Press.

Manson, Marshall. 2004. Written testimony to the House Government Reform Committee Hearing on 'The Supersizing of America'. 3 June. http://www.cfif.org/htdocs/legislative_issues/state_issues/supersizing_america.htm

McCarthy, Anna. 2004. Stanley Milgram, Allen Funt, and me: Postwar social science and the 'first wave' of reality TV. In *Reality TV: Remaking television culture*, ed. S. Murray and L. Ouellette, 19–39. New York: New York University Press.

Ohmann, Richard. 1998. *Selling culture: Magazines, markets and class at the turn of the century*. New York: Verso.

Osbourne, David, and Ted Gaebler. 1992. *Reinventing government: How the entrepreneurial spirit is transforming the public sector*. New York: Plume.

Ouellette, Laurie. 2002. *Viewers like you? How public TV failed the people*. New York: Columbia University Press.

Ouellette, Laurie, and James Hay. 2008. *Better living through reality TV: Television and post-welfare citizenship*. Malden, MA: Blackwell.

Palmer, Gareth. 2004. The new you: Class and transformation in lifestyle television. In *Understanding reality television*, ed. S. Holmes and D. Jermyn, 173–90. London: Routledge.

Rabinow, Paul, ed. 1997. *Ethics: Subjectivity & truth*. New York: New Press.

Rom, Mark Carl. 1999. From welfare state to Opportunity, Inc. *American Behavioral Scientist* 43, no. 1: 155–76.

Rose, Nikolas. 1996. Governing 'advanced' liberal democracies. In *Foucault and political reason: Liberalism, neo-liberalism and rationalities of government*, ed. A. Barry, T. Osborne, and N. Rose, 37–64. Chicago: University of Chicago Press.

———. 1998. *Inventing ourselves: Psychology, power and personhood*. Cambridge: Cambridge University Press.

———. 1999. *Governing the soul: The shaping of the private self*. 2nd ed. London: Free Association Books.

Sender, Katherine. 2006. Queens for a day: *Queer Eye for the Straight Guy* and the neoliberal project. *Critical Studies in Media Communication* 23, no. 2: 131–51.

Watts, Amber. 2006. *Queen for a Day*: Remaking consumer culture one woman at a time. In *The great American makeover: Television, history, nation*, ed. D. Heller, 141–58. New York: Palgrave.

Websites

ABC Television. Shaq's Big Challenge official website. http://abc.go.primetime/shaqsbigchallenge/index

'Healthy US' website. http://www.whitehouse.gov/infocus/fitness/

President's Council on Physical Fitness. http://www.fitness.gov/

Shaq's Big Challenge. Family Challenge website. ShaqsFamilyChallenge.com

You're It, Get Fit website. http://www.presidentschallenge.org/

Economy and reflexivity in makeover television

Guy Redden

This paper examines theories that may help to explain the social rationale of makeover television, viewed as a genre concerned with the evaluation and modification of citizens. It considers the usefulness of models of reflexive modernization to help account for the reflexivity that participants display in the construction of lifestyle projects. However, I argue that a materially grounded notion of reflexivity is necessary to account for the overarching logic of makeover narratives: i.e. the social production of value through consumption. In this respect, makeovers can be seen as consistent with other textual forms of consumer culture that symbolically invest commodities with promises of personal life-improvement.

In the spirit of the shows themselves, makeover television is subject to continual modification. Media industry efforts to keep programming fresh mean that new angles and topics appear on our screens continually. At the same time these innovations seem to constitute exercises in creative recycling of what has worked previously (Morris 2007). Accordingly, while the makeover is a specific genre of lifestyle television that emerged in the 1990s (Moseley 2000), it can also be thought of as a kind of meme, an idea that catches on in a given context through its appeal to a wide array of 'hosts' that help to replicate it and adapt it successfully (Blackmore 1999). The fact is that after initially being confined to familiar lifestyle concerns of the appearance of body and home, the makeover has proved to be a device that is useful for the portrayal of almost any social practice, from hotel ownership to debt management and toddler taming.

Whatever the issue, the core elements of the makeover show centre around what Jack Bratich (2007) refers to as the fairytale-like 'powers of transformation' that develop through the narrative. Makeovers are inherently optimistic. They rely upon a clear contrast between before and after, whereby the after is always seen as better than what went before. Ordinary people are presented as beneficiaries of consumer advice about 'improving practices' (Bonner 2003, 106). Questions of what to do and how to act are applied to their personal cases by figures who have privileged authority to judge: lifestyle experts (Powell and Prasad 2007). These are not detached talking heads, but advisors determined to solve the problems inherent in one particular life situation. After having broken down the larger problem into its parts and explained each necessary step in the improvement plan, the overall effect is shown in the narrative climax, the 'reveal'. This is the point where we see the combined effect of all changes for the first time: in the toddler tamed, the post-surgery body, the beautiful home. Despite the great entertainment value often derived from the dramatization of the change process, there is a pedagogic rationale in this. People are represented as learning (whether or not they really do) from experts various skills and items of knowledge that enhance their ability to act in the world.

My interest here is that the notion of well-being entailed by all this is a particular contemporary sense that people can do things well by choosing well. The very narrative form is predicated on pathologization of inadequate abilities to make choices. What we see is people who apparently couldn't choose properly before becoming able to do so. Although participants may end up following decisions made by the experts, the process is not one of simple emulation or conformity to universalized conceptions of propriety. The discourse pores over the whys and wherefores of choices and their relevance to the lives of specified individuals.

This paper examines social theories that may have some power to explain the allure of this makeover logic in a contemporary setting. In the first part it considers models of reflexive modernization which posit that the need for individuals to choose courses of action reflexively is a characteristic of contemporary social life. However, I go on to question the sense that makeovers merely depict processes of self-fashioning that are at large in the population. Instead, I argue from a materialist perspective that the overarching imperative of makeover narratives is the production of subjects who can signify their value to others in the social contexts of their lives. While individual choice is the focus, it is mediated by expert discourses that moralize about the ends to which it should be put, and which also specify means for fulfilling them. As those means largely involve consumption, theories of consumer society prove useful in explaining the ways in which reflexivity is mobilized in makeovers. Their depictions of personal development are consistent with other textual forms of consumer culture which symbolically assign commodities an exaggerated capacity to improve individuals' lives.

Choosing well

Makeovers teach one to be reflexive about the rights and wrongs of action, in the name of creating a coherent lifestyle capable of satisfying the individual's expressed needs. As has been previously noted (Lewis 2007; Redden 2007), there are affinities between this representation of reflexivity on lifestyle television and that seen as typical of individuals in late modern life in theories of 'reflexive modernization' and 'individualization', of which Ulrich Beck and Anthony Giddens are the most well-known proponents. Makeovers project a kind of 'examined life'. To be on a show is to admit one has deficiencies that one cannot fully overcome, but can at least identify. The examination of the person's lifestyle that follows generates the feedback about their condition that is necessary for them to change. If the end is transformation, the means is a process of self-reflection enabled by interactions with those around them.

The theory of reflexive modernization stresses how technological change and institutional specialization have created a complex social environment. The continual production of new information about the world and possible ways of living is seen to loosen previous collective ties and certainties. Individuals are thrown 'back upon themselves' to work out how they should live, having to filter the information and options they are presented with – a condition also referred to as 'individualization'. In *Risk Society* (1992), Ulrich Beck famously characterized late modern life as full of 'precarious freedoms'. In this view, people are transformed into managers of their own affairs who have to negotiate challenges while adapting to variable conditions in labour markets, education systems and state welfare. For Beck, it is rapid changes in institutions that ensure that uncertainties, risks and opportunities are new in character, such that previously stable solidarities of family, community, and class are themselves transformed and become less useful in providing individuals with reference points and sources of guidance for action. For instance, Beck depicts the pursuit of personal health as a complex matter of citizens trying to make sense of a mass of information and options derived from science in order to make decisions about their conduct (1992, 53). Likewise, in work, the decline of the lifelong job and of employers who recruited from local communities into stable roles (factors that together constituted socially predestined work life) have forced people to consider how to fit themselves into a more flexible labour market (139–52).

Essentially, Beck sees the new demands to create and live a reflexive biography, rather than a socially prescribed one, as diffused across spheres of social life. Whatever the issue:

> As the range of options widens and the necessity of deciding between them grows, so too does the need for individually performed actions, for adjustment, co-ordination, integration. If they are not to fail, individuals must be able to plan for the long term and adapt to change; they must organize and improvise, set goals, recognize obstacles, accept defeats and attempt new starts. They need initiative, tenacity, flexibility and tolerance of frustration. (Beck and Beck-Gernsheim 2002, 4)

The sub-genre of makeover programming dealing with health issues, for instance, illustrates how concern with reflexive control of one's own biography is often foregrounded within lifestyle discourse. Shows such as *You Are What You Eat* and *Diet Doctors* present people struggling to achieve health amid all the risks that are borne of freedom to live one's life. They do not, of course, venture into the territory of serious illness, but isolate the travails of smokers, drinkers, junk food addicts, the overweight, the sedentary: those who can be seen as victims of their own lifestyle choices. Not surprisingly, given the topic, the narratives contain medical conventions of diagnosis, prognosis, and treatment plans. Perhaps most importantly the aetiology of conditions is explained in simple language. The makeover subject is not a passive recipient of expertise but someone who is enjoined to understand the causes of their health so as to better effect their own improvement. The programmes illustrate how one can turn one's health around by being informed and self-disciplined. We may or may not believe that shifts in lifestyle are maintained after the show. But at least for the duration of the episode the subject is an exemplar of the kind of personal filtering of information, risks and practical options that Beck describes. From this point of view makeovers can be seen to make television out of the kinds of life challenges faced by contemporary people. Being reflexive about appropriate choices to make for one's own welfare is presented as both the problem and the solution.

Creating value

However, before assuming that makeovers are a straightforward window onto processes of reflexive individualization in society, it must be noted that these theories have limitations. Whereas Beck and Giddens suggest people live reflexively only as social influences upon them diminish, against this position other theorists have argued that reflexivity can be understood only in relation to traditions, social structures and cultural contexts which shape the lives of individuals (Alexander 1996, 136). For instance, Lisa Adkins (2003) argues that Beck and Giddens depict reflexivity as a cognitive property of the subject that empowers them to act with freedom from lifeworld constraints of class and gender. She argues that this is a simplistic opposition that belies the ways that it is actually grounded in communal experiences and shared meanings associated with an actor's social situation. Similarly, Lewis finds that the reflexivity displayed by young people in health consumption varies significantly depending on different classed social experiences and expectations (2006).

If one of the major flaws of reflexive modernization theory is its suggestion that all citizens are similarly positioned as agents of their own welfare, another is that it includes very little recognition that the reflexive pursuit of lifestyle optimization is mediated through discourse. That is to say, Beck and Giddens do not consider that the sources of knowledge that citizens draw upon may express generic social imperatives about how one should use one's freedom to act. In *Modernity and Self-identity*, Giddens (1991, 70–108) briefly discusses self-help, but views it as little more than a resource that individuals may draw upon in the course of making choices. An alternative understanding is offered by governmentality theorists. For Nikolas Rose (1993), reflexivity is a central concern of contemporary liberal governance that is manifested in practices of self-management of the citizen. The critical difference is that Rose (1996) explicitly rejects any notion that subjects are 'left to themselves' to determine courses of action. The rationale of 'techniques' of self is that they are constructs of a political rationality of advanced liberalism which enjoin certain kinds of performance. A key point in governmentality readings of self-improvement discourses is that agency is mobilized and directed through them. As Rose puts it: 'The language of autonomy, identity, self-realization and the search for fulfilment acts as a grid of regulatory ideals' (1996, 320).

Considering these more critical understandings of contemporary practices of self-fashioning, I want to argue that makeovers represent a specific mode of the social management of reflexivity. This is that in addressing the 'precarious freedoms' of citizens they mobilize participant reflexivity as something to be guided towards the creation of instrumental value through consumption and conduct. In makeovers there is no simple notion of an individual 'living a better life' defined on his or her own terms. Rather, the search for self-improvement is an interactional process in which the meanings of the subject's current social position and possible courses of action are evaluated. The 'right' choices are represented as ones through which the participant may both claim personal satisfaction and demonstrate their enhanced worth to others. This is not only to affirm private responsibility for welfare outcomes, but it is an economic logic that works through the moralization of options for living, binding the subject into regimes of status-value that operate through acquisition of cultural capital.

A youth makeover programme illustrates how actual narratives of transformation direct subjects towards performances intended to yield personal benefits in particular social situations. *Make Me a Grown Up* (Maverick/Channel 4, 2006) is a British series in which young people are scrutinized by a panel of three experts who advise them on changes in their behaviour and appearance that they should make to fulfil their dreams. At the beginning of each episode the participant sets out their hopes for the future. Quite often these involve intended careers or getting by in their existing jobs, but they also involve relationships with peers, family, work associates and potential partners. Their advisers (a psychologist, a fashion stylist and a magazine editor) diagnose the mismatch between the subject's desires and their ability to fulfil them, create an action plan to improve a range of skills, and construct tasks to test their acquisition.

In programme five we meet Cameron Hypolite, who is, according to the narrator, 'a teenager who wants to make it in the world of modelling, but at the moment is struggling to make so much as a conversation' (S01E05, 25 September 2006). After leaving school at 16, Cameron has been unable to hold down any job requiring interpersonal skills. Overall, he is unable to manage the impressions he makes on others to his advantage. Part of the problem is the image he communicates through 'fitting a stereotype', being a black man who only wears tracksuits, trainers, silver earrings and a neck chain. Stylist Gok Wan affirms that he finds Cameron 'intimidating', and Cameron himself confesses that he may look like a 'thug, criminal or yob'. This is confirmed by an exercise where Cameron has to ask passers-by a question on the street, and is given the brush off without exception. All agree that 'things will have to change if he's going to get on in life'.

After six difficult weeks of styling and confidence coaching aimed at imbuing him 'with personality', Cameron is ready to put what he has learned (from engaging in small-talk to dressing to reveal his figure) to a final test. He manages to straddle the social distance between the council estate that is represented as his home ground and swish photographer's studio. He holds his own at a casting and is one of three models selected for a photo-shoot. Afterwards the photographer attests to his modelling ability. We are told that one month later Cameron is 'still loving standing out from the crowd' in a professional milieu that has no room for 'shrinking violets'. His happy girlfriend, who was opining his sense of inadequacy at the beginning, rounds off the observer testaments to Cameron's turn around with a statement of how much better life is now.

As always in the genre, Cameron's predicament is that he has desires, but he cannot yet fulfil them. In his case he is trying to decide what to do after leaving school, having tried a few jobs without any clear compulsion to take on a particular kind of work. He has chosen modelling, but if he is to succeed he must reorganize his conduct to adjust himself to the demands made of successful models. Thus, Cameron is not choosing freely. The expert advice he is given is prescriptive in that it stipulates what he must do if he wants to be accepted by others. The experts articulate their privileged insights into the social meanings of the things that Cameron has consumed and done in the past, and could in future. In so doing they are not simply sharing information that may help an ordinary person make independent choices about how to live. Rather, they are offering methods for him to accrue social status through mastery of cultural codes. In this case they are those concerning appropriate appearance and behaviour in an image-oriented sector of the service economy. His new style is offered up for the admiration of peers and potential paymasters in the modelling industry as well as his expert advisors, random members of the public, and his girlfriend. But this is not admiration for its own sake. It is represented as having practical benefit in Cameron's life, strengthening his personal relationship, as well as advancing his career prospects.

Make Me a Grown Up is part of a discernible trend, in British makeovers at least, towards shows directed at improving young people. Indeed, it is classified as part of Channel 4's educational programming output for schools. Other examples might include *The Bank of Mum and Dad* in which parents and experts conspire to bring financial discipline to spendthrift young adults, *Ladette to Lady*, in which 'blokey' working-class teenage women are sent to finishing school to learn their airs and graces, and Amir Khan's *Angry Young Men*, in which the role-model boxer teaches aggressive young men to be manly in more constructive ways. Yet despite the particularities of this sub-genre, which is heavily overlaid with reality television conventions in relation to the tasks through which the performances of the young are surveilled, *Make Me a Grown Up* articulates a general feature of makeovers. Central to these shows is a concern with the production of value through social practice.

This logic pervades the genre. Improving oneself or one's possessions pays dividends in life. People are ostensibly enhanced in the playing of the social roles they inhabit in the shows. Modified lifestyle practices make them better family members, mothers, cleaners, homeowners, workers, lovers, pet owners: with their success being validated in the eyes of observers who witness the transformation. The better use of symbolic resources allows them to achieve recognition, whether in showing off a beach body, a home, or an obedient toddler. For instance, home makeovers always rely upon some sense that the existing tastes of homeowners are not creditable. By participating in the show, the homeowners open themselves up to others' definitions of what constitutes a nice house. Proof that the new look is more socially impressive comes from the consensus of all involved, and often in the form of actual sale of the property.

As such, makeovers do not indicate a new form of sociality where individuals fashion themselves apart from any moralities of social acceptability, as reflexive modernization may suggest. Rather, they serve to illustrate the mediation of self-making processes by collective forces. By the end, the subject embodies particular social definitions of what it means to be a good person with a good life. That is to say, their apparently enhanced lifestyle literacies serves to make them successful in particular situations by being the kind of person who can accrue status in associated social networks – from housing markets to modelling.

This can be understood as an economic logic, in the sense, established by Bourdieu, that the pursuit of social interests can take place through the exchange of markers of cultural taste for social recognition. For Bourdieu, economic calculation applies to 'all the goods, material and symbolic, without distinction, that present themselves as rare and worthy of being sought after in a particular social formation' (1994, 173; emphasis in original). The empowerment of the individual offered in makeovers comes in the form of squeezing cultural capital out of the practices of everyday life. By capitalizing on conceptions of what is right and wrong in matters of lifestyle, the reflexive self demonstrated is, above all, a negotiator of the value that social relations may yield for the person.

The textual forms of consumer culture

It has become a commonplace that as lifestyles themselves are increasingly based around commodified forms of leisure, television plays a crucial role in mediating consumer culture. It is a relatively low-production cost, moving-image medium that is particularly suited to representing ways of life as spectacle. In the words of Ellis Cashmore, 'Television has become the central apparatus of the consumer society; it promotes not just products, but a culture in which products have value' (1994, 80).

It is important to note that in makeovers social value is generated in the course of the material practices undertaken during the programmes. The codes of propriety that are depicted as leading to personal betterment are largely applied to, and rationalize, consumption. Actions undertaken centre upon the correct use of commodities, from goods like food, clothes and paint, to services such as surgery and financial advice. The experts are professionals who have come from and are agents of the commercial sectors germane to the given task of refashioning; many, like the parenting experts, fall into the class of 'life coaches' whose own advisory services are for sale.

The makeover is, quite literally, a vehicle through which experts communicate with the public directly as advocates of the power of consumer-based lifestyles to fulfil people's needs. This is not a conspiratorial reading of the logic of consumer culture onto media texts, nor a political economy view that sees all media as indissolubly in the pocket of commercial forces. It is about the influence and interests of a class fraction that leads innovations in taste literacies in an environment of choice and continual innovation. The experts are part of the occupational group often referred to as 'cultural intermediaries' (Bourdieu 1984) that has developed with forms of work which fashion the symbolic, whether in design, marketing, leisure services or the media. It is their paid job to create and communicate about the changing meanings of goods. It is through makeovers and other lifestyle media that they present their determinations of the social significance of commodities through case studies of particular lives.

There is a strong emerging literature (including in this issue of *Continuum*) about the cultural politics of identity-transformation/normalization through consumption in the shows. A good example would be the debate over the extent to which *Queer Eye for the Straight Guy* disrupts or confirms heteronormativity and stereotypes of the gay male in its presentation of the improvement of straight men (and their social interest in coupling) through exposure to the 'superior' consumer literacies of gay men (see Clarkson 2005; Di Mattia 2007; Lewis 2007). A genre predicated on the importance of change itself is bound to feature apparently drastic processes of becoming different. Cameron from *Make Me a Grown Up* is enjoined to eschew a previous racially coded, working-class masculine style in order to achieve something. In his case, he is asked to swap black male urban clothing for a sophisticated male-model look, with one of the challenges given to him being to 'wear pink while looking manly'. It is through this particular moralization of consumption that he comes to signify in a narrative of social mobility as the right kind of person to get by in a new milieu. As such, his is one of the more palpable examples of the 'Cinderella-cum-makeover narratives' that Kathryn Fraser identifies as promising a transition from a problematic self to one that is open to the supposed power consumption has to promote social mobility (2007, 178).

However, it can also be argued that change can reinforce social norms expected of certain roles and the identities associated with them. When presenter Kim Woodburn (*How Clean is Your House?*, Channel 4, 6 December 2007) says 'hold this up and be shamed' while handing a dirty cloth to a housewife who should have kept her surfaces cleaner, she applies pressure to conform to a very conventional form of gendered personhood. The premise of a show such as *Ladette to Lady* is precisely that young women who act 'like men' (through heavy drinking, swearing and so on) need reforming into conventional 'ladies' through more refined consumption and associated behaviour. The facts that the participants are all working class and their mentors upper middle class is not incidental either. Working-classness and aberrant gender identity are often dysfunctions to be resolved by induction into middle-class, feminized dispositions.

However, whatever regimes of identity they are directed towards, makeovers inscribe consumption as leading to value increase. Learning to identify and deploy more successfully the opportunities of commodity culture is the modus that leads to supposedly improved personal productivity. In this the pressure to conform is combined with the imperative to change. Whatever the constructions of identity promoted, the shows share the feature that the cultural standards achieved by the end are new to the person in question. There is a gap in social space between the dysfunctional subject 'before' and the functional state achieved as a result of the reorientation. Only after the makeover does the person appear to have a lifestyle fit for social purpose.

In this the makeover shares family resemblances with other textual forms that have figured the social value of consumption through representing the power of commodities to fulfil needs and wants. It can be thought of as a genre that extends familiar tropes and narratives that invest commodities with imagined power beyond any notion of their literal uses. Theories of consumption have emphasized the industrial practices of the symbolic manipulation of the meaning of commodities that have developed in recent decades. Since conventional markets for mass-produced items became saturated with adequate goods in the 1970s, consumption has arguably superseded production as the central organizing principle of advanced capitalist economies (Slater 1997, 174–6). The creation of desire to consume became a system imperative of capitalist production (Ewen 2001). Spending on marketing has superseded that on research and development. The corollary of these changes has been the aestheticization of consumption, as products have increasingly become differentiable from each other on stylistic appeals to consumer choice, rather than functional grounds (Lash and Urry 1994). This is both in matters of product design, and in the promotional discourses that make products known to target publics.

One of the most widely noted shifts in marketing communications has been the rise of 'transformational' advertising. In the past most advertisements were 'informational'. Despite basic use of cultural icons and themes, persuasion was dominated by explanation of utility, or 'describing the use-value' to a potential consumer. While the informational mode still exists, the transformational mode became dominant in the later twentieth century (Leiss, Kline, and Jhally 1986). This saw advertising itself become an art and a psychological science in which, through fantasy, metaphor and use of cultural references and social associations, commodities are assigned meanings beyond their functional utility, invested with symbolic power to transform the imagined user's life. This is selling ego-ideals that become associated with products rather than being immanent to products themselves. As Judith Williamson puts it in her classic *Decoding Advertisements*: 'Advertisements are selling us something else besides consumer goods: in providing us with a structure in which we, and those goods, are interchangeable, they are selling us ourselves' (1978, 13).

Yet the textual construction of need-fulfilment in consumer culture is not only marked by the obvious genres of marketing communications aimed at selling particular brands. In a society where so many practices involve consumption of commodities there are other rationalizations about how their use can be imbricated with everyday life. Lifestyle television fits the mould of a more general advocacy of commodity-based living that Wernick (1991) identifies as pervasive in societies where commodity exchange is involved in a wide range of social relations.

As a form of television in which commodities are put to work to fulfil apparent needs identified in participants' lifeworlds, makeovers take consumer advice to a level where consumption is intimately associated with personal growth. Commodities are invested with what might be called life-value. The makeover extends claims about the benefits of use-value to specify the social interests that such transformations may further serve in actual narratives of personal living. This is a calculative, more productive hedonism which imagines consumption as being useful at the level of the whole life of the person, which is palpably transformed because of consumption adjustments made.

Another way to put this is that makeovers are vehicles of what Sam Binkley terms lifestyle morality. In his study of the 1970s lifestyle movement, Binkley (2004) proposes that the then-emergent class fraction of cultural intermediaries working in the informational areas of the economy eschewed traditional middle-class moralities of self-constraint for morally purposeful hedonism in the 'learned capacity for self-realization through highly individualized lifestyle choices' (73). This is precisely a controlled, rationalized, project-like hedonism directed towards personal progress, rather than episodic abandonment to pleasure. The sectional interests of this class lie in developing advanced consumer literacies to sustain consumption growth in contexts where it is no longer a necessity, and where previous needs are met. It is this that requires the inscription of new commodities as capable of effecting life change. Accordingly, makeovers present a mode of investing in one's life for multiple yields of pleasure (use-value) and profit (exchange for various kinds of social recognition and cultural capital) in such a combination that appears most advantageous not only to the individual's present but also to their life trajectory.

Of course, this may be construed as normalization in the 'name of' the individual. As Palmer (2004, 188) notes, one of the main functions of lifestyle television may be the teaching of middle-classness to participants by experts, but in the name of individual self-development. However, I would argue that the 'lifestyle moralization' of consumption in makeovers is more complex than a reinforcement of generalized middle-class tastes. The interests of the lifestyle advisors lie in appealing to contextual definitions of aspiration (a kind of need for something better), in ways that are intimately tied to understanding differences between members of the whole population and how commodities may mediate improvement for those in a range of situations. This is not the emulation of higher status consumption patterns that have a primary signification of being middle class in the way that owning a fridge or going on foreign holidays might have been as mass consumer markets were emerging. Cameron donning his pink V-neck sweater in modelling circles, or a mother being able to feel good on the beach again by wearing a certain cut of bikini that is not 10 year's out of date and makes the most of her current body shape, express a highly nuanced understanding of the signification of status-improvement in different social spaces, for different people. The cultural intermediaries who convene the makeover process are, above all else, expert in applying their symbolic reconstruction of the cultural value of an ever-changing field of commodities to the refashioning of people – people who face the challenge of negotiating that field in socially useful ways in their lives, which is, in turn, a challenge we might label 'reflexivity'.

Conclusion

This paper has examined social theories that shed light on why the makeover has arisen in a particular socio-historical context, and why it is has proliferated across television schedules to address a range of dimensions of lifestyle. It started by acknowledging that these shows are preoccupied with the reflexive construction of lifestyle by ordinary people. Personal dysfunction in the ability to identify and orchestrate the elements of a life well-lived is the core problem that is apparently solved by expert intervention. This is a therapeutic concern with the well-being of subjects that was absent in the 'relatively simple televisual lessons in how to choose' in earlier forms of lifestyle television (O'Sullivan 2005, 31–3).

Theories of reflexive modernization and individualization suggest the travails and opportunities of choosing how to live are distinctive of contemporary social life. One can argue that the simple number of options they are presented with forces people to live reflexively (Chaney 1996, 52). However, reflexive modernization has been criticized for suggesting that actors are free to fashion their lives because of the withdrawal of social influences over them. Alternative understandings of reflexivity emphasize its embeddedness in social relations and its mobilization in discourses which enjoin people to direct it towards certain means and ends of living. Along these lines, I have argued that the makeover is a textual mediation of material practice in a consumer society. It depicts the passage of a person's life from being worth-less to worth-more through elective consumption. Consumer practice is rendered socially productive in that transformations of appearance in the body, person or home are investments that rely upon being exchanged for the recognition of others in broader, collective, if unstable, economies of value (a more saleable house, a more attractive body ...). Traditional pressures on identity performance may be reinforced, reconstructed, or, perhaps, transcended: above all, moral concerns are deployed in the service of the cultural logic of continual growth economics. Whatever, the meaning of being a better person may otherwise be, it is consistent with expansion of economic value through the amplification of those concerns about social value. That is to say, the industry representatives who host the shows are valorizing the supposed capacity of commodities to fulfil social interests, supplying the viewing population with reasons to buy and use them.

Charlotte Brunsdon (2003, 19) calls for a debate about what is good in lifestyle television. There is no doubt entertainment value in a narrative of change, but any claim that the good life can be achieved by particular means deserves critical scrutiny. Makeovers could be perceived as progressive in their depictions of ordinary people imbued with desire to fashion successful lives by manipulating elements within their spheres of control. However, the control of the discourse of improvement by expert intermediaries who see the need for change everywhere and find that the guaranteed solution to radical betterment lies largely in the commodities over which they preside, at least gives reason to question Bratich's passing contention that 'no one can own powers of transformation' in popular television (2007, 21). Whatever else they are about, makeovers are about what it means to be a socially productive individual in consumer society, a valued and valuable consumer-citizen.

References

Adkins, L. 2003. Reflexivity: Freedom or habit of gender? *Theory, Culture and Society* 20, no. 6: 21–42.
Alexander, J. 1996. Critical reflections on 'reflexive modernization'. *Theory, Culture and Society* 13: 133–8.
Beck, U. 1992. *Risk society: Towards a new modernity*. London: Sage.
Beck, U., and E. Beck-Gernsheim. 2002. *Individualization: Institutionalized individualism and its social and political consequences*. London and Thousand Oaks, CA: Sage.

Binkley, S. 2004. Everybody's life is like a spiral: Narrating post-Fordism in the lifestyle movement of the 1970s. *Cultural Studies/Critical Methodologies* 4, no. 1: 71–96.

Blackmore, S. 1999. *The meme machine*. Oxford: Oxford University Press.

Bonner, F. 2003. *Ordinary television: Analyzing popular TV*. London and Thousand Oaks, CA: Sage.

Bourdieu, P. 1984. *Distinction: A social critique of the judgement of taste*. Cambridge, MA: Harvard University Press.

———. 1994. Structures, habitus, power. Basis for a theory of symbolic power. In *Culture/power/history: A reader in contemporary social theory*, ed. N.B. Dirks, G. Eley, and S.B. Ortner, 155–99. Princeton: Princeton University Press.

Bratich, J. 2007. Programming reality: Control societies, new subjects and the powers of transformation. In *Makeover television: Realities remodelled*. ed. D. Heller, 6–22. London: I.B. Tauris.

Brunsdon, C. 2003. The 8–9 slot on British television. *International Journal of Cultural Studies* 6, no. 1: 5–23.

Cashmore, E. 1994. *And then there was television*. London and New York: Routledge.

Chaney, D. 1996. *Lifestyles*. London and New York: Routledge.

Clarkson, J. 2005. Contesting masculinities makeover: *Queer Eye*, consumer masculinity and 'straight-acting' gays. *Journal of Communications Inquiry* 29, no. 3: 235–55.

Di Mattia, J. 2007. The gentle art of manscaping: Lessons in hetero-masculinity from the *Queer Eye* guys. In *Makeover television: Realities remodelled*, ed. D. Heller, 133–49. London: I.B. Tauris.

Ewen, S. 2001. *Captains of consciousness: Advertising and the social roots of consumer culture*. New York: Basic Books.

Fraser, K. 2007. 'Now I am ready to tell how bodies are changed into different bodies …' Ovid, *The Metamorphoses*. In *Makeover television: Realities remodelled*, ed. D. Heller, 177–92. London: I.B. Tauris.

Giddens, A. 1991. *Modernity and self-identity: Self and society in the late modern age*. Stanford: Stanford University Press.

Lash, S., and J. Urry. 1994. *Economies of signs and space*. London and Thousand Oaks, CA: Sage.

Leiss, W., S.R. Kline, and S. Jhally. 1986. *Social communication in advertising: Persons, products and images of well-being*. New York: Methuen.

Lewis, T. 2006. DIY selves? Reflexivity and habitus in young people's use of the internet for health information. *European Journal of Cultural Studies* 9, no. 4: 461–79.

———. 2007. 'He needs to face his fears with these five queers!' *Queer Eye for the Straight Guy*, makeover TV and the lifestyle expert. *Television & New Media* 8, no. 4: 285–311.

Morris, N. 2007. 'Old, new, borrowed, blue': Makeover television in British primetime. In *Makeover television: Realities remodelled*, ed. D. Heller, 39–55. London: I.B. Tauris.

Moseley, R. 2000. Makeover takeover on British television. *Screen* no. 41: 299–314.

O'Sullivan, T. 2005. From television lifestyle to lifestyle television. In *Ordinary lifestyles: Popular media, consumption and taste*, ed. D. Bell and J. Hollows, 21–34. Maidenhead: Open University Press.

Palmer, G. 2004. 'The new you' class and transformation in lifestyle television. In *Understanding reality television*, ed. S. Holmes and D. Jermyn, 173–90. London: Routledge.

Powell, H., and S. Prasad. 2007. Makeover morality and consumer culture. In *Makeover television: Realities remodelled*, ed. D. Heller, 56–66. London: I.B. Tauris.

Redden, G. 2007. Makeover morality and consumer culture. In *Makeover television: Realities remodelled*, ed. D. Heller, 150–64. London: I.B. Tauris.

Rose, N. 1993. Government, authority and expertise in advanced liberalism. *Economy and Society* 22, no. 3: 283–99.

Rose, N. 1996. Authority and the genealogy of subjectivity. In *Detraditionalization: Critical reflections on authority and identity*, ed. P. Heelas, S. Lash, and P. Morris, 294–327. Oxford: Blackwell.

Slater, D. 1997. *Consumer culture and modernity*. Oxford: Polity Press.

Wernick, A. 1991. *Promotional culture: Advertising, ideology and symbolic expression*. London: Sage.

Williamson, J. 1978. *Decoding advertisements: Ideology and meaning in advertising*. London: Marion Boyars.

Insecure: Narratives and economies of the branded self in transformation television

Alison Hearn

What is real? Whose lives are real? How might reality be remade? (Butler 2004, 33)

Introduction

In a world marked by deepening political, economic, cultural and environmental insecurity, it is little wonder that fairytale stories of personal and material transformation proliferate on the airwaves. Transformation, or makeover, television might be seen as narrative palliative for the psychological and physical precariousness of life in the West under the post-Fordist mode of production – a life made even more complex and volatile by increasing technologization, mediatization and globalization. Reality television shows produced in North America, such as *What Not to Wear*, *Ten Years Younger* and *Style by Jury*, claim to offer useful instruction and aid to downtrodden, unfashionable, insecure people. As the insecure 'other' is massaged back into the fold in the story, we, as viewers, get helpful hints about how to become productive, stable, culturally legible individuals ourselves. Indeed, the meta-message of these shows is that cultural legibility and high visibility *is* productive work and we had all better get cracking at constituting our own attention-getting self-brand. But what is the nature of the labour performed by the individuals whose bodies and senses of self are fodder for these programmes? This paper will explore the theme of insecurity, or precariousness, in the narratives and metanarratives of North American transformation reality television, and will consider this theme in relation to the shows' material practices of production. It will argue that the message of self-branding narrated and produced on transformation television ultimately exacerbates the very conditions of personal and material insecurity it claims to address.

Precariousness in life and work

There is little doubt that the modern world is in a state of perpetual insecurity and flux. We can speak of insecurity and instability in most areas of life and in all kinds of human relationships. Judith Butler, citing Emmanuel Levinas and writing about conditions in the United States after 9/11, makes the case that insecurity, or precariousness is, in fact, an ontological category, potentially applicable to all humans and all human relations. When faced with the radical difference of the 'other', we are all insecure (Butler 2004).

Unfortunately our response to this insecurity often involves ritualized exclusion from political rights and cultural representation. Butler, Edward Said, Stuart Hall and many others point to the ways in which dominant forms of representation often do violence to the 'other' – by reducing them to broadly drawn caricatures – in order to alleviate insecurity. Those who suffer this 'violence of derealization' (Butler 2004, 33) do so at the hands of brutal material practices wrapped in gauzy legitimating discourse. These discourses, in turn, strictly limit modes of cultural legibility and access to them. So, Butler argues, even as precariousness marks a common lived experience, it is not evenly distributed across the population; certain kinds of individuals are purposefully and systematically excluded from 'reality' more than others.

Precariousness and insecurity also mark conditions of labour in the post-Fordist economy. Critics such as David Harvey, Luc Boltanski and Eve Chiapello have noted the shift in recent decades to a new capitalist mode of production. 'Flexible accumulation' describes a mode of production marked by 'time-space compression' or speed-up and involving strategies of permanent innovation, mobility and change, subcontracting, just-in-time delivery, and decentralized production (Harvey 1990). In response to the legitimation crises of the 1960s and early 1970s, Boltanski and Chiapello argue that capitalism has reconstituted its 'spirit' in the form of networked organizations, marked by flexibility, casualization, segmentation, work intensity, and increased job competition and precarity. These processes have led to the formation of a 'dual market': one side marked by a stable, qualified high-waged workforce, the other by unstable, unqualified, underpaid, and unprotected workers (Boltanski and Chiapello 2005, 229).

Autonomous Marxist critics, such as Antonio Negri, Michael Hardt, Maurizio Lazzarato, and Paolo Virno, have also noted the rise of the precarious workforce within current conditions of production in the West. The flexible, small-scale systems of production favoured by post-Fordism in turn produce 'flexible, mobile, and precarious labour relations' (Hardt and Negri 2004, 112). The increasing production of immaterial commodities, such as design, symbols, knowledge and communication, necessitates new forms of labour, which involve creativity, innovation, and the manipulation of personal emotion and affect. This 'immaterial labour' (Lazzarato 1996) demands that the worker put his or her own life experience, communicative competency, and sense of self into the job. In this way, we see 'the very stuff of human subjectivity' (Neilsen and Rossiter 2005) put to work for capital.

As the lines and boundaries between working and non-working life break down, it becomes more and more difficult to find ways to assign monetary value to the jobs being done. The result is that people are working more intensely, investing more of themselves into their jobs, and are often inadequately recognized and compensated. Feminist activists Precarias a la Deriva note that precarious work involves new varieties of employment and innovations in contract labour, dislocation of work times and spaces, the intensification of the production process, the forced incorporation of affective, unquantifiable qualities into the work performed, and a more general lack of workers' rights (Precarias a la Deriva 2003).

This description applies to many workers in privileged fields of the First World economy – media and information technology, advertising and marketing, the creative industries, service industries and corporate environments – but this is only a small fraction of what we can call 'precarious' labour in the world today. Brett Neilsen and Ned Rossiter argue that there is no model precarious worker. Indeed, the term 'precariousness' can refer 'to all possible shapes of unsure, not guaranteed, flexible exploitation: from illegalized seasonal and temporary employment to homework, flex and temp work to subcontractors, freelancers ...' (Neilsen and Rossiter 2005). Unwaged labour, most obviously domestic labour, is also precarious; as Precarias a la Deriva crucially argue, precariousness is a specifically feminized state of being.

Precariousness may be defined, then, as 'the juncture of conditions, both material and symbolic, which determine an uncertainty with respect to the continued access to the resources necessary for the full development of a person's life' (Precarias a la Deriva 2003). The twinned processes of labour insecurity and ontological insecurity enacted at the level of politics and in media representations play out most aggressively in the lives and on the bodies of women, the poor, immigrants, migrant workers, the disabled, and gay, lesbian, and transgendered people. The most precarious individuals and groups are situated on the borders of psychological, material, geographic, political, gender, ethnic, or creative difference; as they are subject to the indiscriminate flow of power, they are forced to maintain perpetual flexibility and mobility.

Branding and the rise of the self-brand

If precariousness is 'the subjective counterpart' (Neilsen and Rossiter 2005) to the post-Fordist regime of flexible accumulation and neoliberal political practices, then the recent phenomenon of 'self-branding' must be understood as post-Fordist capital's palliative to problems of work/life insecurity. But what does it mean to suggest that the 'self' has become a brand?

Branding is a distinct form of marketing practice intended to link products and services with resonant cultural meanings through the use of narratives and images. The practices of branding work to install definite and highly circumscribed 'sets of relations between products and services' (Lury 2004, 1) and the consumers who use them. A brand refers to an entire 'virtual context' for consumption; it 'stands for a specific way of using the object, a propertied form of life to be realized in consumption' (Arvidson 2005, 244). In a world marked by increasing flexibility and flux, branding works to fix, albeit temporarily and tentatively, cultural meanings around consumption, producing aestheticized modes of justification for life under capital (Goldman and Papson 2006). While the material form of the brand as an image, logo, or trademark was initially intended to guarantee quality, it has now become the sign of a definite type of social identity, which then summons consumers into relationship with it. In this way, brands, both as trademarked image-objects and as sets of relations and contexts for life, become the ground and comprise the tools for the creation of 'self' and community (Arvidson 2005; Holt 2002).

A brand is also a value-generating form of property in its own right; brand equity is measured by the extent to which consumers 'live' through the brand: 'the autonomous immaterial productivity of consumers is simply commodified as it unfolds "naturally"' (Arvidson 2005, 249). As flexible accumulation has come to rely heavily on the production of knowledge and symbolic products, emphasizing packaging, image, design, and marketing over concrete material production (Goldman and Papson 2006; Harvey 1990), branding has become an 'institutionalized method of practically materializing the political economy of signs' (Goldman and Papson 2006, 328). As such, it is now 'a core activity of capitalism' (Holt 2006, 300).

Andrew Wernick's work on promotional culture provides an especially useful lens through which to understand the recent phenomenon of 'self-branding'. For Wernick, promotionalism is a culturally dominant condition; it 'is a mode of communication, a species of rhetoric … defined *not by what it says but by what it does*' (Wernick 1991, 184, emphasis added). A culture marked by the ubiquity of promotional discourse is a truly postmodern one, signalled by a lack of trust in language. Here what matters most is not 'meaning' per se, or 'truth', or 'reason', but 'winning' – attention, emotional allegiance, and market share. Goods, corporations, and people are all implicated in promotionalism; not only are they commodified but they must also generate their own rhetorically persuasive meanings. They must become 'commodity signs', which 'function in circulation both as an object(s)-to-be-sold and as the bearer(s) of a promotional message' (Wernick 1991, 16).

The 'branded self' is a commodity sign; it is a body that works and, at the same time, points to itself working, striving to embody the values of its corporate working environment. Here we see the 'self' as a commodity for sale in the labour market, which must generate its own rhetorically persuasive packaging, its own promotional skin, within the confines of the dominant corporate imaginary. This 'persona produced for public consumption' reflects a 'self, which continually produces itself for competitive circulation' (Wernick 1991, 192) and positions itself as a site for the extraction of value. As I have argued elsewhere, 'self-branding' must be understood as a distinct kind of labour, involving an outer-directed process of highly stylized self-construction (Hearn 2008b).

The practices of self-branding are most clearly expressed in popular management literature of the late 1990s. Claiming to provide a 'communicative response to economic uncertainty' (Lair, Sullivan, and Cheney 2005, 309), writers such as Stedman Graham, Tom Peters and Peter Montoya offer self-branding as a way to compete and gain power in the volatile work world of flexible capital. In this literature, success is dependent not upon specific skills or motivation but on the glossy packaging of the 'self' and the unrelenting pursuit of attention.

The practices of self-branding involve a whole way of life. Workers are encouraged to distil their top 10 qualities into a few outstanding attributes, or 'braggables', that might help them achieve 'top of mind' status in their target audience. As Chuck Pettis writes: 'In creating your Personal Brand, Me. Inc., ideally you want to use those skills and talents that are highly valued by your customer' (Pettis 2006). Those in quest of a personal brand are encouraged to expose their braggables in every venue available to them by launching a full-on 'personal visibility campaign' (Peters 1997, 83). Carefully crafted appearance and maximum image exposure, such as writing in newsletters, giving talks, or appearing on television, are crucial.

Gurus of self-branding are careful to dress up the practice in the rhetoric of self-improvement and self-care. As Stedman Graham writes, 'building a life brand is not about achieving status, wealth or fame. It's about taking responsibility for your own happiness and fulfillment. It's about creating a life of value by putting your gifts to their highest use' (Graham 2001, 22). And so, in this literature, self-branding is configured as both a 'public projection of ... personality and abilities' (Lair, Sullivan, and Cheney 2005, 325) *and* 'a way to improve yourself and serve others, a means for achieving a "transcendent self"' (Graham 2001, 24).

As personal branding literature celebrates the freedom and radical individual empowerment involved in creating the personal brand, its numerous edicts, strictures and rules seriously delimit the field of possibilities within which any imagined 'authentic self' might be performed. It reduces the 'self' to a set of purely instrumental behaviours and circumscribes its meanings within market discourse. These practices are the epitome of a process Norman Fairclough has called 'synthetic personalization' (Fairclough 1993). What is actually being sold in this literature, then, is expertise in crafting a potent synthetic *image* of autonomous subjectivity.

Self-branding on transformation television

It is precisely at this conjuncture of ontological insecurity, precarious labour and promotional discourses of self-branding that reality television comes on the scene. Reality television, it can be argued, is the paradigmatic productive post-Fordist workplace – ground zero for the socialization of labour. This is evidenced in its flagrant disregard for unionized writers and performers, its exploitation of unpaid 'real' volunteers enticed by the mythologized glamour of Hollywood celebrity to simply 'be themselves', and in its growing promotional synergies with sponsors and corporations (Hearn 2008a). Reality programming also formally enacts these processes of commodification and promotion, not only marketing goods but also people; providing the means by which contestants can become saleable image commodities or branded selves.

Personal makeover shows, in particular, can be seen to promote this mode of persuasive self-presentation, or 'self-brand'. As will be shown in the analysis that follows, the self-brands produced on these programmes are designed for recognition on both the labour market and the more general market in social status and domestic success. Before the self-brand can be produced, however, the insecurity of the participant must first be established.

Shows such as *What Not to Wear* (WNTW), *Ten Years Younger* (TYY), and *Style by Jury* (SBJ) ruthlessly mine the expressed psychological insecurity of their nearly always female participants for narrative fodder as they work to produce the self-brands ostensibly required to secure a job or re-ignite a marriage. If no real insecurity is apparent on the participants' part, the shows' ritualized forms of humiliation handily create it. The experts and hosts who guide participants through the makeover procedure are representatives of the imagined authoritative gaze of the television image industry. This gaze, however, is displaced onto the generalized figure of the audience via a series of frighteningly apt and intentionally humiliating narrative props: the 360 degree mirror, the see-through soundproof box, and the corporate-style focus group or 'jury'.

'We're right and you're wrong!' Shopping as disciplined pedagogy on 'What Not to Wear'

What Not to Wear (The Learning Channel, 2003) is the most overtly pedagogical and disciplinary of the three makeover programmes chosen for examination here. The US version of this show focuses almost exclusively on the ways a participant's appearance is contributing to her work insecurity and offers very specific information about what to wear, and, more importantly, how to *shop* for what to wear. WNTW emphasizes the fact that shopping *is* work, and, as such, is the key to creating an effective self-brand.

Produced by The Learning Channel, the North American version of the show features Clinton Kelly, an 'out' gay man who generally plays the good cop, voicing clichéd forms of patriarchal male approval ('look at that tuches!'), and Stacy London, a svelte New York girly-girl who is the strict, straight-shooting disciplinarian. The credit sequence involves Clinton and Stacy magically transforming individuals on the street into glossy, movie star versions of themselves.

The first half of the programme involves the relentless exposition of the bad taste or slovenly dress habits of the participant. A narrator puns on the connection between wardrobe and work: 'Forty-two year old Rebecca is a C.P.A. whose style is a liability in the workplace' (WNTW, Rebecca). Clinton and Stacy then ambush the 'makeoveree' in front of her friends, family and co-workers. They present the participant with $5000 and a trip to New York in exchange for following their 'rules' and agreeing to allow them to go through her wardrobe and throw out whatever they deem necessary. The humiliating exposition continues as the assembled crowd watches footage of the participant taken over the past weeks by a hidden camera. Clinton, Stacy and the group make fun of the participant's fashion choices, but also attempt to address the source of her wardrobe problems. Usually the problems identified involve low self-esteem, lack of sartorial knowledge, and, most commonly, fear of shopping.

The participant is next shown in New York modelling her wardrobe in front of a 360 degree mirror for Clinton and Stacy. Again she is subject to withering critique: 'I actually fear for your safety – someone may try to stick a branch in you and roast you over an open fire wearing that … this really doesn't make any statement other than "I'm crazy" … Let's face it, you're just a mess' (WNTW, Carrie). This segment is interspersed with clips of Clinton and Stacy going through the participant's wardrobe, making scathing comments while dumping the clothing into a large garbage can. These scenes of humiliation are interrupted by bouts of rigorous pedagogy where Clinton and Stacy lay down their rules for effective self-branding, urging the participant to consider how 'your style is a tool to help propel you toward your goals. It can really hold you back or it can really move you forward' (WNTW, Annie). Whenever participants dare to voice objections they are invariably shut down: 'No one's going to think anything about you except that you have a really big mouth and you don't follow instructions' (WNTW, Rebecca).

The next section of the show features the participant wandering the stores, confused and overwhelmed by the choices. Clinton and Stacy follow the participant's progress on a television monitor, and, after the first day, swoop in to rescue her from herself, providing lessons on how to become a better shopper along the way. The makeoveree then meets with stylists Nick and Carmindy for hair and makeup lessons. The reveal features a recap of the shopping lessons and a montage of the participant posing brightly for the camera, while the narrator notes how the participant has been effectively branded through smart shopping choices: 'Carrie looks chic and put together is this blouse for fifteen dollars and straight leg jeans for two hundred and twenty' (WNTW, Carrie).

The makeoveree then heads home to show off her new look to friends, family and co-workers. As the participant poses for the camera in a final modelling sequence, she narrates what she has learned on her 'journey'. Without exception, the participant claims that she is more confident, has conquered her fears and insecurity, and has come to appreciate shopping as a way to express her new-found sense of self: 'I used to think it was indulgent to spend money on yourself, but now I see that there's really no reason not to. I really do have the shopping bug' (WNTW, Carrie). All of this is set within the context of garnering attention and enabling future employability as a potent branded self: 'This experience has helped me to sell myself' (WNTW, Annie).

'How did you feel in the box?' Domesticity, sentimentality and self-care on 'Ten Years Younger'

Ten Years Younger (The Learning Channel, 2004) also exploits the insecurity and lack of confidence of its participants but does so in a far more sentimental, less doctrinaire manner than *What Not to Wear*. The show mines the clichéd female obsession with age, working to make its participants look 10 years younger. All of the participants on TYY represent a very traditional version of femininity; they work inside the home and claim to be stressed and exhausted by their domestic situations. Kim has a disabled husband and three children to look after. Christine had a traumatic childhood, suffers from depression and wants to 'give more to her husband'. Rebecca lives with her mother and three children and is 'exhausted and always worrying'. Where WNTW teaches participants how to shop as a way of generating an effective self-brand in the workplace, TYY stresses self-care as the foundation for effective work in the home. Unlike the rigorous pedagogy of WNTW, the hosts and experts on TYY are extremely solicitous of their participants, constantly asking them how they feel and what they need.

The insecurity of the participant must still be established, however, and, just as in WNTW, humiliation is employed for its disciplinary force. On TYY this is accomplished with the use of a see-through soundproof box placed in the middle of a busy street in Santa Monica. The makeoveree stands in the box, while the host surveys 100 people for their opinion about her age. As those surveyed ruthlessly dissect the participant's appearance, the participant stands stock still in the box. Here, she is rendered literally and figuratively abject, socially decontextualized, reduced only to her appearance and to the scathing judgement of her fellow humans. The scene is positively medieval.

The participant then sits down with the host for a heart-to-heart talk. The tone is serious, if not flat out maudlin, as the host cloyingly asks: 'What was your experience *like* inside the box?' (TYY, Christine). The participant invariably talks about how vulnerable and insecure she felt, and goes on to recount the intimate details of her difficult life situation. She works hard for her family, but she forgets to 'take time for herself' (TYY, Christine, Anna, Kim, April, Rebecca). She feels life is passing her by (TYY, Anna, April, Rebecca). She has forgotten how to smile (TYY, Christine, April). The host and the participant review pictures from an earlier, happier time. To add insult to injury the host then submits a current photo to 'scientific age progression', showing the participant what she will look like 10 years from now if she does not get help. Finally, he reveals the average age people guessed her to be; it is always significantly older than her real age.

The next section of the programme focuses on re-(im)aging the insecure participant. Depending on the problems identified, the participant visits a dermatologist, an eye doctor, or a dentist to receive treatments. The doctors maintain the sentimental tone of the programme by expressing how 'proud' they are to be a part of the participant's journey. The makeoveree then meets with the show's 'glam squad', who provide her with a new wardrobe, hairstyle and makeup, offering a few tips and tricks for the viewer along the way. After the inevitable tears and elation that come with the makeover reveal, the participant is ushered back into the box. Again, 100 passers-by are surveyed about her age. This time the comments are all positive. Husbands and families are brought in and the new average 'younger' age is revealed.

Like WNTW, the show concludes with the makeoveree reviewing the process. Consonant with the programme's traditionally feminine tone, these comments are highly sentimental and are framed in the form of advice directed to a presumed audience of female domestic caregivers: 'Don't give up on yourself. Take care of yourself!' (TYY, Kim); 'Embrace your womanhood! Find time to spend with your husband!' (TYY, Christine). On *Ten Years Younger* we see the message of self-branding in its guise as self-care. The insecure female domestic labourers on this programme are encouraged to take responsibility for their own lives by taking care of their appearance, and to 'put their gifts', being pretty and youthful, 'to their highest use' by taking care of their families.

'She looks like a cracked-out Cindy Lauper!' Judgement and impression management on 'Style by Jury'

Style by Jury (W Network, 2004), a Canadian transformation programme aired on The Women's Network, mixes generic conventions borrowed from across reality television; it is part prank show, part court show, part face-your-fear challenge, and part traditional makeover programme. As a result, the tone of the programme is carnivalesque, moving from melodramatic seriousness to light-hearted comedy, with some sentimentality thrown in for good measure. The participant is variously positioned as the butt of a joke, a criminal, someone with major life obstacles to overcome, and an image disaster, while the host plays the part of judge, prankster, disciplinarian, friend, and style guide.

The central conceit of the show is the television courtroom, a la *People's Court*, complete with stern music, pounding gavel, and the jury seated in a red leather jury box. The narration relentlessly reinforces the legal theme. During the credits the host explains that the participant will come in contact with 'two separate but equal groups: the experts who transform them and the juries who judge them'. The jury is a 'group of nine strangers' who will adjudicate the participant's ability to make a good first impression. On SBJ, 'making a good first impression' is key to a stable and fulfilling work and family life.

As with WNTW and TYY, tactics of overt humiliation establish the participant's insecurity. The show begins with deception; while the participant thinks she is simply auditioning for a makeover show, she is actually being watched and judged through a two-way mirror by a 'jury'. The 'jury' is made up of anonymous people described only by their job titles: 'On today's jury, a singer-songwriter, a paralegal, a handbag designer ...' (SBJ, Bernice). As the participant enters the room, the jury members make scathing comments on her looks and attitude: 'She looks like a bag lady' (SBJ, Lisa); 'I want to say "nerd-alert!"' (SBJ, Sharon). The unwitting participant is eventually made aware of the jury and is forced to listen to their commentary. Often she is devastated by what she hears, but, as the tears flow, the host announces that the participant has 'won' the makeover after all.

In addition to the standard attention to makeup, hair and wardrobe, and dental and dermatological treatments, the SBJ participant is also asked to meet a challenge based on their stated life goals, such as singing in front of a crowd, going on a blind date, or making a sales pitch. No matter how the participant does, the challenge is always presented as a success, a sign that the participant is learning 'confidence'. SBJ glosses over some of the very serious economic and social issues that underlie the contestant's insecurity, as the challenge is made to stand in for a real education, better income, or meaningful relationship. On one particularly upsetting episode, for example, Lisa, a single mother on welfare, has been given the services of a nutritionist to teach her how to eat properly. As the nutritionist goes through Lisa's food cupboards pointing out the poor food choices, Lisa, humiliated and ashamed, explains that she simply cannot afford to buy healthy food. Rather than acknowledge the class issues at work here, however, the nutritionist simply ignores them and takes Lisa out for some 'retail therapy' on the show's dime.

During the final reveal a different jury is in place to pass judgement, and their comments are always positive. But, in the final moments of the programme, the participant is 'pranked' once again and told that someone she knows has been a secret member of the new jury. As participant and her loved one are reunited, the jury claps politely and the host dismisses them.

The participants featured on SBJ tend to be far more diverse than the relatively generic career-seeking middle-class women on WNTW or the conservative domestic workers of TYY. But, no matter how atypical the participants are initially, they are effectively 'normalized' by the end of the programme. The jury here functions more like a focus group for a brand or commodity. They invariably, across episodes, use the same clichéd phrases to describe the impression they get from the made-over participant; she is 'glowing', 'confident', 'friendly', 'a go-getter', 'put-together', 'modern', 'sexy' – in other words, a bankable, standardized female brand.

Conclusion

Transformation programmes address insecurity in the culture at large by staging, over and over again, fantasies of incorporation into a stable, dominant cultural imaginary in the form of self-branding. The lessons in self-branding repeated on these shows contain and delimit discourses of 'self' and modes of self-presentation within the strict aesthetic templates of the corporate culture industries and the instrumental logic of the market, offering secure and disciplined forms of cultural legibility. Self-branding may be post-Fordist capital's answer to the generalized cultural condition of precariousness, but whose lives serve as fodder for the inscription of this security?

Transformation television depends on cultural conditions of precariousness to provide a steady supply of makeover subjects. Most often female, underemployed, unemployed or positioned as domestic workers, and identified as physically 'borderline' in some way, these women define precariousness. The shows actively exploit the insecurity of participants for narrative effect; they discipline participants into compliance through the use of an array of humiliating devices with the goal of finally producing a relatively homogeneous array of subjects who have been reinserted into the image logic of post-Fordist capital. The personal insecurity thematized and ostensibly 'fixed' in these shows' narratives can thus be seen as a precondition for transformation television's more general economy of production.

The women on *What Not to Wear*, *Ten Years Younger* and *Style by Jury* labour *as* the image of their insecure selves *for* an image, or viable self-brand. They also labour *in* the image, inside the precarious and unstable world of reality television production. Reality television production models routinely bypass traditional unionized workers, especially writers and performers, in the effort to produce cheap, flexible programming that can be mobilized just in time across platforms and networks and incorporate high levels of promotional content (Magder 2004; Raphael 2004; Deery 2004). The affective labour performed on these programmes, which often involves emotional and physical pain and the public display of the most private or intimate feelings, is not adequately remunerated; participants receive a small appearance fee at best. Indeed, the work of the participants is not recognized as labour at all. Instead, producers and networks position themselves as benign corporate benefactors and the participants as their grateful beneficiaries. Here we see a prime example of post-Fordist capital's perpetual effort to 'escape from labour' and the always-problematic labour relation (Wright 2005) by externalizing its labour costs – downloading them onto individuals and figuring this practice as a gift.

But reality television *is* a promotional factory, a site of production, and participants do labour inside it, both as narrative figures and as self-brands. The branded selves that emerge from this process of production have truly suffered the 'violence of derealization' in their reduction to thoroughly instrumental image commodities. The threatening insecure 'other' is literally and figuratively 'wrapped up' inside the gauzy, insubstantial, legitimating discourses of post-Fordist flexible accumulation, which assert that image savvy and flexibility, consumer prowess, and attention-getting confidence is the means to self-fulfilment and success.

Finally, because the women featured on these programmes labour to perform their insecurity under precarious working conditions, the self-brand produced in the process is an ephemeral, unstable commodity, viable only so long as contextual material conditions make it so. There can be no certainty about the participants' future after they leave the programme. On transformation television, then, 'reality' has been remade in a highly aesthetically circumscribed, promotional form; its material modes of production and its promise of an effective self-brand actively exacerbate any insecurity they claim to palliate. The transformed 'reality' of these women's lives includes only a new wardrobe and the shadowy after-image of their momentary, insecure celebrity.

References

Arvidson, Adam. 2005. Brands: A critical perspective. *Journal of Consumer Culture* 5, no. 2: 235–58.
Boltanski, Luc, and Eve Chiapello. 2005. *The new spirit of capitalism*. London and New York: Verso.
Butler, Judith. 2004. *Precarious life: The powers of mourning and violence*. London and New York: Verso.
Deery, June. 2004. Reality TV as advertainment. *Popular Communication* 2, no. 1: 1–20.
Fairclough, Norman. 1993. Critical discourse analysis and the marketization of public discourse: The universities. *Discourse and Society* 4, no. 2: 133–68.
Goldman, Robert, and Stephen Papson. 2006. Capital's brandscapes. *Journal of Consumer Culture* 6, no. 3: 327–53.
Graham, Stedman. 2001. *Build your own life brand! A powerful strategy to maximize your potential and enhance your value for ultimate achievement*. New York: Free Press.
Hardt, Michael, and Antonio Negri. 2004. *Multitude: War and democracy in the age of empire*. London: Penguin.
Harvey, David. 1990. *The condition of post-modernity*. Cambridge and Oxford: Blackwell.
Hearn, Alison. 2008a, forthcoming. Hoaxing the 'real': On the metanarrative of reality television. In *Reality TV: Remaking television culture*, eds. S. Murray and L. Oulette. 2nd ed. New York: New York University Press.
———. 2008b. Variations on the branded self: Theme, invention, improvisation and inventory. In *The media and social theory*, eds. D. Hesmondhaulgh and J. Toynbee. London and New York: Routledge.
Holt, Douglas. 2002. Why do brands cause trouble? A dialectical theory of consumer culture and branding. *Journal of Consumer Research* 29: 70–90.

64   *A. Hearn*

————. 2006. Toward a sociology of branding. *Journal of Consumer Culture* 6, no. 3: 299–302.

Lair, Daniel J., Katie Sullivan, and George Cheney. 2005. Marketization and the recasting of the professional self: The rhetoric and ethics of personal branding. *Management Communication Quarterly* 18, no. 3: 307–43.

Lazzarato, Maurizio. 1996. Immaterial labour. In *Radical thought in Italy: A potential politics*, eds. P. Virno and M. Hardt. Minneapolis and London: University of Minnesota Press.

Lury, Celia. 2004. *Brands: The logos of the global economy*. London and New York: Routledge.

Magder, Ted. 2004. The end of TV 101. In *Reality TV: Remaking television culture*, eds. S. Murray and L. Ouelette. New York: New York University Press.

Neilsen, Brett, and Ned Rossiter. 2005. From precarity to precariousness and back again: Labour, life and unstable networks. *FibreCulture Journal*, no. 5, http://journal.fibreculture.org/issue5/neilson_rossiter.html (accessed 1 December 2007).

Peters, Tom. 1997. The brand called you. *Fast Company* 10: 83.

Pettis, Chuck. 2006. Building a personal brand identity: The brand called Will and Lydia, http://www.brand.com/frame9.htm (accessed 28 July 2007).

Precarias a la Deriva. 2003. First stutterings of 'Precarias a la Deriva', http://www.sindominio.net/karakola/precarias/balbuceos-english.htm (accessed 25 June 2007).

Raphael, Chad. 2004. The political economic origins of Reali-tv. In *Reality TV: Remaking television culture*, eds. S Murray and L. Ouelette. New York: New York University Press.

Style by Jury. 2004. W Network.

Ten Years Younger. 2004. The Learning Channel.

Wernick, Andrew. 1991. *Promotional culture*. London, Thousand Oaks, CA and New Delhi: Sage.

What Not to Wear. 2003. The Learning Channel.

Wright, Steve. 2005. Reality check: Are we living in an immaterial world?, http://info.interactivist.net/article.pl?sid=05/12/27/0513241 (accessed 1 December 2007).

Property and home-makeover television: Risk, thrift and taste

Buck Clifford Rosenberg

There has been a veritable explosion in home and property shows in the last two decades, swamping television schedules with tips on how best to revamp kitchens on a budget, build outdoor entertainment areas, and select the best paint colours to increase property prices. These programmes have emerged within a world dominated by consumer capitalism and risk, in which the home is promoted as simultaneously a site of shelter and sanctuary, identity production and taste presentation, and as a commodity. While much of the literature on lifestyle and makeover television programmes to date has emphasized consumption, this paper demonstrates, alternatively, that such programmes often employ a discourse of thrift to control, but never remove, consumption. In addition it analyses the 'aesthetic education' offered by such programmes, which, it argues, frequently promote a contemporary design or 'soft modernism' targeted at the anxious middle classes. Such an aesthetic, which removes signs of individuality, also serves the purposes of the property market in that it can both increase property prices and the speed of property sales.

The rise of home and property shows

The boom in home and property shows has occurred across the Western world in the last two decades. It began in Britain with the success of *Changing Rooms*, *Ground Force*, *Home Front*, *Location, Location, Location* and *Property Ladder*. Such programmes marked a disjuncture in style and method – notably the increased use of the close-up – from older and more didactic British home, garden and DIY shows. Such shows included those hosted by Barry Bucknell during the 1950s and 1960s, like *Do It Yourself*, *Bucknell's House*, and *The ABC of Do-It-Yourself* (O'Sullivan 2005, 31) or *Gardener's World* from the 1970s (Brundson 2003, 10–11). These programmes were screened on the British public broadcaster, the BBC, which, as Lewis notes in her essay in this issue on the history of lifestyle television, has played a significant role more broadly in the production and screening of lifestyle makeover formats.

Traditional American home shows such as the long-running DIY show *This Old House* also focused more on didacticism than entertainment. American lifestyle television, unlike Britain, is dominated by commercial interests. It first emerged on cable television at the turn of the millennium, via publicly funded British imports, before moving onto the networks (Kavka 2006, 211). American television initially converted British programmes such as *Changing Rooms* into *Trading Spaces*, but soon developed home-grown home-makeover programmes such as

Design on a Dime, *While You Were Out* and the American ABC's spectacular *Extreme Makeover: Home Edition* (see Palmer 2007; Kavka 2006).

In Australia, home-lifestyle television first emerged on the national public broadcaster, the ABC, before becoming the exclusive possession of commercial television by the late 1990s. The first home/DIY programme, *Handyman*, screened on the ABC in 1976. Yet the home did not make a major return to the screen until the mid-1980s with Channel Nine's *Burke's Backyard*, hosted by horticulturalist Don Burke. This programme had a magazine-style format with scenes on DIY and gardening and other domestic concerns such as cooking and pets, a format that Channel Ten's *Healthy, Wealthy and Wise* would run less successfully with the following decade. By 1990 the national broadcaster returned to focus exclusively upon the home and lifestyle with *The Home Show*, hosted by the defiantly middle-class Maggie Taberer and her partner Richard Zachariah. This lifestyle format was copied successfully by Nine's *Our House* (Harrison 1994). By the late 1990s, and with the exception of Channel Seven's magazine programme *Better Homes and Gardens*, home-makeover shows began to dominate Australian home-lifestyle programming. Like the United States, Australia screened local versions of popular British shows such as *Ground Force* (Seven) and *Changing Rooms* (Nine). Seven screened the less popular local programmes *Room for Improvement* and *Auction Squad*, while Nine had great success with *Backyard Blitz*, *Renovation Rescue*, and *The Block*, which saw couples pitted against each other as they renovated apartments rather than the iconic free-standing suburban house.

Why has there been such a proliferation of home-related lifestyle television? Firstly, these programmes reflect the economic pressures on television networks to produce cheaper programmes, mostly lifestyle and reality shows. But more importantly they reflect wider social processes of lifestylization, individualization and consumerism in late capitalist Western society. Increasing emphasis is placed upon selves and the objects and practices people hold close: commodities such as houses, cars, interior furnishings or hobbies such as gardening and cooking, not to mention pets and families. These objects, practices and relationships are more easily managed, contra the 'wider world'. In this section I argue that there are two socio-cultural reasons for the proliferation of home shows. First is the notion of a persistent home-ownership ideology which operates within Australia, Britain and the United States. Second is the pressures of the risk society which turn people's attention inward upon themselves and their homes.

Ostensibly, home shows reflect what has been termed the home-ownership ideology (Kemeny 1983) and highlight the special role that the owner-occupied home plays within the economic and cultural contexts of the three nations. In Australia and the United States – two pioneering nations – it reflects the conquering of the natural world (and by extension indigenous populations), as free-standing housing spreads in ever-larger suburban waves into the (now outer-urban) frontier: literally a nation-building exercise (see Davison 1993; Davison and Davison 1995; Garreau 1991; Fishman 1987). And all three countries reproduce the privatized, middle-class discourse that underpins the maxim 'a man's home is his castle'. In Australia, writers such as Kemeny have argued that the Australian obsession with owner-occupied housing feeds into the circularity of a home-ownership ideology at the expense of all other forms of tenure (Kemeny 1983). Consequently, home ownership has become a key component of cultural citizenship to the extent that its possession flattens out cultural difference, and becomes the path to national belonging.

Of course, the home programmes, particularly in Britain and Australia, also reflect the increasing commodification of houses and the increasing economic importance of the property market. Brunsdon sees the British property shows as reflecting an increase in home ownership, with two-thirds of the population now living in owner-occupied dwellings (Brunsdon 2003, 7). In Australia, with similar rates, the rise of property and home-makeover programmes overlapped with figures which claimed that the median monthly repayments increased by nearly one-third in real terms between 1996 and 2006 (ABS 2007), resulting in a greater financial and cultural preoccupation with housing. The property market is also crucial here, for as Brunsdon puts it: 'The last 20 years of the 20th century saw the consolidation and proliferation of everyday discourses of value and investment associated with the purchase of housing' (2003, 8). This is reflected not only in the home-renovation programmes but also in those dedicated to the property market such as *Hot Auctions*, *Hot Property* and *Auction Squad* in Australia, and *Location, Location, Location*, *Property Ladder* and *Trading Up* in the United Kingdom. This concern over property prices and locations finds particular voice in the United States, through Mike Davis' facetious remarks about Los Angeles' homeowners loving their children, but loving their property values more (1990, 153).

The second socio-cultural reason for the intense focus on the home in everyday life and television shows is the risk society in which many critics claim we now live. Risk society, as both Giddens (1990, 1991, 2002) and Beck (1992) point out, underpins our globalized modern times. They argue that citizens live in a perpetual state of anxiety, driven by economic instability, the threat of nuclear war, terrorism, and environmental destruction. The risk society, however, is not restricted to nuclear, environmental, or terror threats. It resides more subtly in the advance of late capitalism, and the social retreat from the public sphere. As a result of modernity, capitalism and neoliberalism, Western society has become increasingly privatized, leading authors such as Zygmunt Bauman (1998, 2001) to write of a retreat both metaphorically and actually away from 'the public sphere' – as we have known it – to the home. Thatcher's denial of the existence of society, whilst overstated, has some resonance here: we are truly becoming individualized; society is increasingly DIY (see Tomlinson 1990; Rosenberg 2005). Our generalized ontological insecurity stems, partly, from the decline in the collective institutional support mechanisms of the state, the workplace or the family as social life becomes increasingly the survival of the fittest. It is this insecurity that is transforming how citizens are approaching the home.

This risk-induced anxiety has produced a renewed interest in the idea of home, both in terms of national homelands and cultural security (see Rapport and Dawson 1998; Harvey 1990) and the physical security of houses (see Davis 1990). The house has become a sort of refuge against the runaway world (Giddens 2002), a space of control in a world of flux, offering symbolic protection from the vagaries of the modern world in as much as the house protects one from the elements (see Rosenberg 2004). Yet the home as the symbol of shelter is not unique to global modernity and late capitalism. The house has long been what Bachelard describes as 'a major zone of protection' (1994, 31), offering both physical and symbolic shelter. But today we employ lifestylization processes to mask the signs of (in)security. Through making over our homes we can symbolically erase or dislodge the build-up of risk from the very walls we hope will protect us. Risk then becomes managed through consumption and lifestyle.

Home makeovers and the paradox of consumption and thrift

Much scholarly research on lifestyle television has been critically concerned with the role of consumption. June Deery argues that makeover programmes offer a space for capitalism to appropriate and commodify all manner of experiences and sell them at a profit. She suggests that such programmes function primarily as platforms to advertise goods and services which 'promote an all-encompassing and infallible consumerist ethos' (2006, 159). Lifestyle television has proved to be a boon for television networks and advertisers, as product placement and sponsorship opportunities come to the fore. Property programmes in particular offer enormous possibilities for promoting and advertising a raft of domestic goods and services such as home loans, DIY tools and commodities, décor and furniture wares.

In relation to the American programme *Extreme Makeover: Home Edition*, Palmer writes that sponsors play a particularly important role in the construction of community and promote their role as good corporate citizens. This radical programme makes over the houses of 'needy' families and draws upon a large group of neighbours and national and local businesses to help rebuild their lives by rebuilding their homes. Yet it goes beyond much of makeover television's 'renovation on a budget' theme, often building structures which are much larger and more up-market than those in the neighbourhood, which may cause future conflict. Corporate sponsors, such as the retailing giant Sears, gain fantastic PR from helping these 'needy' families. They use the show as a platform to demonstrate the company's benevolence, that it has the best interests of Americans at heart, a benevolence that can be repaid through shopping at its stores. Local businesses and churches also place themselves at the centre of communities through the assistance they offer the show through advertising or sponsorship or, as in the case of the churches, through spreading the good word about the programme, the network it is on (ABC) and the programme sponsors (Palmer 2007). Hence the programmes promote not just consumption in general but also target consumption via the purchase of sponsors' goods and services, promoting not only the circulation of financial capital but also attaching what I would term a moral capital to this spending.

Morality and consumption loom large in home-makeover shows that 'work' in the service of self or community improvement. As Deery goes on to argue, they:

> promote the capitalist credo that one can buy happiness, that through consumption you or your life experience can be fixed or improved. What is being depicted in the makeover show is not change for its own sake ... but change for the better. So there is a deep psychological and even a residual moral component to this transaction. Consumers are urged to improve self and environment or be perceived as both materially and ethically lacking. (2006, 160)

Guy Redden agrees, seeing makeover television as an important component of a wider consumer culture with its optimistic narratives about life getting better, which 'constitutes a moral vision of consumption' as an act leading to improvement (2007, 152). He goes further, regarding makeover shows as constituting 'the modification of attitudes, behaviour and lifestyle so as to enhance personal wellbeing to a putatively life-changing extent. This is effected largely via participants learning how to select and consume goods and services appropriately' (150).

Softening the approach somewhat, Francis Bonner writes:

> Lifestyle television addresses an individualised viewer with advice about consumption practices ostensibly designed to improve the quality of life. Actual audiences are addressed inasmuch as they recognise themselves and their desires within what the program is offering, but the fantasies on offer are structured to be inclusive wherever possible. In the overwhelming majority of cases, the advice given aims to bring viewing consumers up to date with recent practices and fashions so that they may maintain an appearance not too out of step with their peers. (2000, 106)

What such criticisms fail to recognize is that, despite this centrality of consumption, most home-makeover programmes do not take it to the extremes witnessed on the aptly named *Extreme Makeover: Home Edition*. Most home-related programmes work not within a sphere of uncontrolled consumption but within a discourse of thrift. Hence they promote consumption as a key ingredient for self-construction and upward social mobility, as witnessed by Redden's statement above regarding appropriate consumption. Yet, paradoxically, they also offer suggestions for controlling consumption, for employing thrift.

Australian home-related programmes such as *Better Homes & Gardens*, *Auction Squad* and *Renovation Rescue* frequently employ a discourse of thrift, offering makeover tips for those on a budget. The most famous home-makeover programme of all, Britain's *Changing Rooms*, was likewise structured upon a budget of £500 for couples to transform each other's rooms. The website of the American series *Design on a Dime* clearly states its intent for aesthetic transformation combined with thrifty consumption by working within the relatively small budget of US$1000. It describes its *raison d'être* thus:

> *Design on a Dime* makes over a space for design-conscious home dwellers who want lots of style but may not have lots of money for the project. With a budget of $1,000, a design team tackles a problem area such as a boring bedroom, lackluster living room, cluttered dining room or outdated office space. Together, the team transforms the ordinary into the awesome. And what fun to see the residents' reaction to their new room! The budget isn't big, but the payoff sure is! (http://www.hgtv.com/hgtv/shows_dod/)

How do programmes combine this sense of thrift and consumer advice? *Auction Squad* combines the two. Interior designer Candy Day argues that renovation does not have to mean complete transformation. A similar effect can be achieved by what she terms 'low-cost but big impact changes', which can vastly improve a house's appeal on auction day. In regards to a kitchen, she replaces old blinds with modern Venetian blinds, installs contemporary halogen lighting and 'simply' updates some handles on the cupboards. Candy is adamant that such small low-cost cosmetic changes can have a big impact in the home's saleability. Hence such programmes promote thrift and consumption by offering consumer advice for 'low-cost but big impact changes', suggesting a means by which to control, but never escape, the centrality of consumption.

This discourse of thrift, and its complicated and paradoxical relationship with consumption, brings class and status to the fore. These programmes offer solutions to the problem of aesthetic lag and lack of what Bourdieu terms 'cultural capital', that is, a stock of knowledge about aesthetic objects and practices, such as Art or Design (Bourdieu 1984). They offer the lower and middle classes quick-fix solutions to achieve a passable level of cultural capital relating to questions of taste and domestic aesthetics, and achieve the appearance of 'style' with a minimum of time and money. They are targeted at Bourdieu's most despised class fraction – the new petit-bourgeoisie – who are 'predisposed to play a vanguard role in the struggles over everything concerned with the art of living, in particular, domestic life and consumption' (366–7). The new petit-bourgeoisie seek to bypass the long process of knowledge accumulation and take 'illegitimate' short-cuts to possess 'legitimate culture', a short-cut provided by these programmes. The programmes are, as Gareth Palmer describes in relation to British television, 'the bearers of old middle-classness ... bringing apparently effortless "good taste" to the new and more insecure classes' (2004, 178).

Auction Squad: Modernization and the mockery of taste

This section explores this in relation to the Australian property makeover programme *Auction Squad*, which screened from 2002 to 2005, in a primetime slot on Channel Seven. This programme focused upon houses up for auction, to demonstrate how minor aesthetic transformations can improve the resale value of one's home. Whilst experts are central to this programme, *Auction Squad* is dominated by the non-expert, lower middle-class host Johanna Griggs. Despite her lack of expertise and cultural capital, Griggs has no trouble airing her opinions on matters of style and taste.

The taste education provided to audiences and participants in *Auction Squad* revolves around a specific aesthetic that I term 'soft-modernism'. If we understand modernism to be an aesthetic that is minimalist, tonal, anti-decorative and functional, then soft-modernism is a popularized and democratized version of that, which is less strict in terms of palette and form. Palmer describes it as a necessarily limited aesthetic:

> the style on display here also measures the limits of acceptability for a class who may be 'new' to the whole idea of 'décor'. Thus the affordable, sensible and colour co-ordinated solutions offered by the new experts offer style with minimal aesthetic involvement for a newly risen class who may be uncomfortable about making 'artistic' choices. (2004, 181)

Yet this limited style serves two key purposes for such classes. Firstly, it offers a sense of status and possible social mobility because of its connections to elite modernism. It operates as a key mode of what Jim Collins calls 'high-pop', which refers to the transmission of high-cultural products through a mass-cultural medium, such as television, to a mass market (Collins 2002), a process which paradoxically problematizes the notion of distinction. Secondly, the transmission of this form of cultural capital via the screen can be converted into financial capital, for this aesthetic has become central to the property market. It can serve to increase the sale price, or at least the speed of the sale, which has real economic effects. Because it is also relatively bland it de-personalizes spaces, removing any idiosyncratic aesthetic (and clutter) which may offend any potential buyers who have their own personalization schemes to imagine for the space. *Auction Squad*'s employment of soft-modernism then functions to cleanse or purify (see Douglas 1978) the home of the previous owner, and allows the space for creative thinking on the part of the potential new owner. The deployment of this aesthetic, then, has become central to the machinations of the property market, either through increasing property values or through speeding up the sale process.

Whilst some property makeover programmes reward 'deserving' recipients, *à la Extreme Makeover: Home Edition* and its focus on poor and needy families, *Auction Squad* often merely emphasizes the process of aesthetic transformation. The makeover recipients in the episode I examine here were an elderly Anglo-Celtic divorced couple who needed to sell their house for financial reasons, but nothing too dire. If anything was deserving of the show's renovation gift, it was the house. Because it had been lying aesthetically stagnant for decades, its problems were aesthetic rather than structural, but this would still require a maximum makeover effort to correct its 'bad' and outdated taste.

Prior to the makeover the house was a seemingly featureless 1950s suburban brick-veneer – until you see inside, where the interiors have not changed since the 1960s, featuring orange and brown wallpaper, floral printed furnishings, brown leather easy-chairs and a 'garish' shaggy aquamarine carpet. The house lacks any sense of being what Palmer notes as 'co-ordinated'. It shocks potential buyers who we see inspecting the house before auction day. They comment that the house is 'pretty dated', the colours are odd, and the wallpaper is a 'bit much'. The shaggy aquamarine carpet both shocks and amuses, with one woman claiming that the house is 'before her time', adding that she has never seen a house like this before, whereas another notes that it is a flashback to 'grandma's house'.

This house was chosen for its ability to be mocked, made explicit in the programme's lead-in promo: 'turn down the volume on loud décor and impress buyers with *Auction Squad*'. The house's décor was indeed 'too loud', both for the makeover team and the potential buyers who were bemused by its petrified and neglected aesthetic state. This ridicule served as a disciplinary tool, and continued with host (and non-expert) Johanna Griggs during a 'mocking tour' of the house. She quips that once inside, one enters a 'perfectly preserved time-capsule' dating to an age when wallpaper was cherished, facetiously adding, 'whether it clashed with the carpet or not'. She states that such homes were boxy with 'lots of small separated rooms all focusing in, rather than out as we do now', and that in the 1950s 'durable, no non-sense surfaces were favoured over earthy timbers and natural floorings', in contradistinction to the now-dominant fashion of parquetry. This is technical advice for viewers on how modern homes should look.

The promotion of 'good taste' through signs of the contemporary is articulated both visually and verbally, by experts such as designer Will Dangar, who declares that he will demonstrate 'how to turn brassy into classy' for the frontage by 'toning down' the colour scheme and strategically planting trees to 'smart up' things. Inside, Griggs describes the use of a colour called 'mudpack' for the walls, a light tonal colour, a mixture of beige, grey and brown – a sort of grey café-latte. She says: 'This new colour, "mudpack", is probably the first truly contemporary look, the interior has seen in fifty years'; suggesting that the house has been in virtual aesthetic decline since then, and valorizing contemporary style over personalized decorative schemas. Dangar then offers some interesting aesthetic education. Colour choice is, he claims, one of the most difficult decorative decisions. He warns against using fashionable colours that, whilst fine at the time, can date and end up 'ugly'. The difficulty lies in choosing between personal preference, fashion, and aesthetic longevity, a decision framed again by questions of class, taste and social distinction (Bourdieu 1984). Dangar replaces the extremely unfashionable bright yellow on the front door and window trims with a combination of white (which Le Corbusier declares is *the* modernist tone; see Leslie and Reimer 2003) and steely-blue. He states that whilst such colours may not be at the height of fashion now, they are durable, but, more importantly, will always look 'smart'. He declares that fashion is not as 'good' or 'effective' as good design, and part of good design, he maintains, is the right colour choice. Hence good design and stylistic longevity trump fashionability. Such a scene also highlights the difficulty in determining what colours *are* 'good design', with stylistic longevity, and what are merely 'fashionable'. For example, will the soft-modernist fashionable colours such as 'mudpack' or chocolate brown have aesthetic longevity, or will their very fashionability destroy their chance at 'good design'?

Throughout the hour-long show, the viewer watches the transformation process, listens to the experts' advice, and sits through their demonstrations, waiting for the final scenes when the makeover is revealed to recipient and audience alike. It is important to note that the recipients do not undertake any labour. They are, like in many home-makeover programmes, removed from the house during its transformation, which heightens the importance of the reveal. After the revelation to the recipient, the focus shifts solely to the house and its aesthetic transformation through the use of before-and-after shots. These disembodied shots concentrate on the aesthetic transformation and are reminiscent of serious high-end design magazines and programmes such as the Australian LifeStyle Channel's *Home*, where domestic aesthetics become revered like art (see Moseley 2000). These before-and-after scenes were the slowest moving in the programme, accompanied by slower, more introspective music compared to earlier fast-paced reconstruction scenes. The segment was long too, more than double the average, which underscores the importance of the aesthetic transformation with the ratio of 'after' versus 'before' shots being approximately 2:1.

During these conversion shots we are given another voiceover tour by Griggs. She uses the programme's cultural authority to judge the recipient's house with statements suggesting that pre-makeover, the house was 'neat, predictable, a little dull', but post-makeover, it is 'softer', and paradoxically, more 'individual'. The language of rebirth and renewal are also constantly employed, witnessed again in her comments about the meals area which she refers to as 'a space that's really quite funky after painting, de-cluttering and re-furnishing', favouring the modern ideology of simplicity over cluttered and un-modern personalized spaces. Yet despite the transition to rooms which are 'quite modern', Griggs also claims that they are still 'lovely sort of living areas'.

And because *Auction Squad* reproduces this modern de-personalized aesthetic to increase financial returns, its effectiveness is demonstrated by positive responses from potential buyers who were also present prior to the makeover. One young woman says that she likes the new paint colour which she describes as 'very modern', and a middle-age woman regards the new decorative order as 'much more today'. Whilst such 'ordinary' folk do not use modern design language, preferring a commodified real estate language, all regarded the changes as positive, necessary for the house to gain a good price, which it eventually does. *Auction Squad* then provides insight into an emerging property market aesthetic, which relies of the minimal use of colour (except where heritage laws apply), and the reduction of virtually anything which provides information about the sellers. With increased mobility in the property market, this raises questions as to whether individual aesthetic regimes will be subordinated to the homogenizing cultural logic of the property market.

Conclusion

This paper has sought to demonstrate some of the contributing factors surrounding the rise of property shows in Australia, Britain and the United States. In addition to being cheap to make, the paper suggests that the proliferation of home and property shows has been partly driven by a combination of two factors. Firstly, it explores the manner in which the risk society has produced an anxious citizenry who increasingly turn to the home for personal and cultural solace. Secondly, it suggests that the proliferation has been the result of an emergent home-ownership ideology within the three countries, where the home has become central to national identity. Yet the present state of their property markets has resulted in homes becoming less the 'family nest' than a crucial part of an individual's financial portfolio. The paper suggests that television home shows promote aesthetic transformation and a taste education that overshadow the didactic nature of the programmes. This aesthetic education leads to the accumulation of cultural capital that can be converted into financial capital through the property market. The paper also explores how such programmes promote a 'correct' form of consumption. Yet it suggests, contra much of the research into lifestyle television, that a discourse of thrift is equally present. Thrift, it suggests, allows individuals not only to consume in the present but also become financially prudent, lifelong *consumers*. Thrifty consumption then, operates to ease potential risk that may arise from over-consumption, which could threaten both an individual's ability to own a home, and the stability of the three national cultures, built upon the home-ownership ideology. Hence property and home-makeover shows promote the centrality of the home and home ownership to both national and political culture. They offer guidance on matters of taste, which produces cultural capital that can be converted into financial capital through the property market. Through the promotion of thrift they teach individuals to be prudent, but lifelong *consumers*, which will ensure the reproduction of the home-ownership ideology, which supports both national culture and the stability of the present capitalist political economy.

References

Australian Bureau of Statistics (ABS). 2007. *Australia's big picture: Census highlights the changes in Australian society.* Census of Population and Housing, Media Release and Fact Sheet no. 2914.0.55.002. 27 June.

Bachelard, G. 1994. *The poetics of space.* Boston: Beacon.

Bauman, Z. 1998. *Globalization: The human consequences.* Cambridge: Polity Press.

———. 2001. *Community: Seeking safety in an insecure world.* Cambridge: Polity Press.

Beck, U. 1992. *Risk society: Towards a new modernity.* London: Sage.

Bonner, F. 2000. Lifestyle programs: 'No choice but to choose'. In *The Australian TV book*, ed. G. Turner and S. Cunningham, 103–16. St Leonards: Allen & Unwin.

Bourdieu, P. 1984. *Distinction: A social critique of the judgement of taste.* Trans. R. Nice. London: Routledge.

Brunsdon, C. 2003. Lifestyling Britain: The 8–9 slot on British television. *International Journal of Cultural Studies* 6, no. 1: 5–23.

Collins, J. 2002. High-pop: An introduction. In *High-pop: Making culture into popular entertainment*, ed. J. Collins, 1–31. Oxford: Blackwell.

Davis, M. 1990. *City of quartz: Excavating the future in Los Angeles*. London: Verso.

Davison, B., and G. Davison. 1995. Suburban pioneers. In *The Cream brick frontier: Histories of Australian suburbia*, ed. G. Davison, T. Dingle, and S. O'Hanlon, 41–50. Clayton: Department of History, Monash University.

Davison, G. 1993. *The past and future of the Australian suburb*. Urban Research Program. Canberra: ANU.

Deery, J. 2006. Interior design: Commodifying self and place in *Extreme Makeover, Extreme Makeover: Home Edition*, and *The Swan*. In *The great American makeover: Television, history, nation*, ed. D. Heller, 159–74. New York: Palgrave Macmillan.

Douglas, M. 1978. *Purity and danger: An analysis of concepts of pollution and taboo*. London: Routledge & Kegan Paul.

Fishman, R. 1987. *Bourgeois utopias: The rise and fall of suburbia*. New York: Basic Books.

Garreau, J. 1991. *Edge city: Life on the new frontier*. New York: Doubleday.

Giddens, A. 1990. *The consequences of modernity*. Cambridge: Polity Press.

———. 1991. *Modernity and self-identity: Self and society in the late modern age*. Cambridge: Polity Press.

———. 2002. *Runaway world: How globalisation is reshaping our lives*. 2nd ed. London: Profile Books.

Harrison, T. 1994. *The Australian film and television companion*. East Roseville, NSW: Simon & Schuster.

Harvey, D. 1990. *The condition of postmodernity*. Cambridge: Blackwell.

Kavka, M. 2006. Changing properties: The makeover shows crosses the Atlantic. In *The great American makeover: Television, history, nation*, ed. D. Heller, 211–29. New York: Palgrave Macmillan.

Kemeny, J. 1983. *The great Australian nightmare: A critique of the home-ownership ideology*. Melbourne: Georgian House.

Leslie, D., and S. Reimer. 2003. Gender, modern design, and home consumption. *Environment and Planning D: Society and Space* 21, no. 3: 293–316.

Moseley, R. 2000. Makeover takeover on British television. *Screen* 41, no. 3: 299–314.

O'Sullivan, T. 2005. From television lifestyle to lifestyle television. In *Ordinary lifestyles: Popular media, consumption and taste*, ed. D. Bell and J. Hollows, 21–34. Maidenhead: Open University Press.

Palmer, G. 2004. 'The new you': Class and transformation in lifestyle television. In *Understanding reality television*, ed. S. Holmes and D. Jermyn, 173–90. London and New York: Routledge.

———. 2007. *Extreme Makeover: Home Edition* An American fairytale. In *Makeover television: Realities remodelled*, ed. D. Heller, 165–76. London and New York: I.B. Tauris.

Rapport, N., and A. Dawson, eds. 1998. *Migrants of identity: Perceptions of home in a world of movement*. New York and Oxford: Berg.

Redden, G. 2007. Makeover morality and consumer culture. In *Makeover television: Realities remodelled*, ed. D. Heller, 150–64. London and New York: I.B. Tauris.

Rosenberg, B.C. 2004. 'Safe as houses': Risky cities, consumption and the home. *Antithesis Forum*. http://www.english.unimelb.edu.au/antithesis/forum2004/rosenberg.html (accessed 3 September 2005).

———. 2005. Scandinavian dreams: DIY, democratisation and IKEA. *Transformations*, no. 11, http://transformationsjournal.org/journal/issue_11/article_02.shtml (accessed 25 May 2008).

Tomlinson, A. 1990. Home fixtures: Doing-it-yourself in a privatized world. In *Consumption, identity, and style: Marketings, meanings, and the packaging of pleasure*, ed. A. Tomlinson, 57–73. London and New York: Routledge.

Website

Design on a Dime. http://www.hgtv.com/hgtv/shows_dod/ (accessed 29 October 2007).

Media-bodies and screen-births: Cosmetic surgery reality television

Meredith Jones

'What was it like when you saw the new you?'
'Shocking. Absolutely shocking. There was this person standing in front of you. It was kind of almost like you weren't in your own body.' (Rachel Love-Fraser, winner of *The Swan*, series one, *Larry King Live* 2004)

Even in reality TV, where, in the live telling of the story, in the immediate televised acting, we witness the confusion of the existence and its double … One enters one's life while walking onto a screen. One puts on one's own life like a digital suit. (Baudrillard 2005)

Introduction

Cosmetic surgery reality television (CSRTV) is not merely about cosmetic surgery, nor merely about reality television: it is a blend of these two areas and hence both media and bodies must be analysed when examining it.[1] I suggest that this genre sits at a nexus of transformed bodies that are at once fleshy and digital, three-dimensional and two-dimensional, on the screen and in the living world.

Reality television has been derided as exhibitionistic and banal: a sad indictment of 'low' culture at its most superficial. Salman Rushdie famously described it in 2001 as an 'inverted ethical universe [where] worse is better' (2001). However, as other writers, including those in this issue show, it is also meaningfully interactive and empowering for audiences (Roscoe 2001). While it is panoptic – self-regulating, disciplining, normalizing – it is also pleasurable and seductive. Indeed, its 'surveillance is not only tolerated, but frequently sought after' (McQuire 2003, 116). Further, its mass appeal and global reach are important parts of contemporary culture (Andrejevic 2003; Holmes 2004; Huff 2006; Heller 2007).

Similarly, cosmetic surgery entails far more than the common stereotype of a wealthy and vain woman seeking a surgical procedure in order to look younger or more beautiful. It begs questions to do with authenticity, agency, popular culture, and changing meanings of ageing. Cosmetic surgery is intricately entwined with gender construction (Fraser 2003), is often about seeking 'normality' rather than beauty (Davis 1995), has very different meanings according to national contexts (Edmonds n.d.) and is part of a growing and global 'makeover culture' (Jones 2008).

CSRTV has lately been made up of US shows such as *Extreme Makeover*, *The Swan*, *I Want a Famous Face*, and *Dr 90210*, with other programmes surely to come. The United Kingdom has *10 Years Younger*, Japan has *Beauty Coliseum*, China has *Lovely Cinderella*. In these programmes reality television and cosmetic surgery are entwined for the purposes of modifying bodies and making entertainment: when surgical modification takes place within the highly surveilled space of reality television some profound intersections occur. I suggest that the bodies modified by CSRTV are 'media-bodies' that come about via 'screen-births'. They traverse boundaries between representation and reality, and between skin and screen. They are therefore potentially both radical and terrifying.

The argument presented here is based on a close reading of *The Swan*'s reveal scenes. I suggest that *The Swan*'s reveal is the quintessential example of a rebirthing metaphor that permeates all CSRTV. I trace cinematic links between the reveal and some contemporary horror films in relation to metaphors of birth and rebirth, and show that horror and CSRTV genres share concerns about human hybridity, and about the blending of flesh and media.

'The Swan'

The Swan, created by Nely Galán (a well-known Hollywood producer who is also the programme's 'life-coach'), is a CSRTV programme in which participants are removed from their everyday lives for a period of months during which they undergo multiple cosmetic surgeries. They also submit to brutal grooming, diet and exercise regimes supervised by an army of experts from makeup artists to fitness instructors. Two women, usually white, feature in each episode. They are introduced to the audience as deserving, interesting, and somewhat pathetic in their un-madeover states. We are encouraged to feel sorry for them and to barrack for them in their quests to improve their lives through cosmetic surgery. Each episode climaxes with a dramatic 'reveal' ceremony where newly created bodies and faces are displayed to friends, families, and the world. *The Swan* is a little different from its most famous counterpart, *Extreme Makeover*, because it adds an element of competition between the participants: a beauty pageant. At the end of each episode the two makeover recipients are pitted against each other to see who has made the most dramatic transformation. The winner remains to compete in the pageant; the loser goes home. Another important contrast to *Extreme Makeover* and most other CSRTV shows is that on *The Swan* the contestant is revealed to herself at the same time that she is revealed on television. Crucially, mirrors are completely banned for the period of production: for three months, from surgery to reveal, *The Swan* contestants live in a reflection-free world. So crucial is this rule that one contestant, Tanya (episode seven, series one), was disqualified for having packed a mirror in her suitcase.

Reveals and screen-births

In Bernadette Wegenstein and Geoffrey Alan Rhodes' excellent documentary film *Made Over in America* (2007) a young woman looks at her new and old selves on a computer screen after competing in *The Swan* and having a nose job, a brow and mid-facelift, 'cheek refinement' fat removal from below her eyes, lip augmentation, liposuction, shortening of the chin, a facial resurfacing procedure, hair removal, collagen injections, Lasik eye surgery, breast augmentation, liposuction of the inner thighs, and an abdominoplasty (tummy tuck). As she gazes at the images Cindy is serious and thoughtful: 'well, I definitely like the new better. But seeing the old I'm glad that old is there too because it was, it was me' (she becomes tearful) 'and I can't forget that, I shouldn't forget that.' She recalls her reveal, before which she hadn't seen her body or face for months:

> There is this huge dark red burgundy type curtain and it's the only thing that's between me and the mirror. The only thing between the last Cindy I saw and the new Cindy I'm gonna see. And then the curtains open and then I see myself for the first time and I'm kind of doing what I'm doing now [bending forward, hands on face, crying]. But I just, you know I'm so surprised and I just immediately put my hands over my face and I'm not real sure that it's me. It looks like me but I'm not real sure. And so, and then I just, like I have to know for sure if it was me so I walk up to the mirror, I get close, and then I touch it and I know that it's me and it wasn't something fake on the other side and that it's really me ...

Cindy's extraordinary experience – of almost magical transformation and having to recognize a new self – is the stuff of fairy stories and horror movies. CSRTV has more in common with these older narratives than we might first think, sharing with them themes of rebirth, transition, hardship, endurance, and eventually reward and fulfilment. Philosopher Cressida Heyes points out that in fairy stories and in most CSRTV narratives 'frightening transitions culminate in a stable perfection that bears no traces of earlier trauma' (2007, 102) while cultural theorist Brenda Weber has described *Extreme Makeover* as 'a modern-day Pilgrim's Progress where worthy subjects must undergo humiliation and endure multiple tests in order to arrive at a better place' (2005, bit 19; see also Gailey 2007, 111).

The Swan's narratives of transformation and self-recognition are told directly through contestants like Cindy but also by way of its settings and cinematography: this is particularly clear in the programme's most dramatic moment, the reveal. The reveal's set is luxurious, floored in marble. One wall is sumptuously draped with wide, red, ceiling-height curtains. On either side of the curtains sit antique bedside tables topped with small vases of roses and softly glowing bedside lamps. The *mise-en-scène* evokes both boudoir and cinema: the heavy brocade curtains are cinematic but the style and scale of the furnishings signal the intimacy of a bedroom; in fact, the vertical curtains replace the horizontal bed that would usually appear between the two bedside tables. This theatrical yet intimate set is itself a hybrid, signalling that the reveal is both a public and a private moment, happening in communal and in secret spaces.[2] The action at the reveal is, significantly, a mix of embraces, tears, laughter and *applause*: a heady mix showing how performance and intimacy are intertwined.

The cinematography is also highly expressive in the reveal scenes. As the woman stands before the closed curtains the camera at first sweeps in from above, from behind, from afar. The curtains are looped with tassels and all is anticipation as they rise and separate. But the camera's omniscience quickly becomes personal: highly mobile, it swoops down and moves *behind* the mirror that the curtains have uncovered. Then, it continues to film *through* the mirror. This cinematographic transition from transcendence to immanence again signals an important oscillation between private and public, secret and shared experiences.

Once the camera is established behind the mirror it captures every tiny facial expression, every tear and quiver. Crying, laughing, the woman tentatively touches her face and her body. This is an orgasmic moment, in the centre of the 'bed' where ecstasy is achieved via interactions between old self and new self. This rebirth may have been facilitated by all of *The Swan*'s experts but is finally about connection between one person's selves. Media theorist Mark Poster has suggested that CSRTV exemplifies a form of media culture that carries Baudrillard's concept of the hyperreal to new levels and illustrates a landscape of 'hitherto unimaginable combinations of humans and information machines' (2008 in press, n.p.). It is about representation and simulacrum whilst remaining utterly corporeal. It manoeuvres inside an aesthetic and visual system where two-dimensional images and three-dimensional 'realities' are profoundly intertwined, and where flat images and actual embodied form beg to be reconciled. In the reveal body and body image are finally one: feeling, affect, and movement match – for once, and however briefly – appearance, exterior and reflection. This is the moment when two-dimensional and three-dimensional selves are reconciled.

The reveal is also a birthing moment: the endometrial richness of the curtains, their slow vulval parting, the long labour of sweat and blood and tears leading up to this revelation. Here the woman is both mother and child: giving birth to herself she is powerfully and substantially reborn.[3] And it is absolutely satisfying: the contestant is 'complete' (as so many of them say they are) while at a symbolic level image and flesh have truly melded. Together, body and body image in this moment are about being, about having *become*. Donald Bull, Executive Producer of *90210*, says that being on television is 'a validation of who you are in our culture. If you're on TV then therefore you exist. You are not invisible any longer' (in Wegenstein and Rhodes 2007). At the reveal, then, for a televisual moment, all is well with the world.

As described above, in *The Swan*'s reveal scenes the camera moves behind the mirror in order to film through it. Thus, mirror literally becomes screen – the two are visually inseparable. At the reveal contestants approach the mirror-screen, stare into their own (and our) eyes and touch its reflective surface like infants discovering themselves. This is a revelatory moment between the contestant and the audience, between the contestant's new and old selves, and between the contestant and the mirror-screen-camera. As she contacts the mirror with her fingertips, she simultaneously appears to be touching the inside of the television screen and almost seems to be reaching out to us, to be about to step out of the television world and into the real world. And, in a sense, this is what happens: after their makeovers 'inside' the television, contestants *do* step out into the world, but with newly formed media-bodies. Many declare 'I look like a movie star!' – and indeed, success in this format can lead to a continued suitability for life on and in the screen (the first *Swan* winner went on to be a television personality). This intense reveal scene, then, of mirror–screen symbiosis and of rebirth, is a demonstration of physical and media worlds meshing, of media-bodies coming into being, of actual screen-births.

The look

In her classic 1993 analysis of *Alien*, Barbara Creed tells us that the look has been theorized in three main ways in cinema. Firstly, the camera looks at the filmic action; secondly, characters within the film look (outwards and within the *mise-en-scène*); and thirdly, the spectator looks at the screen. Creed adds another look, specific to the genre of horror: that of the spectator 'looking away'. This look happens during scary moments in which we are simultaneously too frightened to look and also have a strong desire to look. In the same way, many contestants on *The Swan* are at first unable to look at themselves in the mirror. They cover their eyes, hands shaking. Some peek out quickly, glancing, then hide again. So the tension that Creed identifies when we are frightened to look yet *must* look is present in the reveal: this is one of the characteristics that aligns it with horror movies. In fact, contestants on *The Swan* actually experience all of the looks that Creed identifies: because of the camera *being* the mirror in these scenes, and the contestants looking 'through' it, they *are* the camera, hence they have the first look. As characters on screen they have the second look. They are also spectators, looking at themselves, and of course they 'look away'.

This genre is one in which women's bodies are made over, surveilled, and squeezed into rigid gender stereotypes. And yet there is great joy expressed in the reveals and a sense of wholeness conveyed to the audience. I suggest this is partly because all four looks are conflated in the body of *The Swan* contestants. Their ownership of multiple gazes strengthens the reveal as a scene of rebirth or of self-birth: it becomes a kind of parthenogenesis in which woman is further empowered by being witness to her own creation. In this way this genre, repressive in so many ways, offers power to its subjects. Indeed, the combination of power and submission is one of the abiding tensions in CSRTV: Elizabeth Atwood Gailey asserts that CSRTV participants, 'emerging from the ritualized ideal of surgery ... are, paradoxically, both liberated from and reinscribed with their own subordination' (2007, 118).

Skin-screen

The intimate moments between representation and reality and between media-bodies and flesh-bodies in *The Swan*'s reveals have a filmic history. Further, I suggest that parallels between skin (in cosmetic surgery) and screen (in horror) can be identified in order to show that when these membranes are broken possibilities for new bodies are created.

In Jonathan Demme's film *The Silence of the Lambs* (1991) a serial killer, Jame Gumb, uses pieces of skin 'harvested' from his victims to stitch together a new 'true' identity for himself. In parallel, cosmetic surgery – also very much about skin – is linked with expressing one's 'true' inner self. Heyes writes: 'cosmetic surgery is increasingly represented through the resonant discourse of becoming one's true self by having one's body represent the person one feels one is inside' (2007, 89). In other words, by cutting and pasting and rearranging the skin, flesh, cartilage and bone, we manufacture more appropriate physical identities. In cosmetic surgery we put on a flesh suit, in some ways like Jame Gumb's. Similarly, Baudrillard's image of the 'digital suit' donned by participants in reality television (quoted at the start of this essay) is another way of making ourselves a new identity, this time through becoming a media image rather than reworking the flesh. In CSRTV these two modes of transformation merge: participants become media images *and* have their bodies reshaped. Flesh and media combine; skin and screen together help participants to form newly manufactured identities.

Skin plays complex and contradictory roles in cosmetic surgery discourse (see Jones 2004). It is shown to be permeable and changeable but also an essential indicator of the 'true' relationship between inner and outer selves. In surgery it is damaged – cut, abraded, thinned – but only in order to become pristine and poreless, as if it has never been damaged at all (scars are hidden at all costs). Skin is characterized as a stable container for the self but also as something utterly malleable. Similarly, screens are both static and mobile: they are barriers between audience and performance but also conduits by which reality and virtuality can interact.

A convergence of skin and screen can be traced through some Hollywood films of the late twentieth and early twenty-first century. These films' imagery often shows skins and screens blending together as well as stretching and breaking. I suggest that they set up an aesthetic of permeable screen and skin that CSRTV owes some of its roots to. They demonstrate the unstable borders of both skin and screen and enact dramatic mergers between the two. Further, they terrifyingly demonstrate social preoccupations and concerns about the melding of bodies and media.

In Toby Hopper and Steven Spielberg's *Poltergeist* (1982) five-year-old Carol Anne is trapped in an alternative world after being drawn to the television where she talks to 'the TV people'. Her mother rescues her by entering the TV void with a rope (umbilical cord) and they are both metaphorically reborn. The movie's promotional poster shows a little girl with her hands pressed up against a brightly glowing television screen. It is hugely evocative of the ways in which contestants touch the mirror-screen in *The Swan*'s reveals. This material touching of skin to screen is part of the visual language of texts that are concerned with media-bodies.

The hero of David Cronenberg's *Videodrome* (1983), Renn, suffers a series of body – media fusions including developing a vagina in his abdomen into which videotapes can be inserted. He watches himself committing suicide on a television set that then explodes with gore and intestines. Finally he shoots himself in 'real life' and our screen goes blank. The film expresses a profound uneasiness about relationships between bodies and media and between reality and virtuality. Significantly, in *Videodrome* the screen is treated as having an ontological existence of its own – no longer merely a medium, the screen itself has *presence*. In one memorable scene a hand holding a gun presses out of a television screen as if it's made of cling film. In *The Swan*'s reveals the camera ends up almost touching the contestant's face, and indeed, she touches *its* 'face' when she caresses the mirror-screen. Skin and screen here are intimately connected and in some ways serve similar purposes. Both are membranes separating self from other, real from unreal. Both are being integrated, compromised, opened. When recipients of CSRTV makeovers 'step out' of their screens they have stretched both their skins and the screen, joining previously separated worlds. In this way these are hybrid citizens: they have been remade in media and are thus 'born' in two worlds; they are media-bodies.

In Gore Verbinski's *The Ring* (2002), a Hollywood remake of Hideo Nakata's Japanese *Ringu* (1998), the screen's ontological power is violated. Its membranous status as barrier between real and virtual worlds is not merely stretched but broken. An extraordinary climactic scene shows a television that turns itself on, buzzing with static. Noah, one of the main characters, turns it off. It then turns itself on again, to a long-shot of a stone well in a wintry wood. Noah comes close to the television, kneeling before it. A ghostly girl-child, Samara, her long black hair hanging over her face, crawls out of the well and then begins to walk stiffly towards the screen. Noah slides backwards, terrified yet mesmerized. The impossible then happens: Samara crouches and her black hair droops, seaweed-like, out of the television. Her white hand stretches through the screen and she crawls into the room. Importantly, the final shot before she materializes is taken from *behind* the television: in this way the audience is briefly moved from identifying with Noah to identifying with Samara: we identify for just a moment with the killer rather than the victim. This change in camera angle is crucial: it is similar to the far more extended moment of camera-behind-mirror that happens in *The Swan*'s reveals. Although most of *The Ring*'s cinematography invites us to identify with the people Samara is tormenting, this brief shot offers an alternative: we could *be* Samara just as we could *be* a *Swan* contestant, except that in *The Ring* we are invited to identify with a media-body that is deeply malevolent.

Poster, in a fascinating essay about Freudian psychoanalysis, children, and television, suggests that 'the logic of the screen is one of incorporation: of the child by the screen and the screen by the child' (2006, 175). He writes: 'the screen is thus a liminal object, an interface between the human and the machine that invites penetration of each by the other' (175). Analysing the *Teletubbies* programme and the bodies of the teletubbies themselves (cuddly creatures with televisions in their torsos), he argues that 'beings and televisions are one assemblage ... [thus] the viewing child might be a television' (179). In the same way, I suggest that our own body images are connected to and are sometimes dependent upon and interchangeable with the 'media-bodies' that CSRTV presents. CSRTV bodies and similarly presented bodies in other media are far more than just representations: we are as much one with them as our children are one with the teletubbies. These programmes are not just illustrations, they actually have a role in creating bodies and influencing body image and they help to form real bodies (in the case of cosmetic surgery, literally). Scalpels may not push through our screens like the gun in *Videodrome* but CSRTV aesthetics are nevertheless broadcasting out, penetrating the bodies that watch them. Jack Z. Bratich suggests that 'reality television may be less about representing reality than intervening in it; less mediating and more *involving*' (2007, 6–7; emphasis in original). Think of how cosmetic surgery has become an everyday media event: I have argued elsewhere that CSRTV shows such as *Extreme Makeover* work as a kind of 'cultural anaesthetic': we experience virtual surgery by watching them so that the step to real surgery becomes a little bit easier (2008, 53).

Gender and media-bodies

While there are non-horror films that have similar foci to the movies discussed above, my focus on horror is because this genre is renowned for its ability to express and convey deep (and often hidden) social and cultural fears.[4] James Marriott writes that 'at its best the genre speaks directly to the unconscious, bypassing our rational defences entirely' (2004, 2). Horror also works with metaphors of birth and rebirth: Creed writes that 'one of the major concerns of the sci-fi horror film … is the reworking of the primal scene, the scene of birth' (1993, 17). *Alien* is perhaps the most famous horror film designed around birth imagery: the mother ship's pristine white sleeping pods contrast with its belly of dark and dripping, slimy corridors, the former representing an antiseptic, high-tech birthing of full-grown adults and the latter symbolizing corporeal, mucousy and vaginal births (the famous alien itself attacks purely in order to reproduce, using its victims' bodies as incubators). CSRTV is similarly concerned with birth and rebirth, with tensions between the visceral and the technological. For example, the surgical scenes that are part of the formula are condensed and carefully contained structurally and visually in each episode.

Our fears (and hopes) for the joining of high-tech answers with our very bloody and organic bodies express themselves most distinctly and memorably via horror films. Jean-Pierre Jeunet's 1997 *Alien: Resurrection* shows Ripley, herself a clone, coming into contact with her monstrous progeny. There is an extraordinary – horrifying yet deeply moving – scene where she caresses her grandchild (who is half alien, half human) before killing her. They touch, almost nestling. The alien hybrid is oozing, horrifying, but also strangely beautiful, with large, pleading eyes: in her Ripley sees herself in what A. Samuel Kimball calls 'an agony of recognition' (2002, 100). Like *The Swan*'s reveal, this scene is pivotal, a moment of 'contact', a birth and a death, a recognition of both self and other, and a discarding of one self in favour of another. CSRTV expresses the same cultural concerns about birth, technology, bodies and identity as horror and this is one of the reasons it is so engrossing and entertaining.

However, the beings that are 'birthed' through CSRTV are generally very different from those that come from horror. CSRTV men and women emerge from their makeovers looking highly feminine or highly masculine in a typically Hollywood style. In fact, they often look like Barbie or Ken dolls – the women with long flowing locks, thin but curvaceous bodies, big eyes and lips, and smooth skin. The men gain chin dimples, strong square features, muscular torsos, and full heads of hair. Dan, on *Extreme Makeover*, declared 'Oh my god, I look like an action hero' (season two, episode one). In plunging evening gowns and well-cut suits, femininity and masculinity are overplayed and almost cartoonishly exaggerated.

Although she doesn't discuss CSRTV itself, Rosalind Gill sums up the gendered logics behind it nicely, noting that in media 'the body is presented simultaneously as women's source of power and as always already unruly and requiring constant monitoring, surveillance, discipline and remodeling (and consumer spending) in order to conform to ever narrower judgments of female attractiveness' (2007, 255). In CSRTV to be 'feminine' means being sexy in the manner of a pneumatic teenager; a body that bears the marks of having borne and nourished children is unacceptable. Indeed, the popularity of the 'mommy makeover', in which post-pregnancy bodies are (supposedly) restored to nubile form, demonstrates this trend perfectly.[5]

Gender binaries on CSRTV are stricter and more regressive than in any other television genre: youthful femininity is paramount, lesbians and gay men don't exist, everyone craves hetero-romance and women can't even have short hair (hair extensions are popular).[6] And yet, as I have shown, CSRTV *is* radical: it creates hybrid bodies: it joins bodies with objects (implants, scalpels) and bodies with media. I suggest that the highly conservative presentation of gender in CSRTV happens partly because of the ways in which it produces radical media-bodies.[7] Subjects who have had cosmetic surgery, particularly those on CSRTV, cross many boundaries: human/animal (many injectable wrinkle fillers are made from animal products, including cow skin and the combs of roosters), organic/synthetic, normal/celebrity, real/represented, and even the once uncrossable boundary of ugly and beautiful. But hybrid creatures are disturbing: their in-betweenness creates uncertainty and they signal changes to the accepted order. Margrit

Shildrick writes: 'To be out of place, whether in a wholly organic form or as a techno-organic hybrid, is to show up the faultlines in the closure of normativity, and to gesture towards other modes of existence' (2002, 124).

If CSRTV is to be acceptable to the mainstream (and indeed this is one of its commercial aims – to advertise and promote the cosmetic surgery industry) then the bodies on it must never seem monstrous or abnormal. Hybrid bodies are acceptable only so long as they stick to certain rules about containment, presentation and decorum. Most importantly, they must not 'gesture towards other modes of existence' but rather serve to reinforce the hegemonic order. One of the ways to ablate the possibility of disruption to established paradigms is to make CSRTV bodies utterly traditional in terms of gender and utterly conventional in terms of beauty.

Conclusion

Recipients of CSRTV makeovers are not merely *on* television, they also walk out of the television programme and into the physical world with a media-body, one designed as an ideal image. What good citizens these people are then: how perfectly they fit into our media-saturated world, how well they belong. Scott McQuire notes, *pace* John Tagg, that 'proof that "I" am someone worth photographing or filming constitutes a peculiarly modern proof that "I" exist as a unique individual' (2003, 116). The subjects of CSRTV are moulded and shaped as much by the apparatus of television as by the scalpels and liposuction cannulas that slice and penetrate their flesh. Media-bodies come into being when our bodies interact with media – CSRTV is merely an extreme example of this symbiosis –ordinary people *enter* the television and come out transformed into real, living, 'TV people'. Participants declare 'I'm my true self now' and 'this is the real me'. Such pronouncements seem absurd in the context of such a repressive set of aesthetics, but Weber suggests that in an 'image-centered culture, such as ours, perhaps [no statements are] more valid' (2005, bit 12; see also Finkelstein 2007). Thus, these people become featured extras, or perhaps even stars, in a hybrid media-reality that includes their own lives. This was something Baudrillard recognized in 1996: 'reality itself, the world itself, with its frenzy of cloning has already been transformed into an interactive performance'.

CSRTV demonstrates a level of reality in which humans are intertwined with medical and communication machines. Poster argues that subjects on CSRTV 'are not actualizing themselves, achieving their "true" identity, but exploring possibilities of personhood in the age of information machines' (2008 in press, n.p.). The terrifying aspects of these possibilities are explored in horror films: even when wholly in the room *The Ring*'s Samara continues to shimmer and crackle with the blue light of a television screen. She is both electronic and fleshy and is all-powerful because of this. Samara embodies the cultural concerns associated with all hybrids, particularly media-bodies, that make them such good subjects of horror. But so too does *The Swan*'s Cindy, who is as much a surgical and media hybrid as Samara is an electronic one. CSRTV shares concerns and metaphors with horror such as rebirth and the permeability of borders such as skin and screens. Both horror and CSRTV present newly configured bodies and new outlines for the human body. However, while horror addresses the terror that such bodies evoke, in CSRTV the frightening paradigm in which hybrids and media-bodies are born is controlled. The excesses of media bodies and the terrifying aspects of screen-births are rendered less confronting and are domesticated and tamed.

Notes

1. Bernadette Wegenstein argues that body criticism must be part of media criticism because of the 'mutual dependence upon and influence of body and mediation' (2006, 121). For her, discussions and

analyses of the body are only meaningful alongside examinations of those media that comprise embodiment.

2. Hybridity, especially in relation to public/private space, is an important feature of much reality television. Scott McQuire writes that 'The fact that the primary scene of action in *Big Brother* is a hybrid television studio fashioned as a domestic dwelling – a "home" in which people live while being watched by others – brings into focus many issues raised by the increasing mediatisation of what was formerly private space' (2003, 103).

3. Orlan, one of the most interesting artists who has worked with cosmetic surgery, produced a work in 1964 called 'Orlan gives birth to herself, and she loves herself.' The work, a photograph of a nude Orlan coupled with an androgynous mannequin torso, pre-dates the themes of Orlan's later work on the body as modifiable object.

4. For example, Woody Allen's *The Purple Rose of Cairo* (1985) is a benign love story between a 'real' character and a film character who steps out of his movie into the world. In John McTiernan's *Last Action Hero* (1993), characters are transported between the movie world and the real world.

5. 'Mommy Makeovers' usually combine 'tummy tucks' (abdominoplasties) with breast lifting or augmentation, liposuction, and sometimes even vaginaplasty. See 'Rodeo Drive Mommy Makeover' at http://www.rodeodrivemommymakeover.com/

6. Many thanks to one of my referees who pointed out that in fact lesbians and gay men do exist on CSRTV: lesbians are described as tomboys unable to express their 'real' femininity, while many of the fashion consultants, makeup artists and hairdressers are clearly coded as gay men. Paradoxically, they are in the programmes in order to reinforce heterosexuality.

7. I am concentrating on gender here but my argument could equally apply to class or race.

References

Andrejevic, M. 2003. *Reality TV: The work of being watched*. Lanham, MD: Rowman & Littlefield.

Baudrillard, J. 1996. Disneyworld Company. Trans. F. Debrix. *ctheory*, http://www.ctheory.net/articles. aspx?id=158 (accessed 6 June 2008).

———. 2005. The violence of the virtual and integral reality. Trans. M. Lambert-Drache. *International Journal of Baudrillard Studies* 2, no. 2, http://www.ubishops.ca/BaudrillardStudies/vol2_2/baudrillardpf.htm (accessed 6 June 2008).

Bratich, J.Z. 2007. Programming reality: Control societies, new subjects and the powers of transformation. In *Makeover television: Realities remodelled*, ed. D. Heller, 6–22. London and New York: I.B. Tauris.

Creed, B. 1993. *The monstrous-feminine: Film, feminism, psychoanalysis*. London & New York: Routledge.

Davis, K. 1995. *Reshaping the female body: The dilemma of cosmetic surgery*. New York: Routledge.

Edmonds, A. n.d. 'Engineering the erotic': Aesthetic medicine and modernization in Brazil. Unpublished paper.

Finkelstein, J. 2007. *The art of self invention: Image and identity in popular visual culture*. London and New York: I.B. Tauris.

Fraser, S. 2003. *Cosmetic surgery, gender and culture*. London and New York: Palgrave Macmillan.

Gailey, E.A. 2007. Self-made women: Cosmetic surgery shows and the construction of female psychopathology. In *Makeover television: Realities remodelled*, ed. D. Heller, 107–18. London and New York: I.B. Tauris.

Gill, R. 2007. *Gender and the media*. Cambridge: Polity Press.

Heller, D. 2007. Reading the makeover. In *Makeover television: Realities remodelled*, ed. D. Heller, 1–5. London and New York: I.B. Tauris.

Heyes, C.J. 2007. *Self-transformations: Foucault, ethics, and normalised bodies*. Oxford and New York: Oxford University Press.

Holmes, S. 2004. *Understanding reality television*. London and New York: Routledge.

Huff, R. 2006. *Reality television*. Westport, CT: Praeger.

James, C. 2002. It's all in the mix: A plastic surgery reality show. *New York Times*, 11 December.

Jones, M. 2004. Architecture of the body: Cosmetic surgery and postmodern space. *Space & Culture* 7, no. 1: 90–101.

———. 2008. *Skintight: An anatomy of cosmetic surgery*. Oxford and New York: Berg.

Kimball, S.A. 2002. Conceptions and contraceptions of the future: *Terminator 2*, *The Matrix*, and *Alien Resurrection*. *Camera Obscura* 17, no. 2: 68–107.

Larry King Live. Interview with *The Swan* cast aired 24 September 2004. CNN.

Marriott, J. 2004. *Horror films*. London: Virgin Books.

McQuire, S. 2003. From glass architecture to *Big Brother*: Scenes from a cultural history of transparency. *Cultural Studies Review* 9, no. 1: 103–23.

Poltergeist. Directed by T. Hopper. Co-written and co-produced by S. Spielberg, M. Grais, and M. Victor. MGM/UA Entertainment Company, 1982.

Poster, M. 2006. Psychoanalysis, the body, and information machines. In *Information please: Culture and politics in the age of digital machines*, 161–81. Durham, NC and London: Duke University Press.

———. 2008. *Swan's* way: Care of the self in the hyperreal. *Configurations* 14, nos. 1 and 2. in press.

The Ring. Directed by G. Verbinski. DreamWorks SKG, 2002.

Roscoe, J. 2001. Big Brother Australia: Performing the 'real' twenty-four-seven. *International Journal of Cultural Studies* 4, no. 4: 473–88.

Rushdie, S. 2001. Reality TV: A dearth of talent and the death of morality. *The Guardian*, 9 June, http://www.guardian.co.uk/saturday_review/story/0,,503921,00.html (accessed 6 June 2008).

Shildrick, M. 2002. *Embodying the monster: Encounters with the vulnerable self*. London, Thousand Oaks, CA and New Delhi: Sage.

The Silence of the Lambs. Directed by J. Demme. Orion Pictures, 1991.

Videodrome. Directed by D. Cronenberg. Universal Studios, 1983.

Weber, B.R. 2005. Beauty, desire and anxiety: The economy of sameness in ABC's extreme makeover. *Genders online journal* no. 41, http://www.genders.org/g41/g41_weber.html (accessed 6 June 2008).

Wegenstein, B. 2006. *Getting under the skin: Body and media theory*. Cambridge, MA and London: MIT Press.

Made Over in America. Produced and directed by B. Wegenstein and G.A. Rhodes. Brooklyn, NY: First Run/Icarus Films, 2007.

Out for life: Makeover television and the transformation of fitness on Bravo's *Work Out*

Dana Heller

> 'I'm Jackie Warner and this is my world. It's a world of hard bodies and beautiful faces.' (*Work Out* 2006, 101)

With this seductive voiceover, Bravo introduced *Work Out*, a new reality series based on the life of LA entrepreneur and fitness trainer Jackie Warner, and her launching of Sky Sport and Spa, a private, state-of-the-art gym that caters to the Beverly Hills elite. The show's first season, which aired in the summer of 2006, focused on Jackie's determined efforts to get her new business off the ground and to establish productive working relations with her team of professional trainers, a diverse crew whose engaging personalities make them not only readable as character types but also perfect foils for Jackie's dogmatic management style. Additional tensions arose from Jackie's struggles to balance her demanding professional life with her private life, as viewers bore intimate witness to the collapse of her four-year romantic relationship with Mimi, her jealousy-prone Brazilian girlfriend with a penchant for biting.

Although mocked by one critic as '*The Apprentice* in sweatpants' (Fries 2006), *Work Out* emerged as Bravo's most successful new show of 2006. The second season, which aired in the spring of 2007, trained its lens more voyeuristically on Jackie's private life, and in particular her re-entry into the LA dating scene, which prompted some to remark that the show might have been aptly re-titled *Make Out* (*Work Out Reunion* 2007). However, audiences also gained insight into Jackie's strained relationship with her mother, a former Baptist-turned-Mormon who morally disapproves of her daughter's lesbianism. They watched Jackie launch her clothing line of gym-to-street workout attire and became more intimately acquainted with Sky Sport and Spa's clients, mainly through Jackie's launching of Sky Lab, an intensive two-week fitness programme. And fans were saddened, as was the series' cast, to learn of the sudden loss of one of the Sky team, Doug Bladsdell, whose death from kidney failure at the age of 44 provided the season's emotionally climactic conclusion.

A third season of *Work Out* is scheduled to air in 2008, and there is intense speculation on message boards and fan blogs as to what surprises it might hold in store: 'Will Jackie finally meet her match …? Will the other trainers continue to live in fear and mockery of Jackie's bravado? Will someone finally get too much exercise instead of too little? And how much more crying and protein shakes can we really take?' (AfterEllen.com 2007). In fact, viewers can likely rest assured that Season Three of *Work Out* will continue to develop three interrelated themes, which it is the purpose of this essay to consider: Firstly, it will continue to rehearse long-standing American historical tendencies in the social promotion and commercial marketing of physical fitness in the very instance of demonstrating the individual body's capacity to resist and redefine the terms of its conditioning. Secondly, it will continue to reinforce the concept that Ella Taylor has called the 'television work-family' (1989, 14) or the tendency I've described elsewhere

> of American television to recruit its most potent images and forms, to reproduce its foundational myths, and to resolve its most debilitating social contradictions through narrative studies of the unstable boundaries of industry and intimacy, the reproduction of wealth and the reproduction of life, the public performance of labor and the private performance of intimacy, domesticity, and sexuality. (Heller 2004)

And thirdly, it will celebrate 'powers of transformation', a myth system that organizes countless reality makeover formats in markets around the world by manufacturing belief in our individual and shared capacities for radical self-reinvention (Bratich 2007, 8).

Power transformations

In *Work Out*, this latter notion is unequivocally defended by Jackie's ethos that her clients should achieve not just a better body 'but a lifestyle change' (*Work Out* 2006, 101). The belief is further championed by Jackie herself, a working-class girl from Ohio (her father, a Vietnam veteran, committed suicide when she was 18) who got herself to Hollywood and metamorphosed into a glamorous, successful fitness mogul. However, while *Work Out* demonstrates the core strength of the makeover mythos, it also highlights its flexibility, or its adaptability to changing social and televisual contexts. We see this most vividly in the series' handling of Jackie's lesbianism, which throughout *Work Out*'s two years has remained the one aspect of her life absolutely not subject to alteration. Indeed, viewers quickly learn that Jackie is openly gay and uncompromising in her sexual self-definition. In the series premiere, a male client tests her to see if she might be persuaded to date a man, reasoning coyly that 'some people have interests in many things'. 'I'm not one of those people', Jackie responds, with pointed finality (*Work Out* 2006, 101). In a subsequent episode, Jackie lays it out: 'I gotta tell you for the record', she says, looking decisively into the camera. 'People do not choose to be gay' (*Work Out* 2006, 104). From here, *Work Out* continually reinforces Jackie's conviction that while bodies, behaviours, and lifestyles can be positively broken down and transformed, homosexuality remains at least partially genetic, inherent, and wholly compatible with aspirations to individual fitness, social well-being, and national health.

Implicitly, then, the series' focus on Jackie's self-assured sexual identity, her savvy approach to business management and fitness training, her messy break-up with Mimi, and her drama-fraught relations with her real-life television 'work-family' raise a number of questions relevant to recent transformations in health and fitness television programming. For example, how does *Work Out*'s unscripted premise contribute to the repositioning of lesbianism – with its long history of medical pathologization and cultural and religious demonization – as consistent with health and fitness administration? How do audiences and fans negotiate their own viewing pleasures and personal investments in diet and exercise in relation to the day-to-day lives, challenges, and conflicts faced by Jackie, her trainers, and their clients? What does the Bravo series ultimately reveal about the proper management and disciplining of bodies, sexualities, and desires? And how might these revelations reflect broader shifts in the programming and organization of social and national bodies?

To begin with, as social and cultural historian Harvey Green has shown, the proper definition of 'good health' has remained throughout American history a question of unrelenting controversy (1986). Early America's evangelical faith in its own moral perfectibility – and by extension the perfectibility of its citizens – was threatened in the nineteenth century by waves of immigrants from Europe who seemed physically poised to economically outperform the over-indulged and debilitated young men of America's major cities. The natural abundance and industrial prosperity that had been the boast of political orators became, in the vision of social reformers across the nation, a foreshadowing of the republic's undoing, as the sedentary habits, heavy diets, political and religious passions, and nervous stress of middle-class Anglo-Saxon Americans appeared to render them weaker and less able to compete than the new foreigners who were arriving. Fears of 'race suicide' and labour unrest gave way to calls for the nation's men and women to improve their 'edge' through physical strength training and improved dietary habits. The calls emanated from secular medical professionals, faddists and quacks, as well as from non-secular advocates for 'muscular Christianity', such as Luther Gulick who turned the Young Men's Christian Association into a fitness organization. The result of these many calls, and the new programmes, agencies, and activities they spawned, led to a national obsession with fitness and to a growing marketplace for the advertising and consumption of new commercial products, foodstuffs, and equipment for improving the body – and by extension the soul.

In all of this, the health of the individual was understood as tantamount to the health of the nation, and women were not excluded from this moral responsibility. In the pre-Civil War era, middle-class women were encouraged to eschew the fashionable sedentary feminine activities of the time – reading, piano, drawing, and needle-work – and perform vigorous housework as a means of strengthening their reproductive capacities. They were criticized for adhering to the custom of tight-lacing by educators and social critics such as Catherine Beecher, who was among the first to argue for an essential connection between the development of physical fitness and the attainment of natural beauty. The nineteenth-century appearance of this equation, as Green notes, registered a fundamental shift in America's perception of the ideal female form, from ample portliness to a leaner feminine muscularity.

Despite women's participation in callisthenics and other supervised forms of light exercise, serious muscle-building and participation in competitive sports such as football and boxing would remain positive attributes of American masculinity, particularly given their associations with power, violence, and male superiority over those perceived as 'other' to the nation. Still, the twentieth-century development of mass consumer culture often relied upon the image of energetic, sensually vivacious womanhood to promote physical culture products and the promise of bodily transformation to men and women alike. Following on the success of innovators such as Eugene Sandow and Bernard McFadden in linking health to sexual attractiveness and potency, Charles Atlas (born Angelino Siciliano) capitalized upon fears of male sexual inadequacy, distributed through the medium of popular comics, to sell his 'dynamic tension' fitness system, which promised to turn scrawny lads into the heroes of the beach.

With the establishment of commercial radio in the 1920s, boxing matches, college football, and baseball games penetrated into American living rooms with unprecedented immediacy. Television's invention in the 1920s, and its development as an electronic commercial broadcast medium in the 1930s and 1940s, promised a new technological format for the delivery of popular spectator sports and advertising. However, it would not be until after the Second World War, with television's mainstreaming into the mundane fabric of middle-class American domestic life, that 'the godfather of fitness' Jack LaLanne (the son of French immigrants) would see the medium's potential for delivering health and fitness programming to American audiences. In 1951, following on the success of the Oakland, California health and fitness spa that he opened in 1936, *The Jack LaLanne Show* began broadcasting in 1951, thus becoming the first lifestyle health and fitness programme in American television history. It remained on the air until 1984.

Since *The Jack LaLanne Show* first invited television viewers to work out with Jack in the privacy of their own homes, many fitness programmes, gurus, and fashionable methods of weight loss and physical conditioning have come and gone from American television, both network and cable. Adding to this, the popularity of exercise videos, launched by Jane Fonda in the early 1980s, seized upon the entrepreneurial potential of VHS technology as a new inducement for women and men to regard exercise as something uniquely suited to the television screen and the intimate space of the home. These recent developments are part of the long historical view of America's fitness obsession, as we can discern in three recurring motifs: physical fitness remains variously linked to moral ideologies and their management through consumer practices that emphasize ethical modes of identity via what Foucault calls 'technologies of the self' (1992); debates over proper exercise and diet continue to reflect debates over proper gendering and sexuality; which in turn link to questions of social and national fitness (as Ouellette and Hay's essay in this collection discusses in relation to the present-day neoliberal push for a healthy self-governing citizenry); and finally, and perhaps most obviously in its recent forms, our preoccupation with working out – more than simply a register of cultural narcissism or fear of death – remains a technology for the fashioning of identities and 'an expression of the desire for community and emotional bonding in a culture of men and women alone' (Green 1986, 323).

Flexing the family

Work Out amplifies these characteristics in clearly marked ways as it stages, wittingly or not, debates over the ethics of care, morality in the workplace, proper mothering, proper gendering, familial loyalties, and national legacies. Much of this is communicated in the screen time devoted to Jackie's trainers. Only eight out of the twenty-two trainers she actually employs appear on the series. These eight were selected in part as a result of their distinctive personal styles, which produce not only a dramatic sense of 'good TV' but a social microcosm of human expressiveness and human need. They are Brian (the Southern 'ladies' man' and alpha male); Rebecca (the sassy, exhibitionistic flirt); Andre (an African-American former military officer whose traditional values are exercised with quiet tolerance); Jesse (the catty, effeminate gay man, and one of Jackie's closet confidantes); Erica (the reserved and aloof beauty, and a recovered bulimic); Zen (the 'funny' girl, who sidelines as a stand-up comic); Doug (the avuncular elder of the group, and 'everyone's best friend'); and Gregg (an African-American musician and aspiring recording artist who appears only in Season Two). In their first season interviews, they frequently refer to their competitive yet affectionate dealings with one another in terms of natural familial intimacies and rivalries. Brian introduces himself and his co-workers by explaining 'We are like a family here'. Later he dismisses his initial distrust of the new hire, Jesse, by contending that, 'If you wanna be in this family, I will have you in this family' (*Work Out* 2006, 101). Even clients of the Sky Lab two-week fitness programme reiterate the familial ethos that binds them to their otherwise gruelling boot camp sessions and pitiless trainers, as Tess does in admitting 'I really formed a family with these people' (*Work Out Reunion* 2007). In these instances, the concept of family becomes unmoored from its legal or biological meanings so as to suggest that professional labours performed in the name of administering or attaining better health are extensions of the caring bonds and nurturing loyalties that organize the private family. At the same time, the rhetoric of familialism works to naturalize the disciplinary constraints of capitalism and its management of time, bodies, and productivity by suggesting that when we surrender ourselves to workplace governance and surveillance we experience the most meaningful and emotionally gratifying relationships that life has to offer.

In *Work Out*, this idea is reinforced by the near total absence of trainer back-stories or individual histories. Unlike Jackie, whose personal history is a critical part of the series' narrative arc, viewers know comparatively little about where the trainers come from, who their loved ones are, or how they spend time when not at work. The upshot is that the trainers appear to have no serious relationships, sexual or otherwise, beyond the incestuous web of professional affiliation, competition, loyalty and betrayal that the demanding high-stress fitness industry compels. When Zen introduces her new boyfriend to the trainers, she quips 'Welcome to our dysfunctional family' (*Work Out* 2007, 207). The remark serves to intensify the perceived emotional stakes of the trainers' on-camera interactions with one another and with Jackie. This is made more complicated by the fact that Jackie's efforts to nurture intimacy and trust with the crew do not always sit well with her imperious managerial style. 'My place, my rules, and that's how it has to be', she asserts in the series premiere (*Work Out* 2006, 101). Her need to be in control and her tendency to criticize trainers for performing beneath expectations result in frequent clashes and eruptions of pique, many of which direct the narrative arc of episodes as trainers gossip among themselves and offer their individual analyses of the latest scandal or spat. In the premiere, for example, Jackie corrects Brian's training technique in front of a client, which sends him into a rage. He complains about her to the other trainers. Jackie likewise complains about him to the trainers in whom she chooses to confide. Rebecca 'privately' offers her assessment of the situation for the camera: 'I think Jackie and [Brian] are both type A alpha males' (*Work Out* 2006, 101).

Collisions and catty confrontations, many involving complicated tensions around the appropriate performance of gender and sexuality, are central to *Work Out*'s depiction of fitness administration. In this sense, Jackie's gym represents a liminal space, a site of constant negotiation and debate over the proper social posturing and correspondence of bodies, genders, and desires. Jackie admits this to be a general dilemma not only in the gym but also of modern life in LA, when she says 'It's hard to decipher who's gay and who's not in this town anymore' (*Work Out* 2006, 101). In her self-presentation, Jackie likewise resists prescribed sexual and gender scripts and the social codes that organize them. 'A gym is a very different environment', she claims. 'There's flexibility in our environment' (*Work Out Reunion* 2007). Jackie's 'flexibility' is evident in the way she combines 'alpha male' butchness in work-related matters with a chic lipstick lesbian style sense. Politically she identifies as a 'strong woman and feminist' who has 'a hard time with someone … just playing the sex card' (*Work Out* 2006, 102). However, she performs her own sexuality openly and playfully, signifying as queer while showing a marked preference for straight-looking femmes and heterosexual women, around whom she admits to being a sexual predator. At the age of 37 she is happily and even somewhat recklessly non-monogamous ('Being a slut, I've decided, works for me' [*Work Out Reunion* 2007]), yet so invested in her reproductive futures that she consults a doctor about the possibility of having her eggs frozen for later fertilization. In short, *Work Out* traffics lavishly in the seeming contradictory niches and gaps of social gendering, along with sexual, Oedipal, and political identities. But true to Annette Hill's claim that reality television is essentially about 'border territories', or spaces in which relations of information and entertainment, and fact and fiction are tested and re-imagined, *Work Out* revels in subversive border regions that render unrealistic all normative notions of femininity and masculinity, heterosexuality and homosexuality, and butch and femme roles within the stereotypical formation of lesbian subjectivities (2005, 2). Good health, from this standpoint, may require that we reshuffle the conventional codes of gender and sexuality according to our own flexible relational circumstances.

In tandem with this, *Work Out* makes a case for the queering of the neoliberal family by contesting the legitimacy of separate sphere ideology, or the assumption of a long-standing gendered social organization that divides the feminine intimacies of the private home from the brute masculine economics of the capitalist workplace. These debates become contentious in the opening of the show's second season, when, following the obligatory extended recap of the first season's notable interpersonal crises, Jackie's summarizes what she has accomplished thus far: 'My trainers and I bonded like a family', she proclaims' (*Work Out* 2007, 201). From here, Season Two unfolds through documentation of a total boundary breakdown, as Jackie, following her final split from Mimi, begins casually dating her employee, Rebecca, who has heretofore identified as heterosexual. Subsequent episodes follow the bemused and disturbed reactions of the Sky Sport 'work-family' through these incestuous travails. It's 'the most unethical thing that anyone can do' (*Work Out* 2007, 204) says Jesse in relation to Jackie's behaviour, although he later accuses Rebecca of opportunistically dating the 'boss' only to get more screen time for herself (*Work Out Reunion* 2007). It is 'unprofessional', claims Brian, clearly chafed (*Work Out* 2007, 204). And Andre signals his confusion over whether to react caringly or competitively when he admits that no man wants to stand by passively and see 'his [female] boss with women that he secretly desires' (*Work Out* 2007, 204). Through it all, Jackie defends her actions as something she 'deserves', a healthy and joyful stage in her adjustment to single life. Moreover, she understands it to be ethically consistent with the 'flexibility' of the fitness industry. 'Trainers sleep with trainers, trainers sleep with clients', she rationalizes (*Work Out* 2007, 204). However, fans responded very negatively to Jackie and Rebecca's relationship, and in such numbers that Jackie was caught off-guard. 'I had no idea the attention that we would get', she admits, before announcing her decision to continue dating Rebecca only off camera (*Work Out Reunion* 2007).

While Season Two fans of the show, along with Sky Sport and Spa trainers, loudly negotiate their discomfort with *Work Out*'s queering of sexual boundaries and workplace ethics, Jackie's biological family history is narrated contrastingly as a story of bitter silence, national loss, and the failure of traditional family structure to properly manage gender and sexuality. Indeed, a recurrent theme of *Work Out* is Jackie's destructive relationship with her mother, whose strong religious convictions cannot be reconciled with her daughter's sexuality and aspirations one day to marry a woman and have a child. At the conclusion of Season Two, Jackie returns to her home town in Ohio in order to resolve their difficulties and make amends with the painful memory of her father, who returned from Vietnam suffering from severe mental illness. The episode stages the return of the prodigal daughter as putting to rest both personal and national trauma, as Jackie visits her father's grave for the first time with her mother, and as she acknowledges the lasting imprint that US history and politics have left upon them both. Although her father took his life long after the war in Vietnam had ended, Jackie comes to see that 'he was a casualty of that war' (*Work Out* 2007, 207). Meanwhile, back at Sky Sport, Jesse's is similarly faced with a revelation that contradictorily sutures matters of private conduct to public performance and national myth concerning the latest American adventure in Iraq. Jesse is training a male model and actor who works in the gay porn industry. As it turns out, the actor is also a former Marine who served in Iraq on the administrative board for the investigation of accusations of homosexual conduct. The utter irony of masculine identity deconstructed and reconstructed before his eyes absolutely confounds Jesse, as his client confides – between crunches – that his experience in Iraq was nothing except 'pointless' and 'sad' (*Work Out* 2007, 207).

At such moments we begin to get a sense of the multiple meanings inherent in the programme's title. Treadmills, protein shakes, and entrepreneurial growth are mere trace elements within the larger transformational labour process that *Work Out* champions as part of our private and public health consciousness. *Work Out*, Jackie insists on her blog, is really about 'working life out' (Bravotv.com, 'Jackie's blog', 10 May 2007). In other words, life is an extreme sport, the goal of which is to connect the private to the public – the inner self to the outer self – as the key to reinventing ourselves individually and nationally. Indeed, the fitness ethos that the programme advocates is one that requires full disclosure and reconditioning of inner processes. In Jackie's gym, or in her boot camps, physical change matters less than the restored sense of self-worth that disclosure brings about. The 'beautiful faces and hard bodies' that constitute Jackie's world are thus markers of an open and flexible interiority that informs our modern middle-class vision of health and our notions of comprehensive fitness. *Work Out* thus represents physical health and well-being as a set of intimately relational signifying practices, which when flexed properly will reveal and transform our families and communities – beginning with our authentic inner selves.

Outing the real

Another way of putting this is that one's inner 'reality' on *Work Out* is something that needs to be continuously 'outed' in the interests of wellness. Indeed, Jackie's uncompromising openness about her sexuality and her confidence as a gay woman going up against the corporate rat race is entirely consistent with this ethos, as it signals her authenticity and her awareness of the moral obligations that come with it. Fans of the show, both gay and straight-identified, affirm this on message boards and posts to Jackie's personal blog. For example, Cindy writes: 'I watch the show every week and I love your honesty. You just put it out there and it's real' (Bravotv.com, 'Jackie's blog', 1 May 2006). And this from 'Semaj': 'Well tonight was the first time i seen your show and yes … i am just totally in love with it. Why? Well for one it REAL its not some made up stuff that people already whats going to happen. it's REAL people REAL problems, and REAL life. What more could you ask out of a show?' (Bravotv.com, 'Jackie's blog', 4 April 2007). Fans repeatedly claim to be inspired by Jackie's authenticity and the truthfulness of the challenges she faces, and this – they further claim – makes it possible for them to see themselves in a new light and with new hope for retrieving the value of authenticity in their own lives. The external manifestation of this process is physical exercise, as Priscilla suggests in writing: 'Well, I just wanted to let Jackie know that she's really inspired me. I can't wait until the doctor okays me working out again, but when he does, I'm workin' out!' (Bravotv.com, 'Jackie's blog', 20 March 2007).

Also important to consider from an industry perspective is the extent to which the Bravo cable television network (which is owned by NBC Universal) has capitalized on the cultural chic of a simple three-letter word: 'out'. 'Out' has become the veritable signature of Bravo's original reality programming, with niche series such as *Blow Out*, which focused on celebrity hairstylist Jonathan Antin's launching of a salon in LA, and *Flipping Out*, which centres on obsessive-compulsive real estate speculator Jeff Lewis, who buys houses and resells them for profit. This series of shows, along with other popular queer-friendly programmes such as *Boy Meets Boy* (2003), *Queer Eye for the Straight Guy* (2003–), *Queer Eye for the Straight Girl* (2005), the Emmy-nominated *Kathy Griffin: My Life on the D List* (2005–), and *Welcome to the Parker* (2007), caters directly to gay and lesbian audiences and tastes and, in the eyes of *New York Times* television critic Alessandra Stanley, has successfully elevated Bravo to the status of 'premiere gay network, even though it is not labeled as such' (2006).

Moreover, Bravo's slogan 'Watch What Happens' reflects its investment in branding itself as reality, precisely by claiming that its programming is unformulated and spontaneous. Implicit in its slogan is Bravo's recognition that dramatic self-disclosure and submission to surveillance remain the twin guarantors of authenticity and spontaneity, 'the promise of the real in reality TV' (Andrejevic 2004, 108). Like Sky Lab's trainers, clients too become integral players in *Work Out*'s drama of authentic self-retrieval. 'I'm ready to get back to the person I know I am', says Tess in an interview that marks her preparedness to begin a journey towards weight loss, but more importantly towards an ethical unity of inner self and outward performance, a moral obligation that obesity and ill health have seemingly compromised (*Work Out* 2006, 103). Resistance is part of the journey, and on occasions Sky clients do rebel, backslide, question authority, and/or fail. However, they can be redeemed through theatrical emotional candour, by admitting failure and self-revulsion, and by otherwise turning themselves inside out for the camera and for Jackie, who appears to derive tremendous satisfaction from their abjection. 'I get a joy from doing my job well', she admits. 'And I get a joy from just breaking someone down'

(*Work Out* 2006, 101). In one episode, Jackie works Tess out so strenuously she vomits. But even this, which Jackie treats lightly, is seen as a positive step towards weight reduction and even more importantly as a purge of inner toxins that must be outed – in this case literally. As part of this process, Sky Lab clients give up control of their bodies to be tested, measured, weighed, analysed, and monitored, their food input and physical exertion output scrupulously recorded and continuously assessed. Even the trainers are required to surrender their bodies for weigh-ins, fat density checks, and rigorous boot camps, which, as one trainer observes, Jackie orchestrates but never participates in herself.

The information that Jackie exacts from the bodies of clients and trainers at the gym is revealing of how well they care for themselves, and by extension a measure of how well they might care for others. The cultivation and maintenance of fitness is thus coextensive with an 'ethics of care', which Annette Hill locates at the core of much contemporary reality television programming (2005). *Work Out* is a reality programme that is fundamentally about caring for one's own self as the most effective means of caring for others. However, Jackie's proficiency in caring for others does not translate into her private conduct. The challenges she faces in realizing her personal goals – a stable marriage and family – remind viewers that Jackie is neither flawless nor consistently in charge of her own impulses and desires. In other words, she appears conspicuously lacking in certain aspects of self-knowledge – an embodiment of the directive (albeit paraphrased), 'Trainer, train thyself'.

However, it is precisely this inconsistency – the supremely fit and powerful health guru reduced to a chew toy for her petulant girlfriend, and to angry self-condemnation in therapy – that produces viewer interest and involvement with Jackie. Jackie is positioned both as a 'real' individual and as a living symptom of shifting technologies for the screening of sexualities defined as morally deviant. In this way, *Work Out* invites viewers to engage with ethical debates about the normalization of homosexuality and lesbianism in American society. Jackie is in this sense a flashpoint, an embodied site of ethical conflict and transformation. And, indeed, Jackie's celebrity status is rooted largely in the disjuncture between her public function as fitness instructor par excellence and her self-exposure as a less than responsible cultivator of self-knowledge. This encourages fans of the programme to analyse Jackie's ethics, some of them encouraging her to care for her 'self', just as attentively as she does her business and her body. We see this tendency, for example, in the following message from 'a fan': 'In all honesty, I absolutely love this show and I just want to point out that you may be great at everything else in you [*sic*] life, but it has been recorded/filmed that when it comes to relationships, you may need some help ...' (Bravotv.com, 'Jackie's blog', 5 July 2007). Here, the implicit understanding is that health-based reality television lends itself to ethical analysis of what it means to be fit – a condition measured not only by our capacity to care for others, but by 'the self's relation to itself' (Gauntlett 2002, 124–8). As noted above, the push to be physically fit requires that we also commit to our own emotional and psychological improvement through the application of ethical techniques of selfhood (Foucault 1992).

This quest leads Jackie and her girlfriend, Mimi, to seek couple's counselling from Dr Shirley Impellizerri, an LA therapist. In their first session, while discussing the difficulties they have communicating with one another, Mimi's anger is triggered and she abruptly stands up and leaves the office. Jackie is left alone with 'Dr Shirley', who, feigning curiosity, asks her: 'Why are you in this?' (*Work Out* 2007, 201).

'Because I'm fucked up', Jackie blurts out in frustration. She falls silent while the camera lingers over her, maximizing the power and urgency of her confession. But viewers who have been watching the series up to this point will likely be gratuitously affirmed in what they've understood all along: 'This relationship is my addiction', Jackie recognizes. With this admission, she continues seeking individual therapy, claiming that she hopes to discover 'why I attract the people I attract' (*Work Out* 2007, 201).

Reinventing America

Jackie enters therapy in order to resolve her situation with Mimi and to positively transform the quality of her future relationships. Her meetings with Dr Shirley comprise a contemplative leitmotif throughout Season Two, although Jackie's scenes with Dr Shirley provide very little by way of dramatic revelation. Rather, Jackie's decision to pursue therapy is a logical extension of the overarching narrative that frames Jackie as a fitness folk hero, and a distinctively American folk hero at that. Jackie's individual history is evocative of a national makeover mythos, as it rehearses the familiar tale of westward flight towards freedom and new open spaces for the exercise of one's instincts and innermost desires. In this mythos, the American West – and California in particular – represents the pre-eminent locus of self-recreation, opportunity, and youthful experimentation. In national literature, popular culture, and mass media, California has long served as the destination par excellence for all who gravitate towards the farthest western boundaries of the nation and the national imaginary – from Huckleberry Finn to Sal Paradise.

Not insignificantly, this mythology also has a central place in twentieth-century US histories of queer migration, as young gays and lesbians from the nation's more culturally conservative heartland sought refuge in politically and socially progressive locations such as San Francisco in the 1950s and 1960s, and West Hollywood in the 1970s and 1980s. As a receptacle of fantasies that speak to national idealism as well as minority community aspirations, California is where one goes to discover and authenticate new self-meanings – new ways of being. Indeed, Jackie has often attributed the success of her show and the breadth of her fan base to the fact that she is originally from America's heartland, and proud of it. At the same time, she recalls what it meant to grow up isolated, lonely, and closeted in a stifling small town: 'Growing up a gay teenager … I constantly felt that I was going to be exposed' (*Work Out* 2007, 207). That her quest for self-actualization should lead her to Hollywood, to the celebrity fitness industry, and to Dr Shirley's Beverly Hills office is probably no great surprise, but it is ironic that Jackie's teenage fears of lesbian exposure should have led her to become an object of exhibitionistic self-disclosure on national television.

In this respect, no body on *Work Out* is more willingly appropriated, scrutinized, and picked over than Jackie's own. Alongside the glamorous PR photos featuring her famous abdominal muscles and frequent camera shots of her buff body in sports bra and spandex, we see Jackie exhausted and cranky, fidgeting uncomfortably on Dr Shirley's sofa, drinking to excess (the tabloids claim she was arrested for 'driving under the influence' in autumn 2006), making out with women in public bathrooms, puffy-eyed from lack of sleep, and moping about her house in baggy pyjamas. When asked about the magnitude of her exposure on the show, Jackie admits that it often goes too far, but she accepts it all as part of her service to others.

On one hand, Jackie's vision of *Work Out* as a public health service is consistent with her primary passion, 'which is changing people's lives' (*Work Out* 2007, 201). And fans of the show do repeatedly testify to the life-altering influence of Jackie's struggles, as this message from 'Lucy Beard' explains eloquently:

> I have suffered from disabling Fears my whole life, phobias, panic attacks, so on. Jackie Warner has given me permission to accept myself warts and all and see the world as a challenge not a threat. My favorite quote I keep in my purse at all times now is when she spoke at her high school and used the word 'Reinvention.' It gave me hope. Thank you Jackie Warner. (Bravotv.com, 'Jackie's blog', 9 May 2007)

But in conclusion, let's be real: while *Work Out* may improve the health practices of some adoring fans, the success of the programme has contributed as much – if not more – to Bravo's fiscal health, not to mention Jackie Warner's own financial fitness (since the show's success, a private work out session with her costs $400 per hour [*Work Out Reunion* 2007]). This is not to fault Jackie for her success – fitness gurus, like reality programmes, tend to have a short shelf life, and she is entitled to reap the rewards of her labour. Rather, my intention is to stress the fact that fitness television programmes, like all lifestyle programming, produce neither top-down governmentality nor bottom-up resistance in any pure or undiluted fashion. Rather, programmes such as *Work Out* are interesting precisely because they are not ideologically unified but dialectical, marked by incessant and visible border skirmishes over questions of success and failure, secrecy and disclosure, normalcy and deviancy, wellness and illness, subordination and autonomy.

These struggles, as I have attempted to show in this paper, link *Work Out* to a larger, long-standing national mythology that questions standards and technologies of health and self-governance in the very instance of affirming those standards and technologies. And even Jackie Warner herself cannot be understood apart from this mythology, without which television viewers and fans of the show could never believe in her as passionately or challenge her wisdom as righteously as, indeed, they do. Here, a space is opened wherein viewers of lifestyle television 'talk back' to their gurus. Moreover, it is here that the deep ambivalence that Americans have long felt towards health professionals and lifestyle gurus registers in the complex interweaving of conservative as well as progressive beliefs and opinions, disciplined and undisciplined bodies, biological and workplace families, and the categorical blurring of sexuality and gender norms that remain, at the same time, at least symbolically in force. These elements are persistently reorganized in the course of *Work Out*'s narrative, contradictory as it is, to legitimate the transformational powers of discovering one's authentic inner self and 'outing' it, making it manifest.

In the end, I believe that this contradictory process is itself an expression of longing for healthy discussion and community formation against a media-saturated culture that continues to highlight divisiveness by, among other things, compulsively linking homosexuality to illness. This is not the case on Bravo's *Work Out*, where being 'out' functions as a flexible metaphor for ongoing debates over what it means to be healthy and fit at this moment in history, a moment defined by cultural shifts in the perception of normative sexuality and family structure, political shifts resulting from the poor management of the nation's well-being under the failed George W. Bush administration, an economic collapse that will clearly require both disciplined self-management and public assistance to treat, and representational shifts within the television industry itself. Given these conditions, could it be possible that the long-predicted revolution in American health care will be televised? 'Thank you Jackie Warner.'

References

AfterEllen.com. 2007. *Work Out* renewed for a third season. 1 October. http://www.afterellen.com/taxonomy/term/64 (accessed 4 June 2008).

Andrejevic, Marc. 2004. *Reality TV: The work of being watched*. Lanham, MD and Oxford: Rowman & Littlefield.

Bratich, Jack Z. 2007. Programming reality: Control societies, new subjects, and the powers of transformation. In *Makeover television: Realities remodelled*. ed. D. Heller, 6–22. London: I.B. Tauris.

Bravotv.com. 2007. 'Jackie's blog', 20 March. Posted by 'Priscilla'. http://www.bravotv.com/blog/jackiewarner/2007/03/looking_for_a_life_change.p hp#comments (accessed 4 June 2008).

———. 2007. 'Jackie's blog', 4 April. Posted by 'Semaj Taylor'. http://www.bravotv.com/blog/jackiewarner/2007/04/im_never_misunderstood_1. php?page=2 (accessed 4 June 2008).

———. 2006. 'Jackie's blog', 1 May. Posted by 'Cindy'. http://www.bravotv.com/blog/jackiewarner/2007/05/you_can_go_home_again.php (accessed 4 June 2008).

———. 2007. 'Jackie's blog', 9 May. Posted by 'Lucy Beard'. http://www.bravotv.com/blog/jackiewarner/2007/05/until_tomorrow.php (accessed 4 June 2008).

———. 2007. 'Jackie's blog', 10 May. Posted by 'Jackie Warner'. http://www.bravotv.com/blog/jackiewarner/2007/05/its_about_working_life_ out.php (accessed 4 June 2008).

———. 2007. 'Jackie's blog', 5 July. Posted by 'A fan'. http://www.bravotv.com/blog/jackiewarner/2007/05/its_about_working_life_out. php#comments (accessed 4 June 2008).

Foucault, Michel. 1992. *The use of pleasure: The history of sexuality volume two*. Trans. R. Hurley, London: Penguin.

Fries, Laura. 2006. *Work Out*. Variety, 17 July, http://www.variety.com/review/VE1117931098.html?categoryid=32&cs=1 (accessed 4 June 2008).

Gauntlett, David. 2002. *Media, gender and identity: An introduction*. London: Routledge.

Green, Harvey. 1986. *Fit for America: Health, fitness, sport and American society*. New York: Pantheon Books.

Heller, Dana. 2004. States of emergency: The labors of lesbian desire in *ER*. *Genders* 39, http://www.genders.org/g39/g39_heller.html (accessed 4 June 2008).

Hill, Annette. 2005. *Reality TV: Audiences and popular factual television*. London and New York: Routledge.

Stanley, Alessandra. 2006. Sex and the gym: *Work Out* and the gaying of Bravo. *New York Times Online*, 19 July, http://www.nytimes.com/2006/07/19/arts/television/19watc.html?_r=1&oref=slog in (accessed 4 June 2008).

Taylor, Ella. 1989. *Prime-time families: Television culture in postwar America*. Berkeley: University of California Press.

Work Out episodes referenced

Work Out. Jackie does it all. 101. Bravo, 19 July 2006.

———. Untitled. 102. Bravo, 25 July 2006.

———. Weighted decisions. 103. Bravo, 1 August 2006.

———. Jackie's away, trainers will play. 104. Bravo, 8 August 2006.

———. Warm up. 201. Bravo, 20 March 2007.

———. Gym drama. 204. Bravo, 10 April 2007.

———. It's over when it's over. 207. Bravo, 1 May 2007.

Work Out Reunion: Watch What Happens. Bravo, 15 May 2007.

Little Angels: The mediation of parenting

Peter Lunt

Individualization and therapy culture

There has recently been a renewed interest in the question of individualization in sociological analysis of modern societies (Beck and Beck-Gernsheim 2002; Giddens 1991; Rose 1989). Although the relative autonomy of the individual is a long-standing feature of modernity nurtured both by the shift from tradition to enlightenment and the increasingly secular, urban, industrial character of modern life, the feeling is that there has been a significant shift in individualization. New ways of governing that shift the emphasis from sovereign rule to a partnership between relatively autonomous individuals and social institutions, the change in the management of risk and welfare from the collective to the individual level, the move from liberal to neo-liberal economies and the relative importance of consumerism to identity (Lunt and Livingstone 1992) all point to the increasing salience of individuals. Social institutions increasingly address the public as individuals with rights and needs rather than social collectives and, arguably, individuals' sense of themselves is less defined in terms of traditional social roles and origins and more in terms of their personal identity (Giddens 1991).

Furedi (2004) suggests that contemporary society is marked by an increased focus on the internal life, the psychology, of the individual and an increased focus on psychological solutions to social problems. We would expect such social changes to be reflected in culture, and to document this Furedi (2004) maps the rise of psychological terms such as 'self-esteem', 'trauma', 'stress', 'syndrome', and 'counselling' in the British press since the mid-1990s. Before the mid-1990s such terms were rarely used; the term 'self-esteem', for example, rarely appeared in press coverage from 1980 to 1986, slowly rose in use to around 500 occurrences by 1995 and rapidly escalated to over 3000 mentions by 1999. Furedi interprets this increasing circulation of psychological terms in public discourse as reflecting the growth of 'therapy culture' in which individuals increasingly focus on their own vulnerability and at the same time demand that social institutions respond to their psychological needs through the provision of public information and services. For Furedi (2004), therapy culture is two sided since it both increases the focus on internal psychological processes and a sense of autonomy but is also linked to a culture of litigation and complaint and anxiety about the self.

The themes of individualization and the turn to the psychological have been taken up in the analysis of popular culture in response to the proliferation of programmes that enrol the public as participants on popular television shows increasing the mediated visibility of the public. One example is the confessional and therapeutic character of talk shows and reality television (Livingstone and Lunt 1994; Grindstaff 2002; Gamson 1998; Dovey 2000; Illouz 2003; Hill 2005). Another is the development of lifestyle television such as cooking and gardening programmes that shifted into prime-time slots in the United Kingdom during the 1990s (Bell and Hollows 2005; Brunsdon 2003). Brunsdon (2003) interprets the rise of lifestyle programmes against three broad social changes: increasing home ownership, the increasing numbers of women in the workforce and the increase in the age of child bearing. Together these factors have created a new consumer group of single and childless-couple households focused on home ownership, personal and career development and leisure, creating a market for programmes that link identity to consumerism. Such programmes provide an important site for the expression of taste and expertise that responds to the emerging needs of lifestyle consumption. A key element of this focus on lifestyle is the dynamic of transformation (Moseley 2000; Brunsdon 2003) and the programmes provide advice that is sometimes technical (this is how to rag-roll; when do I prune my apple trees?), and that sometimes offers guidance on taste (what counts as quality and value in the transformation of the domestic sphere and the self) (Philips 2005). An important feature of all these programmes, noted by the commentators above, is the significant role of 'expert hosts'; indeed, accompanying the proliferation of the public on popular television has been an equal proliferation of expertise (Taylor 2002; Lewis 2008). Experts of every description now appear on our screens to offer analysis, advice and criticism to individuals concerned to improve themselves (gardeners, interior designers, fashion gurus, a variety of life coaches and therapists).

All these programmes extend the visible public, taking aspects of the private sphere and placing them in a context of public scrutiny. The presence of the public has been a feature of television since its early days but the role that the public plays has changed over time (Livingstone and Lunt 1994). The public presence at televised large-scale public events including sports events and ritual pubic occasions is critical to the sense of liveness that creates a feeling of co-presence for the audience at home. In game shows, audience members are in a different role as they become the main protagonists of the show; appearing 'on stage', their fortunes on the programmes and their reactions are central to programme structure and content (Lunt and Stenner 2005). These programmes are a staged adaptation of an earlier tradition in which *Candid Camera* simultaneously placed members of the public at the centre of the programme whilst ironically distancing them through ironization. These examples, however, were early indications of a trend that has developed rapidly in recent years with the advent of talk shows, reality television and makeover television. In these genres, interactions between members of the public are the core of the content and structure of the programmes. Instead of members of the public revealing themselves in the interstices of a game show or as a mass at a sporting event, these genres put them centre stage and focus on them – on their inner turmoil and their emotional reactions as they live together in a reality television show, or are filmed as they prepare for their weddings, or swap houses or jobs to try a different way of living or working, or are coaxed to open up, reveal and confront difficult personal feelings and relationships.

This therapeutic dimension of the proliferation of the visibility of the public has led to considerable critical scrutiny and there are two competing sociological explanations for these developments. Governmentality theory (Barry, Osborne, and Rose 1996; Dean 1999), inspired by Foucault's writings on the constitution of modern modes of subjectivity, offers an analysis of the enrolment of subjects to institutional discipline through the internalization of normative discourses of the psychological combined with public acts of confession. Under this view the modern subject comes into being through a combination of self-reflection, internalizing institutionally mediated norms of conduct in a society that is understood as a loosely connected network of institutions oriented to governance at a distance. In contrast, reflexive modernity theory suggests that increasing institutional individualization (rather than 'discipline') creates a set of social conditions in which individuals are thrown back on their own resources to manage their identities. This theory offers a different view of the relationship between individuals and society to that of governmentality theory. Under reflexive modernity social institutions establish a set of conditions under which the individual becomes the basic social unit addressed by the state and commercial institutions. The individual then becomes a consumer of goods and services provided by commerce and by public institutions operating as institutional civil society in which resources are made available to the reflexive subject through the provision of advice and information.

These two theories offer different possible interpretations of the proliferation of mediated representations of the psychological life of individuals. Under the governmentality view such programmes are constitutive of a new mode of subjectivity in which governance operates through the dispersal of techniques of the self through which individuals manage and control their own conduct (Palmer 2003; Ouellette and Hay 2008). Under the reflexive modernity interpretation such programmes reflect the way in which the relationship between individuals and social institutions is marked by a number of important transitions. The mode of address (and administrative practice) of social institutions has shifted from the collective to the individual, so that members of the public are increasingly understood, analysed and addressed as individuals rather than members of social groups. The programmes also reflect the situation in which the life chances of individuals are less marked by the chances given to them by birth, with the individual portrayed as having the possibility of constructing different life trajectories which require them to develop self-consciousness related to constructing their life narrative. In turn, these shifts relate to the changing nature of personal relationships in which traditional conceptions of role and duty are less salient and instead the co-construction of relatively socially detached forms of social relationships that are open to scrutiny, review and renewal becomes the norm.

Parenting and childhood

Recent work in the sociology of childhood (James, Jenks, and Prout 1998) has argued that the general proliferation of discourses of the self in late modern society extends to both parents and children. Traditionally the family was studied as a central informal social institution that functioned to socialize children into the norms of the family and society (Parsons 1951). This view of the family has been increasingly challenged and the black box of the family has been opened up to reveal the complexities of interaction between parents and children (James, Jenks, and Prout 1998).

The picture emerges of children as agents in the family in their own right, and as worthy of rights in relation to broader society but also there has developed in parallel an increasing focus on and awareness of the child as victim, or the vulnerable child. The modern family appears as both increasingly democratic in acknowledging the autonomy and needs of children but nevertheless parents still control and threaten children. Consequently, although the focus of concern might be children, the locus of policy initiatives is commonly the parent(s). Ironically, also, although the child has been discovered as a sociological subject in recent years, contributing to the closer scrutiny of childhood in the family, school and locale, an older conception of the child, one that James, Jenks, and Prout (1998) call 'presociological', still provides the means of intervention through therapeutic intervention or advice to parents on parenting. How might the broader framework of individualization versus governmentality apply to an analysis of the social dimensions of the rise of therapy as a major discourse of our age? Is therapeutic culture best thought of as an institutional support for the reflexive subject (the parents dealing with their children through reflection and communication aided by advice) or is it part of a new, subtle form of social control whereby parents both internalize a conception of the child as problem or vulnerable and add insult to injury by adopting a therapeutic frame to 'deal with' their child's 'problems' all in the apparently benign name of therapy (Furedi 2004).

In this paper I focus on an example of makeover programming that explicitly addresses a social issue (concerns about the capacity of parents to bring up their children) as a psychological problem (the problematic behaviour of children). The programme offers 'positive psychology' as a response to the experience of parents living in contemporary society, experiencing the professionalization yet isolation of parenting, moral panics about children being raised outside traditional family structures and the increasing focus on the idea that the provision of life skills and rapid therapeutic intervention is a positive tactical response for a mediated public service. The programme I am focusing on is *Little Angels*, a makeover programme in which a psychologist provides instruction in parenting skills to families with young children. I will discuss an example of the programme in some detail against the background of the arguments above concerning therapy culture, discursive social control through expert mediation and subjective internalization of therapeutic discourse.

'Little Angels'

Little Angels is treated here as a case study in the mediation of therapy culture. *Little Angels* is a series (there have been three series so far) appearing first on BBC3 (the BBC's digital channel) and then repeated on BBC1. The programme runs for half an hour and the basic proposition revolves around parents who are having problems managing their young children (aged three to five). Each episode documents the intervention of clinical psychologists into the family's life with the aim of dealing with a variety of everyday parenting issues; temper tantrums, violent or aggressive behaviour, 'naughtiness' and problems getting children to sleep. On the BBC website *Little Angels* is positioned as part of factual broadcasting on the theme of 'parenting' alongside a documentary series on child development called *Child of Our Time*. The website itself also offers a range of advice for parents. The programme is interestingly positioned in genre terms because it has arisen in the 2000s as part of the emerging makeover format showing the cross-over of reality television into programmes that have an explicitly public service remit achieved by broadening the range of factual broadcasting (Hill 2007).

The programme

Little Angels fits the before and after transformational format of makeover television, starting with the disruption of the home by children behaving badly and the story of the parents' attempts to bring harmony and order to the household by changing their approach to parenting. A variety of material is presented: live-shot material in the homes of the participants filmed on cameras placed around the house; interviews with the adult participants; interactions between the parents and the psychologist; and a narrative voiceover.

The home audience is introduced to the family through a combination of live-shot material of children and parents in conflict and initial interviews with the parents saying what their problems are, along with a voiceover commentary. The narrator tells the audience that these are 'working parents who only have evenings and weekends to be with their kids' (series 1, episode 1) and that the parents are in 'a constant struggle' as images of familial conflict play out on the screen. The narrator tells us that there have been no complaints about the children's behaviour from school or nursery 'but the boys leave Jo and Jason permanently exhausted' (series 1, episode 1). In a talking-head shot, the mother then elaborates the problems as she sees them – the boys squabbling, fighting, screaming (not a 'fun time'). A series of vignettes selected from live-shot material is then introduced to illustrate the points made by the mother – children being wilfully disobedient, fighting, bullying, throwing a tantrum in a shop, refusing to go to bed. In a final talking head of the parents they lay out what they would like to achieve in relation to their children's behaviour. The desires of the parents are presented as modest: 'some time in the evening', 'just peace and quite'.

These examples illustrate well the idea of a social issue presented as a psychological problem as the narration moves from an account of the changing nature of work (dual-career families and the increasing commitments required of workers), taking in the broader social problem of family breakdown and growing ill-discipline amongst children and the changing nature of family life in contemporary society, before introducing the idea that psychological intervention might provide an answer to parents' problems. Several themes are articulated in the show's opening title shots: the use of live-shot material as a document of the state of relations in the household, the central role of psychological expertise in the programme and that the overall story is a transformation narrative emphasizing the effectiveness of therapeutic intervention.

Meet the expert

Following the opening titles the scene switches, and to a background of upbeat music the narrator announces that 'The Bartons have called for some help' over the scene of the expert driving towards the family home. She is introduced as 'Clinical psychologist Dr Tonia Byron [who] works with lots of families, teaching them how to manage their kids' behaviour' (series 1, episode 1). She is a prototypical young professional, neatly dressed, made up and wearing sunglasses as she drives her neat small car. Her aim is presented as going to 'try to help' the parents deal with their children.

Meet the equipment

In the next section of the programme the recording equipment set-up in the home is introduced – the family has agreed to be 'filmed over the summer' and the cameras are shown being fitted into the home 'to capture behaviour as it happens'.

This scene ends with the meeting of the expert and lay participants in a performed 'as live' sequence; the psychologist is seen walking up the path of the family home and being greeted and invited in by the adults. The combination of the deployment of psychological expertise and the saturation of the house with cameras in surveillance mode are key features of the programme (Andrejevic 2004). This combination fits well with contemporary notions of governance – that a social problem can be managed by encouraging the internalization of techniques for behavioural control and the use of surveillance technology that creates a sense of scrutiny which leads the individual to reflect on their own behaviour. Alternatively, we can read the programme as acknowledging the pressures on couples who are attempting to live out relationships of equality in relation to their careers and shared parenting. The role of the psychologist is to provide a resource through which the parents can reflect upon and adjust to the problems resulting from their pressured lives.

Making over behaviour

There then follows a scene that is central to the programme and which raises a range of questions about the ethics of the show. The psychologist has brought video extracts from the filming that has taken place over the previous weeks and she now goes through these extracts with the parents. Examples of particularly problematic behaviour of parents and children are identified. The psychologist offers an analysis examining the link between the parents' behaviour and that of the children with a particular focus emerging on the conduct of the parents. This is an important emphasis – whilst the children and their behaviour is presented as what clinical psychologists term the 'presenting' problem, the psychologist works directly only with the adults in all phases of the programme, focusing on their conduct as parents, making suggestions about the way that behaviour that they see as problematic or bad in their children is either a response to or can be ameliorated by a change in the way they act towards the child.

This scene is a critical moment in the narrative of the programme. On one level the review of live-shot material led by the psychologist can be seen as a version of the 'before' of the magazine makeover but here the before is not simply a photograph of clothes or appearance but a reflective viewing of edited highlights of difficulties between parents and children with commentary by a child psychologist. This is also a critical moment of the programme in the sense that the psychologist offers a vocabulary to the parents as a way of thinking about the relationship between their conduct and their child's behaviour. At the same time an ethic is introduced to the parents which has two dimensions; it is an ethic of reflection exemplified by the psychologist's reflections on the video material but also a practical ethics of parental conduct offered in the form of rules of thumb for behaviour loosely informed by psychological theory.

Here the double meaning in the title of the programme is revealed; the ironic meaning of 'little angels' contrasts with the images of the children being 'difficult' at the beginning of the programme and anticipates what the programme tries to achieve through intervening so as to transform the little devils into little angels. But it also reflects the underlying theory revealed in the focus on the conduct of the parents that children are, in principle, all 'little angels' – inherently good, positive and just waiting for the opportunity that good parenting brings to reveal their positive qualities.

To illustrate the subtle use of psychological discourse to establish norms and the focus on the parents reflecting on their own behaviour, consider the following extract from the first *Little Angels* programme:

> Now, one of the biggest mistakes we make as parents, and we all do it, is we leave them alone when they're behaving nicely and say nothing to them, and when the behaviour gets kind of out of control we come in all guns blazing and they get tons of our time and tons of our attention. Now, if we do that often enough, what they learn is, the way to more of mummy or the way to get more of daddy is to start beating each other up because actually there's no payoff, there's no reward for sitting and playing nicely.

Three more incidents are reflected on in a similar way and discussed, with the narrator summing up as follows: 'So if they want to fix their kids' behaviour it looks like Jo and Jason will have to change their own.'

The video analysis complete, the psychologist then meets with the parents in the garden to debrief them and plan a new parenting strategy. This is another critical phase of the programme because after the surveillance and critical reflection the next phase of the programme involves the formulation of a new parenting ethic that is suggested by the psychologist as a way forward:

> We're gonna set clear limits and clear boundaries around behaviour and you're going to be lavishing praise on your boys at every opportunity you can when they are doing all the wonderful things you want them to do and when they do the things you don't want them to do you're going to, (we're going to,) have two separate ways of managing the two older boys.

In addition to the use of their own conduct as a way of conditioning the behaviour of their children, other techniques for managing their children's behaviour are introduced including the use of a sticker chart for rewarding and punishing behaviour and the use of a 'time-out' procedure for the other, younger child.

In governance terms, at this stage of the programme the psychologist works to train the parents in techniques for managing the conduct of their children. For the sticker chart there are three signs that can be placed on the chart in response to the child's behaviour: a star for good behaviour, a sad face for poor behaviour and a big cross through the square for the day for seriously problematic behaviour. For the time-out procedure the parents are introduced to the 'once nicely, once firmly rule' where instructions or requests are to be made of the child, the first statement said 'nicely', the second 'firmly', and if the child does not stop after this then they are advised: 'If he carries on you take him, with absolutely no discussion, no eye contact, nothing, into another room in the house, and you leave him there for three minutes.'

The psychologist then goes away for a week during which time the parents 'practise her behavioural techniques on their own' in the presence of the cameras. In the next section of the programme the parents are shown applying the sticker chart and time out – the older child is rewarded with stickers for good behaviour and gets sad faces and crosses for bad behaviour. Time out is demonstrated in an episode in which the younger child throws a tantrum because there are no chocolate ice creams and he is removed to another room after which he settles down, gets a cuddle and an ice cream.

After a week another training technique is introduced: 'Tanya's back to give Jo hands on coaching. She's going to teach Jo how to get better behaviour from her boys.' The psychologist sits in the house while the mother plays with the two older boys in the garden. The mother is fitted with an earpiece so that she can hear the psychologist who is also fitted with a headset and has a television screen on which to view the parent and child interacting while not being in the scene herself. In this way the psychologist can give real time coaching in parenting skills. The key skills that the psychologist concentrates on are allowing the children to take the lead and set the agenda in play and for the parent to give positive feedback to the children as they play together.

At this point in the narrative structure of the programme we have reached the point of resolution of the first disruption. However, there are further 'challenges' to be confronted and two further problems are dealt with: bedtime and shopping. In both cases remarkable changes in the children's behaviour are shown to result from the application of similar principles to those used to deal with disruptive behaviour. The splitting up of the problem behaviour into definable and workable behavioural issues reflects a common approach to therapeutic practice which isolates specific behaviours and provides cognitive behavioural solutions by changing the parents' understanding of the targeted behaviour and uses behavioural techniques to initiate change.

In the final scene the parents reflect on the effects of adopting Tanya's strategies and rules: it is more fun to be with their children. As the mother puts it:

> What I think has come to light from doing the programme and taking Tanya's advice and everything, is that it's parents behaviour and attitude towards the children that can make them better behaved. They haven't necessarily become any better behaved from doing this, we've just been able to manage what we like and what we don't like.

The father is very positive also and the final scene is of the parents being able to go out together for the first time in ages in the evening to play bowls.

Analysis and conclusions

Little Angels is a complex production that combines a number of elements of documentary making with a lifestyle transformation reality television format. The programme presents a narrative of transformation through the editing together of a variety of live-shot material and talking heads with an accompanying voiceover narration. The pace of the programme is unremitting – voiceover narrative sections of the programme over fast-cutting excerpts of live-shot material interspersed with interview material with the parents and shots of the psychologist working with the parents.

The programme is tightly structured as a narrative with an initial state of disruption which is confronted with the help of an external heroic figure (the psychologist) who deploys her special skills to enable the participants (the parents) to overcome their problems. As in many hero narratives a series of three challenges are presented and the common focus on the participants going on a journey of self-discovery under the guidance of a guru/teacher is played out. The disruptions consist of problems that parents have with young children such as disruptive behaviour, tantrums and not sleeping.

The moment of reflection, where the psychologist sits down with the parents in front of the camera to reflect on their own and their children's behaviour is a key moment in the programme. It hinges the narrative since it is based on the analysis of the live-shot material collected from the cameras in the household. It provides an analysis of that behaviour, it humiliates the parents to some degree by publicly exposing their doubts and limitations and it affords the introduction of a psychological account of the link between parenting and children's behaviour and allows the development of the plans to be enacted by the parents in the rest of the programme. The shift in the narrative of transformation from a focus on the children's behaviour to the conduct of the parents is also accomplished through this scene.

Another important element of the show's rationale comes to the fore at this critical moment. These scenes are often also moments of public emotional vulnerability for the parents as they experience the shame of having their behaviour dissected and their inadequacies pointed out. The technique that the psychologist deploys is one derived from social skills training and often deployed in clinical contexts: watching videos of one's performance makes visible tacit aspects of conduct and the subject becomes an observer of their own behaviour in a very literal sense. This scene is also important for licensing the role of the psychologist in a particular therapeutic role. The therapeutic intervention takes a very particular form, combining elements of clinical interviewing, lectures, life coaching and role play. This presents an interesting contrast to documentary-style programming in which the therapy would be portrayed as a process going on off air which is recorded and reflected on at key moments. In contrast, in *Little Angels* there is little reference to the work between the psychologist and the parents behind the scenes. Instead, the work is presented as done in front of the cameras (although edited to be sure). This also indicates the centrality of performance in constituting the transformation in the lives of the parents and the children in these programmes. There is relatively little verbal reflection on the programme which consists mainly of live-shot material of parent–child interaction.

Although the expert on the programme is a psychologist, the use of psychological vocabulary is limited and effort appears to be made by the psychologist to talk in lay terms about and to the parents concerning their behaviour and the children's. The words that the psychologist uses – 'reward', 'routine', 'time out' – are all examples of terms that are widely disseminated in vernacular discourse. The adoption of psychological discourse is also conducted as a performance played out in the interaction between the psychologist and the parents. Only briefly does the psychologist directly address the audience at home and this is during the part of the programme when she is communicating with the parents over closed-circuit television and audio link. In the sections of the programmes where the psychologist provides support and commentary to the parents', expertise is adapted to providing advice, encouraging reflection, coaching in parenting skills and emotionally supporting the parents. In other words, the psychologist is present mainly in her therapeutic role and the knowledge that is made public is given in the form of a performance of the therapeutic relationship rather than an expert account of the problems between parents and children. A performance of parenting, loosely informed by psychological principles, is co-enacted by the therapist and the parent and both adjust and orient towards the child in ways that are attuned to bringing about specific changes in the child's behaviour.

In relation to the sociological theories of governmentality and reflexive modernity it is clear that both theories provide illuminating but partial ways of analysing and theorizing both the structure and content of such programming and the broader social significance of the increasing visibility of individuals in contemporary society. Governmentality theory draws our attention to the role of psychological discourse, the use of techniques of training and self-control and the importance of surveillance technology. Reflexive modernity theory provides an emphasis on the transformation of expertise as self-help, the narrative dimension of self-transformation and the role of the media as an institution of civil society. The deployment of psychological discourse and the enrolment of the parents through a training regime into an ethic of self-reflection are recognizable representations of governmentality. However, the ways in which psychological expertise is adapted to the practical concerns of the parents and the narrative conventions of the makeover format aimed at the reflection of the audience at home can be seen as a contemporary form of self-help supporting joint parenting roles for young professionals.

Finally, what does this mean for the public service ethic of the BBC? Something intriguing is happening in relation to the blurring of the boundaries between factual broadcasting and entertainment, the shifting nature of expertise and the proliferation of the representation of everyday life problems (Bondebjerg 2002). Public service television now appears to combine elements of surveillance with self-help resources as part of the mediation of civil society. The question remains whether the best interpretation of such programmes is that they provide a way in which participants and audiences internalize a normative psychological vocabulary under conditions of surveillance leading to docile subjects or whether the programmes represent an institutionalization of civil society that pragmatically facilitates self-help in parents.

References

Andrejevic, M. 2004. *Reality TV: The work of being watched*. Lanham, MD: Rowman & Littlefield.

Barry, A., T. Osborne, and N. Rose, eds. 1996. *Foucault and political reason: Liberalism, neo-liberalism and rationalities of government*. London: UCL Press.

Beck, U., and E. Beck-Gernsheim. 2002. *Individualization: Institutionalized individualism and its social and political consequences*. London: Sage.

Bell, D., and J. Hollows, eds. 2005. *Ordinary lifestyles: Popular media, consumption and taste*. New York: Open University Press.

Bondebjerg, I. 2002. The mediation of everyday life: Genre, discourse and spectacle in reality TV. In *Realism and 'reality' in film and media*, ed. A. Jerslev, 159–92. Copenhagen: Museum Tusculanum Press.

Brunsdon, C. 2003. Lifestyling Britain: The 8–9 slot on British television. *International Journal of Cultural Studies* 6, no. 1: 5–23.

Dean, M. 1999. *Governmentality: Power and rule in modern society*. London: Sage.

Dovey, J. 2000. *Freakshow*. London: Polity Press.

Furedi, F. 2004. *Therapy culture: Cultivating vulnerability in an uncertain age*. London: Routledge.

Gamson, J. 1998. *Freaks talk back: Tabloid talk shows and sexual nonconformity*. Chicago: University of Chicago Press.

Giddens, A. 1991. *Modernity and self identity*. Cambridge: Polity Press.

Grindstaff, L. 2002. *The money shot: Trash, class, and the making of TV talk shows*. Chicago: University of Chicago Press.

Hill, A. 2005. *Reality TV: Audiences and popular factual television*. London: Routledge.

———. 2007. *Restyling factual TV: Audiences and news, documentary and reality genres*. London: Routledge.

Illouz, E. 2003. *Oprah Winfrey and the glamour of misery: An essay on popular culture*. New York: Columbia University Press.

James, A., C. Jenks, and A. Prout. 1998. *Theorizing childhood*. Cambridge: Polity Press.

Lewis, T. 2008. *Smart living: Lifestyle media and popular expertise*. New York: Peter Lang.

Livingstone, S., and P. Lunt. 1994. *Talk on television: Audience participation and public debate*. London: Routledge.

Lunt, P., and S. Livingstone. 1992. *Mass consumption and personal identity*. Buckingham: Open University Press.

Lunt, P., and P. Stenner. 2005. The *Jerry Springer Show* as an emotional public sphere. *Media, Culture & Society* 27, no. 1: 59–81.

Moseley, R. 2000. Makeover takeover on British television. *Screen* 41, no. 3: 299–34.

Ouellette, L., and J. Hay. 2008. *Better living through reality TV: Television and post-welfare citizenship*. Malden, MA: Blackwell.

Palmer, G. 2003. *Discipline and liberty: Television and governance*. Manchester and New York: Manchester University Press.

Parsons, T. 1951. *The social system*. London: Routledge & Kegan Paul.

Philips, D. 2005. Transformation scenes: The television interior makeover. *International Journal of Cultural Studies* 8, no. 2: 213–29.

Rose, N. 1989. *Governing the soul: The shaping of the private self*. Routledge.

Taylor, L. 2002. From ways of life to lifestyle: The 'ordinari-ization' of British gardening lifestyle television. *European Journal of Communication* 17, no. 4: 479–93.

Fixing relationships in 2-4-1 transformations

Frances Bonner

Most makeover shows, whether they take houses, gardens, bodies or behaviour as the site of the transformation to be effected, do so on the assumption that the lives of their subjects will thereby be improved. A life with a redecorated house or a redesigned garden is presented unproblematically as a better life, just as one with larger breasts, a reshaped nose or quieter children will be. The improvement comes not so much from getting the 'free stuff' as from the lifestyle benefit in the way one's identity is more accurately indicated by the new presentation. Occasionally a small comment in the set-up or the reveal will mention easier entertaining in the newly provided spaces, more dates from the enhanced appearance, or a more relaxed family life with the tamed toddlers. For the most part, though, this goes without saying unless there is a very strong component of what I have elsewhere called the 'fairy godmother' role of television (Bonner 2003, 127–8). In these cases, because the recipients of televisual largesse are presented as particularly deserving (the heroic firefighter whose damaged face is rebuilt in a cosmetic surgery makeover, or the family recovering from the early death of a breadwinning father given a full house and garden renovation), the presenters have the opportunity to expatiate at greater length on the consequent non-material benefits of their gifts.

This paper, though, is concerned with programmes that deal with ordinary recipients but are actually designed around a two-part change; there is an explicit acknowledgement that the subjects have more than one problem and that something more than a lifestyle solution grounded in a visible or material transformation is needed. This could be part of a nascent shift in attitudes to consumption. A particular concern is with the way in which the presenters of these expanded programmes handle this situation. For the most part, presenters have expertise in material transformations, so attention will be paid to how these people operate when the makeover is affective. The study will consider four primetime shows, two British and two Australian: in *Trinny and Susannah Undress* (UK, ITV, 2006) the well-known clothing arbiters fixed couples' wardrobes and addressed their relationship problems; in the other British programme, *Your Money or Your Wife* (Channel 4, 2006), Cesarina Holm-Kander got tough on people in debt, also with a view to its benefit for their relationships; the Australian show *DIY Rescue* (C9, 2003) engaged in completing house and garden makeovers started earlier by the owners, and improved the relationships the unfinished renovations had disturbed; and *Agony Aunts* (ABC, 2006) dispensed advice aimed at improving the subjects' finances and sex life. The paper thus analyses two programmes involving conventional material makeovers and two considering matters which aim to transform less material, or at least less visual, concerns. The combination makes it possible to examine the role of the heretofore little considered aspect of time in the makeover programme and its significance in lifestyle television's attempts to direct viewers' developments of the requisite skills to advance as entrepreneurs of the self.

All the programmes investigated concern themselves with relationships. Conventionally, makeover programmes address inadequacies we can see – it is a televisual genre after all. As the attention to houses, gardens, clothes and bodies has all been subject to a degree of programming exhaustion, there has been an expansion of the makeover field to include modifying behaviour, but usually behaviour involving physical display – hence the attention to children, pets and the obese. These programmes may not seem as immediately amenable to analysis centring on their encouragement of consumption (as earlier work, such as Philips' study of interior makeovers, does), but they certainly demonstrate the deployment of services which can themselves be bought by those wishing to follow the advice.

Not just humiliation

A central focus of British analyses of makeover shows in particular is on the modification of class-based tastes and the humiliation of those evincing working- or lower middle-class preferences and behaviours by those possessing middle- or even upper middle-class social capital (see, for example, McRobbie 2004; Palmer 2004). This approach is not just a consequence of the heritage of British cultural studies but also follows from the way in which the British shows evince such a formula with much more clarity than do American or Australian equivalents. An American study of the centrality of humiliation to reality television sees it as emblematic of the 'contemporary status of women in post-human rights societies' (Mendible 2004, 335), without noting much about variations between these women. McRobbie, however, insists on the presence of a 'new virulent form of class antagonism' towards women in makeover shows marking 'the cultural undoing of the social and liberal reforms' of the 30 years up to the 1990s in the United Kingdom (2004, 103–5). So vicious does she see the humiliation dispensed that she refers to the makeover subjects as 'victims'.

Few shows demonstrate class distinctions with greater force than those involving Trinny Woodall and Susannah Constantine, particular targets of McRobbie's argument, since few presenters are as clearly and unashamedly upper middle class as these two women. I want to complicate current readings of their programmes a little since their class position is precisely the point of the programme producers' using them; it is their USP (unique selling point), just as, in conjunction with sex, it is Nigella Lawson's. Viewers do not tune in to watch the couple confirm the right of middle-aged women to wear comfortable shoes and loose-fitting dresses, nor do the subjects offer themselves up for such confirmation. The bossing around was what *What Not to Wear* was about, especially when they were its presenters, and the difference between the knowledgeable and those in need of direction was revealed, this being a British programme, through the gap produced by class. More than enough people judged the potential humiliation of being a subject an acceptable cost for the benefits, not just the advice and free clothes but also the televisual exposure (see Priest 1996 for a discussion of the enhanced self-esteem just appearing on television was found to bring American talk show participants). Viewers and recipients know the form; they have watched the shows and know what occurs, and it is not just a matter of endorsing the humiliation. The viewing pleasure lies largely in the excesses of the presenters, and deriding their behaviour is as much a part of viewers' reception as is condemning the recipient's initial clothing choices and marvelling at the transformation that a properly fitting bra and a haircut can achieve.

Across all their programmes,[1] the makeover subject is invariably found to be dressing in an old-fashioned style that does not make the best of her shape. While the judgements are clearly based substantially in class, the advice is presented in the form of ethical injunctions. For example, if the recipient of the makeover has large breasts, she is failing in her duty to make the most of herself if she does not choose V-necked tops. The requirement to dress in the terms advocated by the presenters is a requirement about living properly, about not being an embarrassment to friends or family, not letting the partner's desire flag, not failing to look right at work. This is very much the kind of work Nikolas Rose is referring to when he talks of

> transforming the ways in which individuals come to think of themselves, through inculcating desires for self-development that expertise itself can guide and through claiming to be able to allay the anxieties generated when the actuality of life fails to live up to its image. (Rose 1999, 88)

The makeover subjects are just such anxious individuals. There is no place on lifestyle television for those confident in their expertise except as presenters or as those who have just been subject to their interventions.

An example from an episode of *What Not to Wear* (BBC, 2001–2006) screened in Australia during 2003 makes the change in self-knowledge clear. At the end of the programme, Vanessa, the recipient of the makeover, tearfully confesses to camera:

> I have trouble in equating what is really tops and trousers and dresses and stuff with what is really something much deeper about me, which is how I express myself outside. I've gone into shops I've never dared to go into before, or if I have I haven't dared try things on. [. . .] They weren't things that people like me wore, they were other girl's things. I didn't wear things like that and then suddenly I am wearing them and it feels like me.

Having brought about this degree of new self-knowledge in their subject, Susannah concludes, over footage of Vanessa at work in her new clothes, with a comment about the continuation of the transformative work she has started: 'I think now she's going to start learning to use her sex appeal and realise that that can be as much a weapon if you like as an armour of masculinity.' Whether or not this is how Vanessa herself is allaying her previous anxieties or intending to operate her new self-knowledge, the comment certainly demonstrates Jane Roscoe's observation about how conservative reality formats are, presenting a 'closed world where morality and ethics seek to preserve the status quo rather than challenge it' (2004, 43). Gareth Palmer inflects this a little differently, arguing that Trinny and Susannah take away the individual's 'self-expertise by encouraging a belief in the norm' (2004, 188). But the matter of the norm itself needs attention. It is heterosexual, certainly, and it is also hostile to comfort, but it is not in all regards quite the same norm evident elsewhere on television on the question of beauty.

As is regularly the case with makeover programmes, the person at the end of *What Not to Wear* is held no longer to be a person out of sync with themselves. They are in their transformed state, now revealing the 'real self' and this is both visually and ethically the right thing to do. To fail to do this is repeatedly presented as morally reprehensible. The usual caveat in popular discussion of Trinny and Susannah is that whatever their 'posh totty' status and bossiness, they really do like other women. This has more consequences than their tactile approach, the women shown on this programme are presented as able to become beautiful without surgery, there are always clothing and hairstyle solutions instead. When women gain this knowledge and are shown to have accepted it, they are regularly declared stunning. In a refreshing change for television as a whole, for Trinny and Susannah, being middle aged and plump is not a hindrance to this declaration being made. It can be seen to represent such a different response to the televisual dominant where beauty and attractiveness is solely the preserve of the young and slim and those willing to ape those qualities surgically, that the critical hostility to the programme's conservatism needs not rejection, admittedly, but some modulation. By not requiring surgical intervention, yet still confirming the fairy tale that under a plain workaday exterior can be found a more beautiful person who is a truer reflection of the inner self, they insist on the power of self-expertise. Trinny and Susannah do not just show a transformation, they teach the rules by which to operate it (and sell books making them ever more explicit, witness the most recent: *Body Shape Bible: Which Shape are You?*).

The practical betrays intimate problems

What Not to Wear represented the older form of clothing makeover which does pay some small attention to the subject's own affective responses to her new appearance; it did not, however, pay much attention at all to the relationships the subjects were in. The new programme, *Trinny and Susannah Undress* expands the previous format by paying attention to (heterosexual) couples whose relationships appear to be under stress. Trinny and Susannah makeover both the couples' appearance and relationships and thus regularly have to makeover men as well as women. Most personal makeovers, including the surgical ones, intermittently transform male subjects, but heretofore the men had been vastly outnumbered by women. The shift to relationships means that the gender imbalance which implied women were more in need of enhanced expertise no longer holds sway. The programme was the first for the duo after their move from the BBC to the commercial network, ITV, which may have caused a shift from their making over, for the most part, individual unremarkable-looking middle-aged women (and the odd celebrity), to couples with a higher potential for sensationalist television based in rather extreme age, height and weight differences, or marginal careers (an ex-stripper married to a club owner). As earlier, the clothing in which viewers first saw them was invariably ill-fitting, unflattering and out of date, but now in each case at least one partner was also suffering very low self-esteem. No longer could the makeover assume expertise in appearance management alone would be enough to transform the subjects' lives. People's incompetencies in managing their relationships needed to be addressed explicitly.

This produced a problem, though, in that while Trinny and Susannah have expertise to pass on about dressing to enhance attractiveness, they had not previously revealed relationship counselling skills. It was necessary for the programme to devise ways to link their expertise in producing subjects capable of informed consumption to this new domain of interpersonal intimacy rather than shopping.

The gimmick in the show and the justification for the 'undress' part of the title was the segment entitled 'The Naked Room'. In this segment, which was designed explicitly to address the relationship rather than the clothing, the couple were sent behind a backlit screen with a miniature DV camera and instructed, while Trinny and Susannah and a nation of viewers watched and listened, to show on-screen and tell one another which parts of each other's body they liked. The bizarre nature of the set-up was much remarked on in reviews and conversations and in a later series it became less evident, but its function at the start of the series – tying both the acknowledged expertise in appearance and the distinctive enjoyment of less than ideal bodies to a counselling role – for the pair was clear. The intimate relationship of the subjects was brought centre stage and the affective reactions of both subjects and presenters became the focus. The moment when a woman who had refused to show her husband her mastectomy scar finally showed it to him and he reassured her that she did not look any different to him, reduced the presenters and a number of newspaper reviewers to tears. It was most absolutely the 'money shot'. Where in *What Not to Wear* the subjects would cry while the presenters' emotions slid only from exasperated to triumphant, in *Undress* the presenters had a wider range of affective emotions, perhaps to index their involvement in this aspect of their subjects' lives. They cried quite frequently.

The transformation of the two individuals as they were shown what was wrong with their existing choices, and how dressing to the presenters' rules improved them, proceeded as is customary for personal makeover shows. The reveal now, though, was only to each other (and Trinny and Susannah), rather than to a group of family and friends, and it included commentary from the presenters about how the relationship, too, had been refreshed. Viewers were left uncertain as to whether the unsuitable wardrobes were symptomatic of, or causal in, the relationship problems. Both financial problems and incomplete renovations seem to have a more obvious causal impact on personal relationships than clothing, but *Undress*, while tending to the causal explanation, not least through the absence of the presenters' qualifications for any other kind of counselling, left the ramifications unexplored.

Even if their right to counsel those with troubled relationships is ill-based, Trinny and Susannah are acknowledged possessors of expertise about appropriate clothing. It is therefore considerable fun for the viewer when a subject challenges their right to pronounce. This was evident in an episode with the ex-stripper who revealed herself as a most resistant subject. Her husband was perfectly happy to follow Trinny and Susannah's suggestions, but the woman disagreed with their rules. Despite her being both working class and with a career background easily represented as abject, she refused to accept their expertise. She rejected their clothing directives and spent their money, to appear in the final reveal dressed on her own terms. The programme's structure was undisturbed, but the unwavering compliance of recipients with presenters' diktats was broken. This is not unheard of on makeover television, but it is usually framed as disobedience, and hence disciplined. Here the presenters praised such of her choices as they felt they could claim to have influenced and noted her feistiness as good for the relationship. No programme that I have seen includes such a challenge to the relationship advice or pronouncements.

The other programme which combined material makeovers with relationship repair was the oldest of my sample, the Australian show *DIY Rescue*. I do not believe that it was its 2003 transmission date which made it so very conservative. Like *Undress* it was an hour-long couples' makeover programme, but hosted by a young relatively unknown presenter, Leah McLeod. The recipients were usually in their late 30s, lower middle class, married with children and with the wife pleading for help about having to live, usually with very young children, in appalling conditions because the husband was an unsatisfactory renovator. Distinctively, relationship problems were seen as the husbands' fault, since they were shown to be incapable of completing one room's renovation before beginning another. This failing meant that the house and garden were able to be convincingly presented as disaster sites.

This may sound like an Australian version of the British *DIY SOS*, but there was no formal relationship between the shows and the difference was provided by the component that makes it of particular interest here – the attention to the state of the marriage. The initial situation presented the marriage and thus the family as in some level of crisis, although this was shown mainly through consequent practical difficulties and the wife's exasperation. In contrast to *Undress* and other shows considering relationships, there was no discussion of the couples' sex life. Roscoe's 'closed world preserving the status quo' was evident not only in the narrowly stereotypical gender roles but also in the way the only show not to feature a married couple involved a couple where the woman had refused to get married until the renovations were completed, and here the programme was able to bring about – and stage – the wedding.

While over half of the show focused on the house and garden makeover, with McLeod occasionally helping the team doing this, the presenter's primary attention was devoted to the couple's relationship. Her previous presenting roles had been on music television and a dating show, so moving to relationship counselling was a significant shift, especially given that there was no indication that she had any relevant training. In the course of each episode, she interrogated both the husband and the wife about how they met, how their romance started and what their wedding day was like.

Before the reveal, which, since the dominant genre was that of a physical makeover show, provided the real climax, there was the culmination of the marital therapy. Each member of the couple sat down individually with the presenter before a monitor and was shown the other confessing what the marriage meant to them. The presenter then interrogated the one shown viewing the confession about what hearing their spouse's words meant to them. Invariably there were smiles, tears and, viewers were led to believe, a strengthened marriage.

Because McLeod was the same age as the couples and, as far as could be ascertained, of a similar background, there was little social distance between them. The technique – requiring the couples individually to recall what they liked about the other – was very similar to that used by Trinny and Susannah, but the lack of distance between host and participant (as well as the presence of clothes) resulted in a greater possibility of this seeming a more natural exchange.

McLeod, then, as presenter revealed to the couple what was good and bad about their relationship and how the external sign of malfunction – the renovation malfeasance – needed to be removed to return the couple's life to harmony. She evaluated the conduct of their marriage and through repetition across the episodes drove home the message of responsible renovation and a marriage marked by communication and friendship between the parties.

The link between large-scale unfinished renovation and an unhappy marriage may seem commonsensical, but the programme's bipartite structure meant that the relationship problems were addressed separately and by a person dedicated to that task. Specialists completed the renovations, but the relationship trouble was located explicitly in poor communication. McLeod required the subjects to recall and recount their intimate history in a version of the speaking cure. Her own expertise was in mediated speaking and so the subjects confessed their feelings not to each other directly but into a camera so it could be replayed to their partner. McLeod sat with each one of them watching the monitor, pausing and requiring comment on instances of heightened emotion like male tears. She did not herself become emotional. The double mediation and her focus on getting a response from the viewing partner to the monitor's revelations were enough. That poor communication was the implicit diagnosis, but direct speaking between the partners not modelled, passed without notice.

Making over the finances

Locating the advice about affective relationships in the midst of conventional makeovers helped to keep both programmes examined so far recognizable lifestyle programming maintaining a broadly (*Undress*) or decidedly (*DIY Rescue*) conservative frame, in Roscoe's terms. The next two shows shift to a financial discourse as the accompaniment to the intimate one, which brings several other aspects into play. The title of the first, *Your Money or Your Wife*, reveals the programme's brief as looking at a relationship threatened by debt; in each case this was shown to be because one partner of a couple (one gay male, but all the rest heterosexual) was concealing the extent of their debt. Clearing up this deception was the main way that the relationship was worked on, but, at the start of each show, one partner was apparently unaware that the relationship was troubled. Presenter Cesarina Holm-Kander's first act was to announce the size of the (unconfessed) debt and bring the problem into the open. Although muted, the programme thus shared with the other programmes a belief in the centrality of good communication to good relationships. One episode foregrounded the possibility of a man's girlfriend leaving him because he believed she had taken up with him for the good life. (She didn't, at least while the show was being filmed.) More commonly the misled partner expressed horror at the size of the debt and was supportive of the presenter's actions to rein in spending and reduce the debt.

Holm-Kander, while having some prominence as a media commentator on financial matters, had little profile as a television presenter and thus none of the aura of known personality to encourage a rapport with the subjects. In the world of lifestyle television, where new goods and services are repeatedly promoted as the path to self-realization, Holm-Kander's crusade against debt and unthinking consumerism seemed almost a counter-discourse. She rejected both the credit economy and the desire to disregard debt as long as one could have the shirts, holidays and cars that give status and act as lifestyle indicators. Contrary to the competing televisual messages from banks and other lenders, this programme operated an old-fashioned ethos of 'living within one's means'. It also appeared old-fashioned when the presenter, Cesarina Holm-Kander, raised the possibility of personal bankruptcy as the ultimate horror. It seemed quite obvious that not only did this not operate as a frightening sign of disgrace to anyone on-screen other than Holm-Kander but also that it had no meaning at all for the subjects. Given that the subjects of *Your Money or Your Wife* appeared middle or lower middle class, it seems likely that the salient difference responsible for the lack of accord between the presenter and the participants was age. All but one of the subjects was younger than the presenter by at least a decade, but the class distinction was smaller than in most British shows. The absence of working-class subjects presumably resulted from the design of the programme, which required that going into debt be treated as the result of individual greed and a lack of self-discipline. Those in debt for more structural reasons would have been unable to be suitable subjects.

As in makeover shows with working-class participants, there were still quite explicit attempts to humiliate the spendthrift subjects, though with these unable to be based in class, exposing financial folly and moral weakness was the trajectory. Several of these moves operated to render visible the otherwise undramatic aspects of indebtedness. Thus the revelation of the extent of the debt to the other partner, and the viewing audience, involved the figures being projected in large size onto a wall, and the 'waste' of money in interest payments was demonstrated by forcing the spendthrift to give equivalent amounts of money away to strangers. Although the show's website advertises for more couples, there has been no sign of a second series, in part, I suspect, because its attitude to debt is so much out of sync with broader popular and institutional perceptions. Bankruptcy did not appear a deterrent and none of the couples (neither those partners in debt nor the previously deceived) appeared at all impressed by the final statements of their being able to get free of debt in three or four years if they maintained Holm-Kander's stringent regime. In this it can be seen to be very different from the formally similar weight-loss programmes like those involving Gillian Keith, most particularly her recent *Gillian Moves In: You are What You Eat* (ITV, 2006–). Here the message to reduce consumption and adopt self-discipline is in tune with dominant explicit discourses on obesity (however much other food discourses may compete). Debt is at least as common as obesity, but its invisibility and the absence of state-sponsored scare campaigns makes the shame, which underpinned Holm-Kander's approach, difficult to operate. Most of the relationships did not appear seriously threatened by the revelations, though the gay couple's plans to operate a business together may not have proceeded. This couple, incidentally, had been explicitly recruited through advertisements in the gay press, presumably to present a less dated impression of the show than its title and the financial attitudes promoted alone would have done.

It is worth comparing it with its more successful counterpart *Did They Pay Off Their Mortgage in Two Years?* (BBC2, 2007). Again, the show's remit involved reducing a couple's debt, but this time it was a 'respectable' one, i.e. a mortgage. Rather than shame the subjects about their spendthrift ways, this programme introduced the couples to expertise aimed at instilling entrepreneurialism as well as financial self-discipline, but with a much more appealing outcome – not just being debt-free, but owning a house (and usually, by the end of two years, a related business) outright. The couple here worked on a visible project, and the two-year period meant that while, for the most part, viewers only saw them in the company of the presenter, Rene Carayol, it was obvious that they were active participants rather than just recipients or victims.

This show demonstrated how a discourse of debt reduction could be produced in accord with contemporary capitalism and highlighted the way in which the troubled relationship unsettled *Your Money or Your Wife*. The deceit and the revelation of one innocent and guilty partner produced an air of melodrama, which, in conjunction with the stringency of the financial advice imparted and the presenter's contempt for status-enhancing consumption, made the programme oscillate strangely between reactionary and progressive positions.

Agony Aunts provides a very different approach to combining financial and affective makeovers. It harks back to the first two programmes in addressing relationships acknowledged from the beginning as under strain. Unlike those shows, though, there was no material makeover involved. This may have been linked to its placement on the Australian public broadcaster, which has not screened regular lifestyle programmes (other than food ones) since a 1994 scandal over the undue influence of sponsors on such shows (see Inglis 2006, 270–3, 319–23).

The show was introduced by the on-camera statement from principal host Clive Robertson, the chief grumpy old man in Australian media: 'This is a programme about middle-aged couples who need a change, [...] and we're here to help them with their health, with their love life and with the big one, money.' He had little precise function other than this and providing a well-known face, since the advice was given by Dr Patricia Weerakoon, a middle-aged sexologist, described as the show's 'love guru', and Sally Wilson, a similarly aged financial adviser. 'Health', which most of the time meant fitness, appeared to be a sub-category of the 'love life'. In each episode a heterosexual couple dissatisfied with their lives was visited by the trio who, after investigating the situation, provided a seven-day course of activities, addressing the identified problems. For the most part the couples were middle class, small business people, though one was retired and another had been retrenched from his job.

The financial problems addressed here were not focused on debt, although they did discuss people who had retired (very) early living beyond their means and needing to return to paid work. More often they involved inept business practices in small enterprises which Wilson addressed through her own expertise, or that of similar business people. Working for a large institution was never mentioned; this was the world of self-employment. Consequently, while the subjects were in need of instruction, they all had levels of independence which gave them a more secure position from which to engage with the presenters and their advice. The only person who could not be so characterized, and who seemed to have strayed from a British programme targeting the working class, was an obese mother of three very young children whose husband had recently been retrenched. She was, however, introduced as the possessor of a maths degree, so that even when she refused to follow the show's (fitness) advice, she could still not be represented as inferior either to presenters or to viewers.

The most significant feature of this show was its different approach to the relationship question. Far from seeing it as subsidiary to the main concern and able to be addressed by people without specialist qualifications, *Agony Aunts* explicitly identified the couples' problems as occurring within the sexual side of the relationship, employed an expert and trumpeted her qualifications ('sexologist, sex counsellor and senior lecturer in sexuality and sexual relations'). While her advice for some of the couples centred on improving their communication, for the most part she addressed what was presented primarily in terms of a loss of sexual interest through requiring participation in practical activities designed to bring the couples into close physical contact in a fun setting, like white water rafting. The self-knowledge and reflection featured in *Trinny and Susannah Undress* and *DIY Rescue* were a very minor aspect – even the main episode, focusing on communication, stressed practical techniques to make the couple hear what each other was saying. The choice of a woman of Indian sub-continental background in a variety of saris as the expert for this component of the programme provided greater visual interest than yet another white woman in fashionable Western casual dress, as well as interacting provocatively with the potentially challenging topic of the sex lives of the middle aged. While there may have been a stereotypical association with the Kamasutra in the sub-text, discussion was characterized by the extreme mundanity of an expert thoroughly at home with her topic who was dealing with what for her were very workaday concerns. There was none of the sniggering component of Trinny's taking the middle-aged husband of the very first couple in *Trinny and Susannah Undress* into a sex shop to buy hand-cuffs. Actual expertise in the area produced advice which, in its practical approach, was much closer to that given for the financial matters.

Considering this group of programmes together brings a number of aspects to prominence. The first is the apparent diminution of the centrality of consumerism. I have entered the discussion of the programmes through the prism of the earlier work of my first presenters in the very consumerist *What Not to Wear*. It would alternatively have been possible to consider them as following on a less or even anti-consumerist line evident in programmes such as *Life Laundry* (UK, BBC2, 2002–2003) and *How Clean is Your House?* (UK, Channel 4, 2003–). This lineage would have drawn more attention to the diagnosing of dirt and clutter as symptomatic of unhappiness and dysfunctional relationships. Certainly, *Agony Aunts* had a number of couples whose financial failings were traced to unsuitable cluttered work sites, which led to their owners being castigated and clean-ups initiated. Holm-Kander never regarded the excess accumulation of possessions as symptomatic of anything other than a spending habit, but her failure to pathologize would have been more obvious set against *Life Laundry*'s Dawna Walter's readiness to do precisely that. Both trajectories would have demonstrated presenters with expertise in one area being ready to pronounce on a very different one, as long as it had an affective dimension.

Although Holm-Kander's advice to reduce debt by restricting the use of private cars, for example, overlaps with much that is given in the new range of green programmes such as *Eco-House Challenge* (Australia, SBS, 2007–) or *It's Not Easy Being Green* (BBC2, 2006), it was not framed in that way, nor would it be productive to consider the programme in that way. Consumption itself was not condemned. Furthermore, the two programmes which combined a physical makeover with relationship advice spent most of their airtime on the material transformation and were very firmly embedded in a culture of consumption. The shift to services does not negate consumption, since that is not bound to the material. Constant monitoring is still necessary to ensure that all aspects of our lifestyle speak of us as we would like them to, but consumption just becomes a less obvious solution to many of the problems presented.

Secondly, the gender of the presenters, even when the subjects are heterosexual couples, remains constant. All the advising presenters of the shows considered here are female (as are almost all in those shows mentioned in passing). Both the domestic and the personal continue to be women's domains. Men may have greater presence there than in the past, but guidance is a female matter. Even the gay presenters of *Queer Eye for the Straight Guy* go no further than setting the stage for marriage proposals and Gok Wan of *How to Look Good Naked* works through the old-fashioned clothing makeover to instil confidence in his subjects. When yoked to relationship matters, even financial advice comes from a woman. The recipients of the advice, though, were not so gendered. When humiliation was inflicted, it was as likely to be of a man as a woman – certainly the allocation of blame in *DIY Rescue* was entirely to the male partner and more men than women were shown as spendthrifts, as the title *Your Money or Your Wife*, however overstatedly, indicates. Perhaps the presenters' being female also inflects the matter of their qualification to advise. As noted above, only *Agony Aunts* called on the services of someone qualified for the relationship advice. Since all four programmes saw improved communication as the prime solution to marital or relationship disharmony, perhaps being a skilled communicator, as a presenter needs to be, was considered enough. Alternatively, or additionally, it might have been an acknowledgement of the belief that skills in communication and relationships are female qualities.

Time and the makeover

I want to conclude by examining the temporal dimensions of the lifestyle advice dispensed by the various programme presenters. As Guy Redden notes: '[t]he received habits that makeover morality enjoins us to transcend are the marks of non-productive clinging to the old ways' (2007, 168). One way of encouraging such transcendence, which is easily seen in the genre as a whole, is linked to fashionability. Elsewhere, I have noted the strength of fashionability as a motor driving lifestyle consumption (e.g. Bonner 2003, 106). Physical makeovers of houses, gardens and wardrobes are overwhelmingly based on the initial appurtenances not suiting contemporary tastes. All they signal about a person is that he or she is out of date, that while time and tastes have moved on, the subject/recipient has failed to keep pace with it. The shopping segments in *Trinny and Susannah Undress* necessarily involve people buying contemporarily available items, so while Trinny and Susannah do not often mention fashion, they do bring their subjects up to date. Since also the new look is linked to a rekindling of desire between the couple, it underlines that aspect of fashion that links the new styles with desirability, that associates sexiness with whatever is currently in mode, while staying with past fashions is seen in terms of letting oneself go.

The wife of a trainee nurse in *Trinny and Susannah Undress* was reproved for wearing embroidered jeans suitable for a woman 10 or 15 years younger and by the end of the programme had been persuaded to jettison them. This example shows not so much the operation of fashion as of age-appropriate consuming – another way of promoting product turnover. Many of the clothing makeover programmes perform their transformations by matching the clothes to the age of the wearer. *10 Years Younger* (UK, Channel 4, 2004–) often chooses its 'victims' (McRobbie's term seems very applicable here) by identifying women who still dress in clothes that may have suited them 20 years previously, but now – combined with a skin raddled by smoking and tanning lounges – makes them look obviously 'mutton dressed as lamb'. In considering the operation of age-appropriate clothing, I am, of course, ignoring one whole field of makeover – that of cosmetic surgery. It does not negate my argument since it merely shifts the variables. A person who has had the apparent age altered still needs to dress for that apparent age and is even more bounded by the passage of time as nip follows tuck.

But it is not just through fashionability and ageing that time enters the world of the television makeover. All of the people in the programmes mentioned here had failed to heed it, whether in their renovations, their accumulation of debt and of clutter, or in the inadequate attention paid to running their businesses. Above all, they had failed to maintain their relationships as the years passed since they were first established. The self-monitoring that the reflexive self requires, itself needs time to implement. Wood and Skeggs draw attention to the inadequate distribution of resources to engage in the project of self, and they nominate social location as the prime variable (2004, 206). They are certainly right and many makeover recipients have no opportunity of themselves affording the recommended products, but time is highly relevant too.

The person not in need of a makeover is a person who has paid attention to the passage of time. They have registered their own ageing and aligned their consumption patterns appropriately. They have noticed and rectified any disjunction between their property and those which are able to command the highest prices in the neighbourhood when sold. If they have started a renovation they have performed it in a timely manner and certainly not embarked on another one before the first is completed. They have registered how interest on loans builds up and monitored their passage into and out of debt; if they are living on retirement income they have gauged the level of expenditure that will allow the principal not to be diminished. If they wish to continue in a long-term relationship they will have engaged in activities to stop it getting stale. They are very aware of the health problems that become more salient at particular ages.

The list sounds an unlikely pattern of perfection, and an impossible level of self-knowledge and expertise to acquire, even for the middle-class subject, but that also makes this collection of areas for advice a very fruitful one for television advisers to operate in. Viewers are more likely to find some of the expertise on display applicable to their own lives. No wonder it is not regarded as wasteful of televisual ideas to provide two types of makeover simultaneously.

Note

1. They appear occasionally in the United States and have recently visited Australia, but their shows screen either as imports or formats. Their advice directly to American women has appeared only occasionally on *The Oprah Winfrey Show* or on *Good Morning America*.

References

Bonner, Frances. 2003. *Ordinary television: Analyzing popular TV*. London: Sage.
Constantine, Susannah, and Trinny Woodall. 2007. *Body shape bible: Which shape are you?* London: Orion.
Inglis, K.S. 2006. *Whose ABC? The Australian Broadcasting Corporation 1983–2006*. Melbourne: Black Inc.
McRobbie, Angela. 2004. Notes on *What Not to Wear* and post-feminist symbolic violence. In *Feminism after Bourdieu*, eds. L. Adkins and B. Skeggs. Oxford: Blackwell Publishing/*The Sociological Review*.
Mendible, Myra. 2004. Humiliation, subjectivity, and reality TV. *Feminist Media Studies* 4, no. 3: 335–8 (as part of Sujata Moorti and Karen Ross, 2004, Introduction. *Feminist Media Studies* 4, no. 3: 333–64).
Palmer, Gareth. 2004. 'The new you': Class and transformation in lifestyle television. In *Understanding reality television*, eds. S. Holmes and D. Jermyn. London and New York: Routledge.
Philips, Deborah. 2005. Transformation scenes: The television interior makeover. *International Journal of Cultural Studies* 8, no. 2: 213–29.
Priest, Patricia J. 1996. 'Gilt by association': talk show participants' televisually enhanced status and self-esteem. In *Constructing the self in a mediated world*, eds. D. Grodin and T. R. Lindlof. Inquiries in Social Construction series. Thousand Oaks, CA and London: Sage.
Redden, Guy. 2007. Makeover morality and consumer culture. In *Makeover television: Realities remodelled*, ed. D. Heller. London and New York: I.B. Tauris.
Roscoe, Jane. 2004. Transformative television: RTV helps you discover the 'real' you. In *Lounge critic: The couch theorist's companion*, eds. A. Rattigan and T. Waddell. Melbourne: ACMI.
Rose, Nikolas. 1999. *Powers of freedom*. Cambridge: Cambridge University Press.
Wood, Helen, and Beverley Skeggs. 2004. Notes on ethical scenarios of self on British reality TV. *Feminist Media Studies* 4, no. 2: 203–8 (as part of Sujata Moorti and Karen Ross, 2004, Reality television. *Feminist Media Studies* 4, no. 2: 203–31).

The labour of transformation and circuits of value 'around' reality television

Beverley Skeggs and Helen Wood

Introduction: Immediacy and intimacy

The current swathe of 'reality' television engulfing our television channels could be seen as the medium ultimately fulfilling its own technical potential. Television as a domestic medium reorients the household space it physically inhabits into the space it covers or represents on television. What Lang and Lang call 'The unique perspective of television' (1982, cited in Scannell 2001) refers to the way in which television's claims to liveness and immediacy create a sense of spatially and temporally 'being there', an experience which a phenomenologist such as Paddy Scannell would describe as an 'authentic' publicness through which we have direct access to the witnessing of events 'out there', or a kind of proximity without presence (Fleisch 1987). In many ways, therefore, 'reality' television represents some of the triumphs of the medium. However edited, scripted or formatted, 'reality' television presents the audience with the tension over an impossibly knowable 'what will happen next', making us part of the unravelling of the 'real' before our eyes. Whilst the staging of events on 'reality' television complicates any ontological claim to the 'real', it *can* make a claim to the 'actual' – the camera tells us this 'actually' happened as a response to an unscripted, if contrived, *actual* situation. According to Kavka and West (2004), the etymological genealogy of 'actual' is related to a temporal sense of 'now', rather than an ontological claim to truth, through which 'reality' television constructs a new sense of 'presentness', arguing that 'reality' television 'is curiously appropriate to its medium because of the way it manipulates time as a guarantor of both realness and social intimacy' (136). This is a process set in motion by the potential of the medium: 'The actuality strengthens the effect of immediacy; immediacy strengthens the effect of social community; and the community creates a sense of intimacy with performers' (141).

Extending intimacy: Domesticity and moral responsibility

What, then, are the implications of this special claim to intimacy produced within 'reality' television? The realm of intimacy is one traditionally associated with the feminine private sphere, but various commentators have marked out how public worlds, institutions and market forces have marshalled the intimate terrain into public spaces for the operation of power, using it to reinforce arguments of 'normalcy' against the ruptures of social and cultural tensions. Lauren Berlant (1998) tells us 'intimacy also involves an aspiration for a narrative about something shared, a story about oneself and others ... set within zones of familiarity and comfort: friendship, the couple, and the family form, animated by expressive and emancipating kinds of love' (Berlant 1998, 1). It seems clear that stories told in various forms of 'reality' television contribute to the tide of ways in which questions of intimacy are transmuted through, for example, the rise of the therapy industry, talk shows and pseudo-psychological advice espoused in women's magazines. Yet often the questions asked about 'reality' television as a genre fail to adequately account for how it sits adjacent to those forms, or explain how these histories have associated connections to the terrain of emotional labour. Eva Illouz (1997) maintains that the 'transformation of intimacy' calls for an extension of notions such as domination and capital to domains hitherto out of reach. Moreover, Patricia Clough (2003) proposes that the promise of normalization is no longer simply trusted to the family, kin groups and other institutions of civil society: it is also a matter of investment in and regulation of market-driven circulation of affect: control accompanies the shift in capitalist accumulation to the domain of affect and attention. 'Reality' television, by sensationalizing women's domestic labour and emotional management of relationships, displays the new ways in which capital extends into the 'private', in which capital is engaged in the socialization of affective capacities. The space and practice of intimacy becomes like other social goods and exchange-values that are socially distributed and allocated. Miriam Glucksmann (2005) has for a long time insisted on the importance of domestic and emotional labour to the maintenance of the economy. She uses the phrase 'the social organisation of labour' to name total social reproduction. But we now see increased attention paid to how the economy and economics have to move beyond the limited sphere of production towards the totality of social life,[1] or what Marx (1973) called general productive power, in which activities assumed to lie outside of capitalism are subsumed within it. Eeva Jokinen (2008) refers to this process as the 'fourth shift', a temporal moment in labour relations in which the borderline between work and home becomes obscure and dissolved. In the fourth shift, the core of creating and accumulating wealth shifts from material goods to immaterial ones, in which knowledge, education, communication, caring and taking care of the chain of services – all kinds of domestic management – are central, and the paradigmatic form of new work is *domestic work*.[2] It is the visualization of this fourth shift, to affective, domestic, emotional and affective labour on 'television' and the process of subsumption by which value is extracted from intimacy, that we address by utilizing some of the data from our empirical research project on 'reality' television and women audiences. We are concerned with how 'reality' television contributes to the transmission, legitimation and promotion of the distribution of unequal resources and domination through its emphasis on intimacy in the location of domesticity. And, in particular, how domestic and emotional labour becomes the mechanisms by which bad subjects are subject to transformation.

In the move to an affective economy, the establishment of moral value becomes more transparent, as caring for (labour) and caring about (affection) are made explicit as responsibilities to be performed. 'Reality' television relies upon attaching signs of value, making good and bad behaviour specific to practices, bodies and people. Some forms of 'reality' and transformation lifestyle television (*Wife Swap, Supernanny, What Not to Wear, Honey We're Killing the Kids*), for example, by sensationalizing women's domestic labour and the emotional management of relationships, foreground the ways in which capital is engaged in the socialization of affective capacities. The space and practice of intimacy becomes like other social goods and exchange-values that are socially distributed, allocated and mediated.

Yet this subsumption is able to utilize a long historical tradition of making women the visible bearers of moral value. Davidoff and Hall (1987) note how in the 1840s a culture of domesticity was established, promoted by middle-class women, who were expected to operate as the relay mechanisms of manners and morality to pass on their influence to others (often in the early traditions of social work) whereby 'the minutiae of everyday life, their personal behaviour, dress and language became their arena to judge and be judged in' (398). During the twentieth century, responsibility was also entrusted to working-class women (see David 1980), but this extension of responsibility also brought with it increased surveillance, as if working-class women could never be fully trusted.

Mary Beth Haralovich (1992) documents how 1950s sit-coms detailed female (often maternal) failure, repositioning domesticity from a practice in which pleasure was previously taken, to one in which women clearly 'need to try harder'. This shift brought into vision a different object: from the middle-class 'polite and proper' family to the dysfunctional working-class family. By extension, what we see now with 'reality' television is the *obsession* with domestic failure and emotional management, in which responsibility for self and family development and control is separated into its constituent parts (cleaning, caring, education, eating, manners) and subjected to surveillance and judged accordingly. Middle-class practices are presented as the standard to be achieved regardless of the necessary resources required to achieve them. By repeatedly distinguishing, defining and attributing moral value to specific intimate practices, 'reality' television (like its predecessors, etiquette manuals, social work interventions, women's magazines and soap operas) makes the schema of moral value apparent as it identifies people in need of transformation – predominantly working-class participants. Our research project therefore attempts to unpick exactly how moral value circulates around reality television's intimate excess.

Audience research project: 'Making Class and the Self'

Our research, funded by the ESRC, 'Making Class and Self Through Televised Ethical Scenarios' (Res-148-25-0040), began with a detailed textual analysis of 10 reality-style television series concerned with self-transformation in an attempt to capture a critical period on British television in the period 2004–2005.[3] We used the generic term 'reality TV' to explore the increased use of working-class women to display the performance of different aspects of self-work.[4] We examined how such a shift to *self*-representation challenges existing paradigms of representation. Since our study began, the range of formats available has multiplied, and the usefulness of the term has been questioned (Holmes and Jermyn 2004). There is considerable mileage in textual enquiries into the distinctions between types and sub-genres of 'reality' television; however, using the phrase 'reality TV' with our audiences mobilized conversations about its generic tendencies. Whilst we generated data on particular programmes, we were also able to compare parallel observations about distinct formats, some of which are explored in this paper.

In addition to our textual analysis we interviewed, watched 'reality' television and conducted focus groups with 40 women, middle and working-class, white, black and South Asian, settled and recent residents from four areas in South London. We gained access to four friendship groups through key informants. The interviews provided information on how the women watched and used television and how it fitted into their lives more generally. We developed Helen Wood's (2007) 'text-in-action' method to explore the viewing experience itself, watching a self-selected 'reality' programme (from our range of 10) with participants (and sometimes their friends) and recording their immediate reactions alongside the television text. Finally, we convened focus groups to take up key themes from our interviews in order to explore how group opinions of reality television might mobilize around the popular public debates circulating at the time.

Before we get to some of our findings, let us locate some useful precedents in audience research that have been concerned with the way in which viewers use strategies of personal identification to interpret television texts. Numerous studies have suggested that proximity to the experience represented in the media shapes the types of responses produced. This has been described as a 'referential viewing mode' where audiences make fiction relevant to their real lives (Liebes and Katz 1990). It has also been related to viewers' establishment of 'para-social' relationships with television characters (Hobson 1982; Livingstone 1990); some studies often describe the inextricable entwining of stories about television texts with personal experiences

(Hobson 1991; Press 1991; Engel-Manga 2003), and one study theorizes the phenomena as a complex process of 'positioning the self' (Livingstone 1994). Audience research has therefore repeatedly highlighted the fact that there are moments when viewers cannot fail to connect to what is happening on the screen as it resonates with and repeats their own experiences. But to incorporate this aspect of viewing into the more traditional model of 'decoding representations' might elude an analysis of the emotional and experiential aspects of television's intimacy. Wood's (2008) research on talk television shows how viewers regularly talk back to television as if in conversation, through interlocutions which weave the people, incidents and problems on television with their own lives. This demonstrates a complex interaction between television texts and subjectivity which is more dynamic than the relationship implied through the analogy of text–reader relations. We want to take some of these observations further, generated through our understanding of the intimate and immanent nature of 'reality TV' discussed above, to explore the genre's relationship with viewers as a 'mediated social/public realm' (Biressi and Nunn 2005).

Speculating about the experience of watching 'reality' television, Justin Lewis (2004) suggests that we make sets of judgements through operating with two discrete sets of criteria: the experience of our immediate environment, and the broader symbolic reality of the world beyond it, where, if we are unable to make judgements in terms of our immediate experience, we make them in terms of our understanding of the codes and conventions of verisimilitude ('realness'), genre and characterization. Often, 'reality' television's particular verisimilitude is related to its relationship to time and the 'actual' as described above, and also through *mise-en-scène* (i.e. filmic framing or composition) which makes use of familiar settings such as kitchens, gardens, living rooms, etc. Jon Dovey suggests that the increased use of the first person across new factual formats on television might invoke a different type of relationship between text and viewer: 'The particular rhetorical structures whereby texts make generalised meaning through specific representations are of less importance than the overall interactive relationships between audiences and texts that constitute public discourse space' (2000, 159). Parallels can be drawn with the work of film theorist Vivian Sobchack (1992, 1999) whose phenomenology of film asks us to move beyond conceptualizing film as an object of vision, towards accepting film as a concrete experience of the viewer. Film thus becomes open to dialogic interpretation as a sensuous experience, rather than conceptualized or cognized through conventional sign systems.

The significance of 'labour'

Through the emphasis on domesticity, relationships and the family as sites for inspection and transformation 'reality' television enables us to identify the aspects of emotional labour that generated viewers' interest. The previous invisibility of emotional and affective labour, once hidden and unacknowledged within the private sphere, is now made perfectly visible on 'reality' television, particular in the case of reality shows centred around transforming selfhood and lifestyle. In different ways our participants regularly recognized the labour required for the requisite transformation to take place. For example, the labour of femininity, made explicit on programmes such as *What Not to Wear* through the amount of effort, skill and knowledge required, was recognized precisely *as* labour and not as natural and inevitable to an essential femininity. Conversations made with the programme in the text-in-action sessions often challenged the unrealistic standards promoted.

As Michelle responds as part of a group of interviewees 'talking back' to *What Not to Wear*:

> Yeah, yeah. And you think … they forget that normal women have just got to go out and go to work and sort the kids out, and you know that does stuff your dresses up a bit.

Whilst Nicola suggests:

> Remember how much hard work it is to look good all the time?

And Lucy comments as follows:

Audio cue	Television text	Participant responses
02.23	Presenter Trinny (introducing potential participants): … the main offenders for closer inspection	Lucy: I bet they have got a nanny. Bev: Yeah? Lucy: I bet they have. I bet they have got a nanny and it's all very well isn't it?
04.27	Trinny (on mothering): There are all those juggling acts that are really tough	Lucy: Oh I think it's true but … But I think that it's true but I don't think people want to hear it from some stuck up posh bird with a nanny. Do you know what I mean?
07.13	Presenter Susannah: it's Sarah, a mother of triplets who not surprisingly	Lucy: triplets?!
07.19	Trinny: because they have triplets	Lucy: and no nanny. Bev: mmm? Lucy: and no nanny
07.45	Trinny: three kids at 23	
07.57	Susannah: … drab, dull, uninteresting woman	Lucy [shouting]: no! you're exhausted, you have got three kids

Lucy assesses the advice of makeover experts Trinny and Susannah in terms of different social location, but also the presumed labour attached to that position. She begins by suggesting the conditions for childcare between the experts and participants are radically different, which leads her to de-authorize the experts in specific class terms as, 'stuck up posh birds'. That the television participant has triplets makes Lucy, as a mother, even more sympathetic and protective of her, hence the strong response, shouting at the television 'experts' in a direct challenge to their assessment and authority. In a later section she is more willing momentarily to listen to their advice:

Audio cue	Television text	Participant responses
33.16	Suzannah: Now we are suggesting clothes which are practical by being in a pattern that'll cover up sick, a bit of tomato ketchup …	Lucy: [laughs] that is quite good.
34.01	Participant: I can't imagine I would ever wear that. I like the style but the whole colour	Lucy: Where is she going to wear that though? She has got triplets? Where exactly? You know, once a year to her husband's Christmas do and it's not going to hide sick is it?
35.20	Trinny: If you come back in the same clothes you are wearing now I will personally strangle you. You have £2,000.	Lucy: She doesn't get it though does she? [reference to Trinny] why women dress like that, it's practicality, you want stuff that washes and dries quick. You want stuff that maybe doesn't need ironing. I have got lovely dresses, I don't wear them to school because I would get snotted on and you know I am getting up and down off the floor and it … because I don't want to be hand-washing and ironing and stuff, you know you have got enough to do. Bev: exactly Lucy: they should be finding them nice stuff that's easy care and it doesn't seem to be.

Lucy begins to think that Trinny understands the issue of clothing in relation to childcare, but then realizes as the programme develops that the speech of the experts is different to their action. Their advice is impractical which leads them to criticize the participant when it is not put into practice. The failure of the 'experts' to understand the labour of different women's lives informs all of Lucy's responses.

What is important to note is that Lucy does not address the programme as if 'deconstructing' a textual representation of the characters as such, but is involved in a dialogic relationship with the text (see Wood 2007, 2008) potentially experienced more like an extended social realm. Her interactive engagement with the television programme in question is governed by the actuality of the setting and the self-representation of a 'real' mother. Thus, Lucy is immanently placing herself as adjudicator of this advice for her own life as well as that of the television participants, locating herself physically within the action: 'I don't want to be hand-washing etc.' We suggest that it is the focus on domestic labour and the labour of femininity that generates this connection, a gendered connection that also brings class relations into the conversation to assess authority (as seen in the dismissal of Trinny and Susannah as 'stuck up posh birds'). These types of responses were frequent in our data, where these programmes provoke recognition of the different types of labour and of the actual energy expended in the labour of femininity.

The connection to the participants through labour is also generated through an assessment of the extent of their efforts. The actual visual performance of labour, which is often central to the dramatic action on 'reality' television, was significant to the ways in which viewers assessed participants. An appreciation of those who 'just get on with it' was a regular theme, and a central criterion for judgement. For example, our Addington group (white working class from south-east London) debate the merits of Jordan[5] on *I'm a Celebrity Get Me Out of Here*:

> Nicola: I always liked Jordan.
>
> Joan: I didn't.
>
> Vik: I didn't either.
>
> Joan: I didn't like her.
>
> Mel: Well not that I didn't like her, I didn't know her, I didn't know anything about her really just what I'd seen on the telly and I think she's got a bad, not a bad name but she adds up, well she did. I really did hear her talking and that, she had quite a lot to talk about, it weren't just about herself. She's quite a funny person as well. You think a person like her, 'cause she's got money and that and she's going to be spoilt: 'me me me', but she weren't. She was like –, she *did the tasks* and that, she didn't think, 'no I ain't doing that', like some of them said, 'I'm not going to do that,' and *she just got on and did it*.
>
> Joan: She had to prove herself and she did.

Our participants' perception of a woman often vilified in the British media transforms after they see her making an effort and not complaining on the programme. For Joan this means she has 'proven herself' to have value in their eyes. Jordan's uncomplaining labour enables a connection to be made by the women to her performance, and using the same value system they apply to themselves to assess the celebrity.

'Getting on with it' is valued and there is a good deal of discussion across our data about the value attached to people 'coping', for example:

> Just to see how other parents are coping like with difficult children and then seeing what her method is in terms of coping with that. (Kathy, Brockley group)

A figure who achieved celebrity status through the programme *Wife Swap* is Lizzie Bardsley from the first series. She was unapologetically loud, clearly working-class, and engaged in a spectacular row with the other wife. Rather than drawing upon the dominant portrayal of Lizzie in the press afterwards,[6] Sharon and Michelle from Addington describe the value they saw in watching how she 'coped' with her life:

Bev: So you remember Lizzy?

Sharon: Just how she managed to cope with what she had. She had loads of children didn't she?

Bev: Yeah, eight children.

Michelle: And she used to have to do all the dinners and I don't know, I couldn't do it myself.

Similarly, Michelle from Addington locates the struggle on television within the context of the 'real world' and again sees the incongruence between the 'professional' role of the expert and the 'coping' role of the mother on *Supernanny*:

Yeah put it in the real world, I mean you are the mum that's left on their own and you're trying to cope with that and a hundred other things on top, it's not quite the same is it. 'Cos looking after a child as a nanny is completely different than looking after a child as a mother, completely different. But you can see its text-book theory. You know, it does work, it would work, but it's very hard to …

Particularly for our working-class participants where the labour of their own lives is lived through similar requirements, value is placed on indefatigability – a survival tactic that has a long history in working-class culture. For example, Paul Willis (1977) discusses the working-class values attached to the physicality and endurance of 'practical' manual labour. The television participants, celebrities or otherwise, are subject to the same judgements applied to themselves, enabling immanence and generating a dialogical effect. The way in which Michelle articulates her disagreement with experts through '*you* are the mum … *you're* trying to cope' again registers an attempt to locate oneself within the narrative of the television text as an evocation of recognition and even co-presence. By speaking to and about participants, our viewers also seamlessly speak to and about themselves, which we suggest establishes a 'circuit of value'.

Class, value and 'authentic' modes of labour

Whilst similar forms of attachments may well be found in audience responses to fiction, we suggest that the way in which the 'circuit of value' is established here is exacerbated by the consequences of self-representation and the generic verisimilitude of 'reality' television. Viewers often draw a distinction between participants on 'reality' television operating as performers taking a part in a television text or event, and those valued as 'real' people inhabiting recognizable lifeworlds who are therefore subject to recognizable constraints. The working-class women in the study are media literate in terms of the staging and editing of television production, but at the same time they make connections to the 'real' through seeking out authentic experience. Therefore, recognition and assessment of effort also directly leads to viewers to make judgements about the authenticity of the participants, for example:

Vik: The ones you can tell like when they're acting, you can see when they're acting for the camera and you can see the other ones that ain't, that are *just getting on with it*.

Our findings replicate those of Hill (2005) and Jones (2003) whereby the pleasures of viewing 'reality' television are generated in the dramatic 'breakthrough' moments when participants 'show their real face'. Audiences are described as valuing authentic displays of emotion in the otherwise inauthentic arena of 'reality' television. But in our data, particularly those drawn from working-class participants, that moment of revelation is directly attached to forms of labour. For participants to be *acting* for the camera is a distraction from the effort required and distances our viewers in terms of the attachments they might make.

This was very different from the responses generated by our middle-class participants in our Forest Hill focus group. Their group reading was created through offering more abstract and critical readings of texts and their construction rather than in terms of immanent attachments. They were concerned with a broader cultural debate about celebrity culture and in particular with a perceived *lack* of labour involved in 'making it': Liselle: 'I think we start to think that you don't have to work hard to get things and don't have to, it's like the kids who just want to be famous', and Orlaine: 'About how people get famous and rich for not having any skills any more.' Effort and labour are directly connected to the rewards of paid work reliant on legitimate skills and education, thereby reproducing a formulation of labour connected to a different value system, which for them cannot be replicated in the television format. (Elsewhere we describe how the middle-class women in our study were often able to distance themselves from 'reality' television by using their cultural capital to articulate quite sophisticated discussions of contemporary culture; see Skeggs, Wood, and Thumim 2008.)

By contrast, a different mediation of the notion of the labour involved in 'making good' on 'reality' television is apparent in the Brockley focus group, whose participants were black and white working-class. The value of participating in 'reality' television is discussed, but as a way of escaping the difficulties of providing for a family within economic constraints; escaping from being a 'ghetto rat' whilst at the same time 'keeping real'. Here the discussion focuses upon another white working-class woman – Jade Goody – who became famous for the vicious attacks made on her by *The Sun* tabloid newspaper.[7] The debates around Goody were based on her perceived lack of propriety: her colloquial direct speech, her size, her lack of education and her humour on the third series of *Big Brother*:[8]

Sonia: Don't get her started about Jade.

Ruby: I kind of like Jade. I kind of like Jade. My little ghetto rat made good, you know what I mean [laughter]. I like her.

Sally Mc: [. . .] This is what it's done for a lot, the ghetto rats that you're all referring to.

Sally: I like Jade.

Sally Mc: About giving them a chance?

Ruby: Before you're struggling, ducking and diving, and then you get an opportunity through 'reality' TV and then all of a sudden you're able to provide for yourself, provide for your family and not go to bed and . . . you know what I mean . . . And not wake up in the morning and think, 'Oh God, where is this going to come from, where am I going to get that from?' 'Reality' TV does that.

Sally: Yeah.

Janet: No, I like Jade.

Marian: I do actually.

Ruby: It's *only* Jade that I like. I think she's done very well.

Marian: She does her own shows.

Sally Mc: *But she does what she did well.*

Sally: Yeah.

Ruby: Because there are some programmes, I mean how could you . . . you did, I don't like you so I don't care. But that's the first, I got to care about, like with Jade I liked her.

Sally: Yeah I like Jade. I do like her.

The connection to Jade is made through an ethic of care, to her proximity to the culture and labour of the group. That Ruby, Sally Mc and Sally are black perhaps produces the particular articulation of 'ghetto rats', but it is also through a shared sense of identification with class and labour. Jade's actual labour is valued and her participation on 'reality' television opens up an opportunity structure, with the possibility of not having to worry constantly about providing for your family. The stressed repetition of 'I like her' from all the focus group participants signals an insistence against the negative value generally attributed to Jade and those like her who are often positioned as the abject working-class (see Skeggs 2004). Here, the group offers a display of defence against the judgement of her/their culture and labour as bad, and the fact that Jade has resolutely refused to accept and perform middle-class standards:

> Marian: Yeah, she's all right. I don't know her but I mean [all talking at once]. She's done well [all talking at once].
>
> Sonia: I suppose we all relate to that don't we?
>
> Sally: With elocution lessons, she's not Jade.
>
> Ruby: Yeah.
>
> Sarah: She's still Jade.
>
> Ruby: I say I like her, she's still got a belly, she's my kind of girl [laughter].
>
> Marian: She has no poshness or no airs and graces.

The fact that they assess Jade's success – 'she's done well' – as a good thing, rather than critiquing her lack of skills, education or qualifications, suggests that members of the Brockley group are bringing a different value system to bear on the composite of the 'authentic' person who also needs to provide. To our working-class groups it is precisely both Jordan and Jade's resistance to certain middle-class forms of transformation that gives them value. Both represent that which is devalued on television and dominant culture more generally: loud, excessive, sexual, large, fecund, local, uncompromising, and without pretensions. Both come from similar economic and cultural positions to the women in the group. Both are seen to be deserving of their success because they are not ashamed of, or apologetic about, their culture.

Applauding unpretentiousness is an older tradition of diffusing middle-class values and authority that is identified by Vicinus (1974) in Victorian Music Hall performances and continues to the present day in some television, music and film (Skeggs 2004). The different value systems and related authorizations that accompany social positions therefore obviously mediate relationships to television. The performance and endurance of labour have long been major values in working-class lives, just as critiques of anti-pretentiousness have structured the challenges to the attempted imposition of middle-class standards and values. We should not be surprised, therefore, that 'reality' television is continuing to generate similar challenges to bourgeois intervention.

'Looking through': Presence and the priority of care

Whilst the focus groups tended to reify discussions of labour into group readings, individual interviews and the text-in-action sessions allowed more intricate explorations of how emotional reactions are generated in all our viewers. Responses were articulated through the experiential resources that viewers have to hand to make assessments of the different forms of labour on television, and these were unsurprisingly worked through the competing and contradictory forces of class and gender. For example, we have argued that Lucy from our middle-class group is assessing the incompatibility between forms of aesthetic labour and her own experience of mothering; members of our working-class groups privilege material labour as a mode of authenticity; and it is the experience of material labour, or the value placed on educational labour, which defines the class differences in the group readings of 'reality' television participants' financial success. Our findings therefore do not paint a picture of working-class women as necessarily more sympathetic, and middle-class women as more condemnatory, towards television participants simply by virtue of proximity. For example, whilst watching *Wife Swap* (a 'reality' show where two families, often from starkly different social backgrounds swap wives) some of our working-class women quite forcefully took the high moral ground afforded to them as non-working mothers by privileging care for children. There were also often quite lengthy attempts made by the middle-class women to reach for a point of connection beyond that which might be obvious, in order to care for, and about, television participants.

Our final discussion explores one of these occasions further in order to draw out some of the workings of these forms of connection. The following extract is taken from a text-in-action session with Liselle (from our Forest Hill middle-class group) while watching an episode of *Wife Swap*. It shows how even when the participants are viewed as a source of shock and humour to our viewer, and are clearly presented as extremely dysfunctional, she is able to '*look through*' the symbolic representation of the person to analyse and value the relationship on display. In this instance, the television participants are a fat, white, working-class couple who constantly swear loudly, whose children behave badly, and who express their aversion to mixed-race marriages. They are swapped with a healthy, fit, semi-respectable black family.[9] Yet when Liselle gets over her shock of their initial presentation she finds something endearing in their relationship:

Audio cue	Television text	Participant responses
05:31	Voiceover: After 18 years of marriage ...	Liselle: Aaah.
		[laughs]
05:46	Voiceover: She definitely wears the trousers, so to speak.	Aaah.
05:59	David: I wouldn't change her for the world.	Aaah.
06:12	David: ... she took me as I was, I took her as she was.	Aaah, oh my God.
		[laughs]
06:29	Woman: ... bubbly like David.	
06.47	... voiceover describing other family whilst focusing on the fat couple eating large dinners in front of the television	Oh my goodness.
		What a picture, that is phenomenal. That is a performance that is amazing
		That is two fat people with a huge amount of food
		[laughs]
		Oh my God.
08.11	Voiceover: It is the day of the swap. The couples hope that the swapping ...	I think what is nice about it is that ... yeah we can laugh at them, but there is actually ... there is something *very genuine* between them
9.08	David: ... I will have a big problem	Did she say if they are black I will have a big problem?!
09.15	David: I am not against coloured people	Oh my God.
09.23	... but I don't believe in black and white together	Aaagh.

Liselle moves in and out of different judging positions, firstly attributing value to the relationship even though everything about the couple has been coded negatively, then displaying shock at the racism expressed. She challenges the bad language and rudeness of the older daughter towards the father. She is critical of the manipulation of the swapped wife and of the programme format itself while reading the husband/father's attempt to wield family power as a product of manipulation:

Audio cue	Television text	Participant responses
49:35	David: I've had enough of Mary's [daughter] language. I told you long before Christmas I have had enough of Mary's language.	Mmm.
50:00	David: Things have to change round here	Ohhhhh!
50:12		Jesus Christ! He has been manipulated so much by her.
50:22	David: I am asking you [to wife] to support me and back me ...	Wow.
50:42	Wife/Mum: 18 years down the Swannee. Go for it.	Wow. They were so together at the beginning. Look at how together they were. > Oh my God. Oh God.

Liselle sees how the apparatus of the television 'set-up' provoked the destruction of their relationship. Before condemning the family, through which it seems only entirely possible due to the way in which it has been represented, she reaches for a point of connection by evoking memories of her similar experiences and considering herself within a similar social dynamic:

> But then again if I look at my family going 'bloody hell' that is the other thing, you can relate to it as well because I remember things like that you know, you know ... I mean I can really relate to the girl who was manipulated by the black woman, because you just want to please the adults. (Liselle, Forest Hill)

Drawing upon the work of Vivian Sobchack, we might refer to these instances of evocation, where viewers conjure a 'presence' in the text, as 'constitutive actualizations'. This phrase comes from her discussion of the distinction between watching documentary and home videos. Documentary consciousness requires comprehension and learning, whereas home video requires the viewer to look through image via the experiential evocation of memory. In this process the images on the screen come to mean so much more than their object; they activate the viewer's sense of the whole person (constitutive) in the present (actuality). One might argue that 'reality' television occupies a curious space between documentary and home video and that its particular verisimilitude and construction of intimacy and immediacy generates recognition in viewers beyond that available in traditional documentary forms.

Such moments, we would argue, reveal a circuitous movement in and out of issues of 'value' where viewers make attempts at attachments with 'reality' television participants. Liselle 'sees through' the negative images of the couple and the manipulative elements of the programme format to contextualize and make the connections to her life, which is actually radically different in terms of class background.[10] In this instance it is the verisimilitude of the unfolding relationships (mother, father, daughter, wife, husband) that generates the types of *connections* she has to 'reality' television. Liselle is alert to how the different couples have been stereotypically valued and positioned and even repeats the positioning, but rather than judging and legitimating the stereotype she instead judges the quality of the relationships.

Liselle evokes a 'presence' in the text which we might say is achieved through the structure of immanence made available in 'reality' television, which we can also see at work in some of our earlier examples. What is consistent across our findings is that viewers, by putting themselves in the place of participants, work to recognize the performances of domestic, material, feminine and relationship labour that are part of their own experience. The 'circuit of value' therefore means that in order to judge you also have to care, and in order to care you need to have 'been there'.

Conclusion

By contributing to a new sense of 'presentness', as Kavka and West (2004) propose, the immediacy and domestic verisimilitude of 'reality' television enables moments of connectedness, which involve both judgement and self-placement. Through the display of domestic and emotional labour, 'reality' television becomes emblematic of the fourth shift, whereby affect and emotional labour become requirements to display value and governance in and of oneself. Yet the increased visibility of domestic and emotional labour follows in a long tradition of attempts to impose bourgeois standards of domesticity and self-governance on the working-class. The formula of 'responsibility given and yet surveillance required' has just found a new outlet and new techniques. That this new outlet for displaying and deriding working-class women enables others to benefit from the display, by converting the imperative to improve into television careers and shareholder capital,[11] should come as no surprise as capital moves its line of flight to extract profit from wherever it can.

But what we think is interesting from our empirical research is the various ways in which our participants make their connections to the television participants through these circuits of value. They see through the 'transformation' narrative of the experts to the labour required and they reject the symbolic violence that is done to participants, whilst simultaneously participating in the assessment of the labour performed, because they too are located in that circuit of judgement. They are not extracting capital from the performance but locating themselves as fellow labourers; it is a collective enterprise. When Hartley (2004) proposes that television now makes the intimate 'I' into public property to be judged by strangers, we answer 'yes' ... but: the intimate 'I' is always dialogical, always explored through social relationships. And this is what we saw in our responses: our viewers watched and judged and were watched and judged through their relationships to others, through an ethic of care. As Williams (2001) contends:

> [C]are provides an important lens through which to make situated judgement about collective commitments and individual responsibilities. In this way it is different from liberal notions of justice, which are based upon legalistic principles that assume individuals are independent and atomistic beings. Instead it recognises us as all interdependent and as having the potential and responsibility to be cared for. (478)

What surprised us from our research was how connections were made through viewers' positions in relationships (be they mothers, wives, partners) and how 'constitutive actualizations' were read through and/or back onto the relationships to moderate judgement. Knowing how 'reality' television is designed to present morality in a particular way, viewers instead decide what matters, showing us the difference between our textual and empirical analysis. Through their immanent relationship to this mode of programming our participants defend against derision, assess labour contributions, continue the de-authorization of middle-class standards, search for redeemable features, value non-transformation and pursue care. Against the almost wholesale denigration of the working-class on reality television, always in need of transformation, our viewers see something quite different. Our textual analysis produced severe pessimism of the intellect; our empirical analysis provides optimism for the will.

Notes

1. Hardt and Negri's definition of affective labour is that which 'always directly constructs a relationship' (2000, 147). However, the gender-specific aspects of these 'new' forms of immaterial labour are rarely addressed.
2. Which is a reversal for the discursive term 'economy', which was initially used to describe domestic management: see Poovey (1995).

3. Selected from British terrestrial television, these shows included: *Wife Swap* (RDF for Channel 4, 2003–); *Faking It* (RDF for Channel 4, 2000–); *What the Butler Saw* (BBC2, 2004); *Get a New Life* (BBC Scotland, 2003–); *The Apprentice* (RTL Talkback Thames, 2005–); *What Not to Wear* (BBC, 2001–); *Supernanny* (Ricochet for Channel 4, 2004–); *Ladette to Lady* (RDF for ITV, 2005–); and *Club Reps* (SMG for ITV, 2004–). We classified programmes into themes (money, holidays/travel, homes, food and health, hygiene, families/relationships, work, sex, appearance, manners, class mobility) that we mapped against 'dramatic techniques' (swaps, passing, challenges, competition, makeover, expert observation, life overhaul, abject).
4. The focus of our textual analysis detailed how a 'moral person economy' was made visible on 'reality' television through a process of metonymic morality. Here we describe how types of behaviour and dispositions (e.g. eating, speaking, manners, tastes, forms of expression) are identified as parts which are loaded with moral value (good or bad, potential or abject) and outlined as in need of improvement in order to transform the whole self (see Wood and Skeggs 2008).
5. Jordan, aka Katie Price, is a British celebrity famous for her enormous breasts, relationships with footballers, her marriage to pop singer Peter Andre, and looking after her disabled child.
6. 'Wife Swap Star Guilty of Benefit Fraud': 'The loudmouth mother of eight, who shot to fame in a hit Channel 4 reality show, pocketed £3,800 for media work while raking in £37,500 a year in state handouts', *Daily Mail*, 26 September 2005.
7. 'By the end of the summer Jade had been described as a nasty slapper, public enemy number one, the most hated woman in Britain and a monster'; see 'The Jade Goody Phenomenon' in *The Independent*, 9 January 2007, http://www.independent.co.uk/news/people/the-jade-goody-phenomenon-431370.html (accessed 21 April 2008).
8. This focus group discussion took place before Jade was ejected from *Celebrity Big Brother* for attacking Indian film star Shilpa Shetty by calling her 'Shilpa Poppadom' and creating a national scandal during which the then Chancellor (now Prime Minister, Gordon Brown) had to apologize for Jade and British racism to the Indian Prime Minister. See full transcript on http://newsvote.bbc.co.uk/mpapps/pagetools/print/news.bbc.co.uk/1/hi/entertainment (accessed 15 August 2007).
9. We add the prefix 'semi-' here because we are told that Vince, the husband, spends £50 per week on weed.
10. Liselle directly identifies herself as 'middle class' through a discussion of her education, housing, family and aspirations.
11. RDF, which makes *Wife Swap*, announced a turnover of £37.5 million and profits of £11.5 million in 2006. See http://www.rdfmedia.com/rdfmedia/rns/.rnsitem?id=1161237679 nRHSS691k&t-popup (accessed 21 April 2008).

References

Berlant, L., ed. 1998. Intimacy. Special issue. *Critical Inquiry* 24, no. 2.
Biressi, A., and H. Nunn. 2005. *Reality TV: Realism and revelation*. London and New York: Wallflower Press.
Clough, P. 2003. Affect and control: Rethinking the body, 'beyond sex and gender'. *Feminist Theory* 4, no. 3: 359–64.
David, M. 1980. *The state, the family and education*. London: Routledge & Kegan Paul.

Davidoff, L., and C. Hall. 1987. *Family fortunes*. London: Hutchinson.

Dovey, J. 2000. *Freakshow: first person media and factual television*. London: Pluto Press.

Engel-Manga, J. 2003. *Talking trash: The cultural politics of daytime TV talk shows*. New York: New York University Press.

Fleisch, W. 1987. Proximity and power: Shakespearean and cinematic space. *Theatre Journal* 4: 277–93.

Glucksmann, M. 2005. Shifting boundaries and interconnections: Extending the 'total social organisation of labour'. *Sociological Review* 53, Suppl. 2: 19–36.

Haralovich, M.-B. 1992. Sit-coms and suburbs: Positioning the 1950's Homemaker. In *Private screenings: Television and the female consumer*, ed. L. Spigel and D. Mann, 110–41. Minneapolis: University of Minnesota Press.

Hardt, M., and A. Negri. 2000. *Empire*. Cambridge, MA: Harvard University Press.

Hartley, J. 2004. 'Kiss me Kat': Shakespeare, *Big Brother* and the taming of the self. In *Reality TV: Remaking television culture*, ed. L. Ouellette and S. Murray, 303–23. New York and London: New York University Press.

Hill, A. 2005. *Reality TV: Audiences and popular factual television*. London and New York: Routledge.

Hobson, D. 1991. Soap operas at work. In *Remote control: Television, audiences and cultural power*, ed. E. Seiter et al., 150–67. London and New York: Routledge.

Holmes, S., and D. Jermyn. 2004. Introduction: Understanding reality TV. In *Understanding reality television*, ed. S. Holmes and D. Jermyn, 1–32. London and New York: Routledge.

Illouz, E. 1997. Who will care for the caretaker's daughter? Towards a sociology of happiness in the era of reflexive modernity. *Theory, Culture and Society* 14, no. 4: 31–66.

Jokinen, E. 2008. Home and work in the fourth shift. In *Home at work: Dwelling, moving, belonging*, ed. H. Johansson and K. Saarikangas. Helsinki: SKS (Finnish Literature Society).

Jones, J. 2003. Show your real face. *New Media and Society* 5, no. 3: 400–21.

Kavka, M., and A. West. 2004. Temporalities of the real: Conceptualising time in reality TV. In *Understanding reality television*, ed. S. Holmes and D. Jermyn, 16–153. London: Routledge.

Lewis, J. 2004. The meaning of real life. In *Reality TV: Remaking television culture*, ed. L. Ouellette and S. Murray, 288–303. New York and London: New York University Press.

Liebes, T., and E. Katz. 1990. *The export of meaning*. Oxford: Oxford University Press.

Livingstone, S. 1990. *Making sense of television*. London and New York: Routledge.

———. 1994. Watching talk: Gender and engagement in the viewing of audience discussion programmes. *Media, Culture and Society* 16: 429–47.

Marx, K. 1973. *Grundrisse*. London: Allen Lane/NLR.

Poovey, M. 1995. *Making a social body: British cultural formation 1830–1864*. Chicago: Chicago University Press.

Press, A. 1991. *Women watching television: Gender, class and generation in the American television experience*. Philadelphia: University of Philadelphia Press.

Scannell, P. 2001. Authenticity and experience. *Discourse Studies* 3, no. 4: 405–11.

Skeggs, B. 2004. *Class, self, culture*. London: Routledge.

Skeggs, B., H. Wood, and N. Thumim. 2008. Oh goodness, I am watching reality TV: How methods make class in audience research. *European Journal of Cultural Studies* 11, no. 1: 5–24.

Sobchack, V. 1992. *The address of the eye: A phenomenology of film experience*. Princeton: Princeton University Press.

———. 1999. Towards a phenomenology of nonfictional film experience. In *Collecting visible evidence*, ed. J. Gains and M. Renow, 241–54. Minneapolis: Minnesota University Press.

Vicinus, M. 1974. *The industrial muse: A study of nineteenth century British working class literature*. London: Croom Helm.

Williams, F. 2001. In and beyond New Labour: Towards a new political ethics of care. *Critical Social Policy* 21, no. 4: 467–93.

Willis, P. 1977. *Learning to labour: How working class kids get working class jobs*. Farnborough: Saxon House.

Wood, H. 2007. 'The mediated conversational floor': An interactive approach to audience reception analysis. *Media, Culture and Society* 29, no. 1: 75–103.

———. 2008. *Talking with television*. Urbana: University of Illinois Press.

Wood, H., and B. Skeggs. 2008. Spectacular morality: Reality television, individualisation and the re-making of the working class. In *The media and social theory*, ed. D. Hesmondhalgh and J. Toynbee. London and New York: Routledge.

Epidemics of will, failures of self-esteem: Responding to fat bodies in *The Biggest Loser* and *What Not to Wear*

Katherine Sender and Margaret Sullivan

Fat people are greatly underrepresented on US television, and when they appear in fictional shows they are usually the objects of derision.[1] Reality television, with its claims to authenticity and endless search for new participants, has offered more opportunities to represent obese people. Makeover television shows, in particular, have included obese people and explicitly addressed obesity as an issue. How do viewers of the US versions of two makeover shows, *What Not to Wear* and *The Biggest Loser*, talk about the representation and treatment of obese people on these shows? Audience responses to the shows suggest that even viewers who consider themselves 'fans' critique them for narrow and unkind representations, and for inadequate or bad advice. Yet audiences concur with the underlying premise of both shows: an obese body is evidence of an inner malaise. In particular, epidemics of the will and failures of self-esteem are seen as both the cause and the outcome of the problems that makeover shows must address.[2]

What Not to Wear and *The Biggest Loser* appeared on US television in the context of increasing concern about growing rates of obesity in the United States, where two out of three people are estimated to be overweight or fat (Ogden et al. 2006). This concern was reflected in press coverage of obesity; one researcher found 2700 US articles in a LexisNexis search on 'obesity' in the second half of 2007 alone (Nagler 2007). Yet although obese people have become the focus of much debate in society, they remain underrepresented on television. In 2003 Greenberg, Eastin, Hofschire, Laclan, and Brownell found a 'comparative neglect of overweight individuals on television and [an] imbalance toward thinner men and, especially, thinner women' (2003, 1346). In their content analysis of 210 hours of primetime network programming they estimate that 'whereas 1 in 4 women in reality are obese, the television figure was 3 in 100, . . . [and] men in real life are 3 times more likely to be obese than their television peers' (1343). Moreover, when larger people are portrayed on television, 'fat women are frequently figures of fun, occasionally villainesses, often "bad examples" of people with no self-control or low self esteem' (LeBesco 2004, 41, quoting Debbie Notkin). Fat men tend to appear on situation comedies (*Drew Carey*, *The King of Queens*) where the 'frequent employment of the soft, fat male to represent the impotence of patriarchal power invests male fat with an effeminacy (or "sensitivity") for which the heterosexual masculine ideal has little tolerance' (Mosher 2001, 187). Except for those few occasions where obese men represent the threat of brute, physical power, as in crime dramas and *The Sopranos*, fat people in fictional shows are 'figures of fun' or failure, and are rarely credited with a subjectivity that isn't entirely constructed by their size.

Reality television, however, needs audience-grabbing topics and characters, both enabling and demanding much greater diversity of images than those found in fictional shows. Yet authenticity and diversity have not protected reality shows from criticism. Health scholars argue that although reality shows that deal with health-related issues, such as *The Biggest Loser*, may be helpful in encouraging people to lose weight, they promote unrealistic – even dangerous – expectations about the methods and speed with which to achieve this (Christenson and Ivancin 2006; Stein 2007).

Communication scholars have also taken to task reality shows that promote what Foucault calls 'governmentality': instilling in participants and audiences a willing acquiescence to surveillance and self-monitoring (Andrejevic 2004), and doing the work of governmental agencies, including the courts, in encouraging audiences to focus on issues of personal responsibility and self-discipline (Ouellette 2004; see also Ouellette and Hay in this present issue of *Continuum*). Lifestyle television, in particular, has been criticized for enforcing bourgeois tastes, especially in the United Kingdom (Palmer 2004), and extolling the benefits of consumption. As Roberts (2007) summarizes, 'Lifestyle television transforms consumption into a form of citizenship, a duty that we are all, as responsible citizens, required to perform for the general good' (228). Through stigma, shame, and financial reward, candidates are induced 'to become fully participant, consuming subjects in the neoliberal economy' (228). This process, moreover, is highly gendered. McRobbie (2004) argues that lifestyle television shows, including *What Not to Wear* (UK), chastise the tastes of working- and lower middle-class women in order to promote the fantasy of upward mobility, while simultaneously containing the threats to traditional sexual and family orders posed by (some) women's greater economic independence.

Most of the current work on reality television is concerned with analysing the programmes themselves. In contrast, our project looks at the perspectives of television audiences and, in particular, whether the governmental critique of makeover shows is born out by audiences' perceptions of two makeover shows: *What Not to Wear* and *The Biggest Loser* (US versions). We consider how viewers discuss the representation of fat bodies on both shows, their appraisals of the instruction offered to large candidates in each show, and their perceptions of questions of 'inner' and 'outer' selves and self-esteem – themes that run through both shows.

The shows: *What Not to Wear* and *The Biggest Loser*

What Not to Wear and *The Biggest Loser* are two examples of the rapid and global expansion of makeover television since the 1990s. Emerging from a longer history of lifestyle television, which includes cooking, gardening, DIY, and other personal and domestic skills shows, the US version of *What Not to Wear* debuted on The Learning Channel (TLC) in January 2003, a franchise of the British Broadcasting Corporation's show of the same name.[3] Contra the class-based expertise of the original British hosts, the upper-crust Trinny Woodall and Susannah Constantine, the US hosts Stacy London and Clinton Kelly, both slim, thirtysomething, and white, mete out advice on the basis of their professional experience in the fashion industries. The British and US versions are also distinguished by the former's framing within the remit of public service broadcasting, which aims to inform, educate, and entertain, in comparison to the expressly commercial format of the US version, with advertising and product placement (see Lewis's overview of the histories and cultural specificity of makeover television in the United Kingdom, United States, and Australia in this present issue of *Continuum*).

The US version of *What Not to Wear* is TLC's most popular show, garnering high ratings by cable standards: 2.3 million viewers by the autumn of 2003, with the highest cable television rating among the advertiser-friendly category of women aged 18–34 (Stilson 2003). The show's message has proliferated to a range of branded products, including books, DVDs, and an ad-supported website. In each episode of *What Not to Wear* a new candidate is made over. Almost all the participants are women, white, lower middle (sometimes working) class, aged between the mid-20s and early 40s, and range from quite petite to size 14 (US), occasionally larger. Each candidate's friends and family nominate and secretly film her, after which Stacy and Clinton make her take a hard look at her clothes and her body on camera and in the notoriously unkind 360 degree mirror room. They teach her new dressing rules, send her out to shop, and then appraise the results before her 'reveal' to friends and family.

The Biggest Loser (2004–), NBC's primetime competitive weight loss series, debuted in the United States and has since been franchised to nine other countries, including India and Australia. The show recruits seven women and seven men from among thousands of applicants who want to lose a lot of weight; these are divided into teams that work with personal trainers Jillian Michaels, Bob Harper, or Kim Lyons. The trainers are all youngish, white, and extremely fit. Their expertise is based on different approaches to weight loss and exercise, and each has authored workout books and DVDs. *The Biggest Loser* selects a diverse group of contestants, including men and women of colour and drawing from a range of ages. Like *What Not to Wear*, these contestants are usually lower middle class: police officers, hairdressers, and paramedics. The contestants spend up to three months at the southern California ranch where they live, eat, and workout, before returning home to finish losing weight.[4] Contestants' starting weights range from mid-200 pounds (about 115 kg) to more than 400 pounds (180 kg), and many candidates have lost more than 100 pounds (45 kg) on the show. The series debuted with almost 10 million viewers (Carlin 2004), and drew 13.7 million to the first season's finale episode (Gough 2005).

The two shows were met with very different responses in the news press. Like many journalists, Rodman saw *The Biggest Loser* as a new low in the reality TV genre: 'Survival and talent are out, and self-improvement by way of self-abasement is in' (2004). She is equally unkind in her portrayal of the imagined audience: 'Even as viewers sitting at home on their butts are lured in by tear-jerking teasers that promise inspiration from these dieters, smokers, and slobs, they are also manipulated into snickering, "Hee, hee, hee, they have fat asses."' *Schadenfreude* – gaining pleasure from others' misery – is the only mode of viewing that Rodman can imagine.

In comparison, press reception of *What Not to Wear* was more positive, especially when compared to cosmetic surgery makeover shows: 'Unlike *Extreme Makeover* and the like, this show doesn't declare someone hopeless unless they have a nose job or liposuction. *Wear* instead provides an instructional look at the way clothes fit us, providing hard-and-fast shopping guidelines for the figure challenges we all face' (Crow 2003, C12). *The Biggest Loser* was seen as exploitative, embarrassing, and cruel; *What Not to Wear* as helpful, necessary, and welcome. To what extent did viewers revel in the humiliation of *The Biggest Loser* contestants, or docilely adopt the instruction of *What Not to Wear*, as these journalists presume? How did both regular and occasional viewers perceive the representation and treatment of obese bodies in the two shows?

Method

Between autumn 2005 and spring 2007 Katherine Sender and a team of researchers at the University of Pennsylvania conducted extensive audience research on *The Biggest Loser* and *What Not to Wear* as part of a larger project on reality television. We collected more than 1800 online surveys,[5] of which 464 responded to *The Biggest Loser* and 623 responded to *What Not to Wear*. Eighty-six per cent of *The Biggest Loser* respondents were women, and 91% of the *What Not to Wear* respondents were women. The modal age of the respondents in both groups was 30–39; *What Not to Wear* also had a large number of respondents in their 20s and 40s. We interviewed by phone 29 regular viewers of *The Biggest Loser* (23 women) and 26 *What Not to Wear* viewers (19 women). We also interviewed comparison groups of five interviewees for each show: these were not regular viewers and were not recruited online. These interviewees were shown a test episode of either *The Biggest Loser*, in which the candidates, mid-way through their weight loss, got makeovers,[6] or *What Not to Wear*, which featured Jeannine, a large blonde woman who was a part-time Anna Nicole Smith impersonator.[7] We coded every episode of two seasons of both shows (2005–2007), as well as numerous press articles on the shows and related makeover programming.[8]

Representing fat

> I never watched *The Biggest Loser* because the one time I was flipping channels and saw it, [my husband] said, 'Oh my God, who wants to look at that?' So we didn't. The thing is, weight is a sensitive issue around the house because I've always battled mine … What's impressed me so much on [*What Not to Wear*] is you get people of all shapes and sizes and that have weight problems, people that are not necessarily model-type figures and all this sort of thing … And they've had some really sizable ladies, and yet the whole thing is that they keep telling them that they're beautiful nonetheless. (Gabby, *What Not to Wear* viewer)

Gabby's response to *The Biggest Loser* and *What Not to Wear* echoes the press coverage of the two shows. Towards *The Biggest Loser* she expresses a combination of disgust and an unpleasant kind of identification; these people look like me (fat) but I don't want to see them exposed like this. Like other *What Not to Wear* viewers, she appreciates that *What Not to Wear* shows a diverse range of body types, making candidates look good whatever their size. *What Not to Wear*'s approach is to elide fat by shifting emphasis to parts of the body that are seen as most attractive: 'There's a lot of reinforcement on what's good about the person. A lot of, "You've got beautiful eyes," "You've got nice skin," or "Look at those legs." Or, "Yeah, you're concerned about this but look, we can camouflage it with this jacket."' With its emphasis on 'dressing the body you have', *What Not to Wear* was generally seen as kinder than *The Biggest Loser*.

Yet regular *Biggest Loser* viewers also valued seeing very obese people on this show. One *Biggest Loser* viewer said: 'I felt like I was bonding with people on the show because I can relate, being a large-sized person, to some of the things they talked about, and the prejudice that people deal with every day.' An interviewee in the comparison group, who had not seen *The Biggest Loser* before, mused that through watching the show audiences would 'feel what other people feel … to be in somebody else's body. It's not everyday you see a big person walking down the street and you're like, "I wonder what she's going through?"' For this person, *The Biggest Loser* had the potential to increase understanding and empathy between normal-sized and obese people by representing not only obese people's bodies but also their experiences.

Viewers of both shows complained, however, that they did not include enough larger women candidates. This was seen as giving the men in *The Biggest Loser* an unfair advantage in the competition because they had more weight to lose, and indeed, men have won *The Biggest Loser* title in the three US seasons to date. *What Not to Wear* respondents also criticized the range of candidates' sizes as too narrow, but for different reasons: 'They do have people who are a little heavier on the show, but I don't think they've ever had anyone who was like *plus*.' A male viewer critiqued the show for a narrow range of male candidates (when they appear at all), and linked this with his awareness of the production demands of the show:

> The people who they select are based more on: 'Will they look good on television?' Rather than, 'Let's really try to use this as an effort to teach people.' Because I've noticed, most of the men who they select are never older than their mid-forties, relatively in shape. You're never going to find a really heavy-set guy on the show, or even a real stocky guy.

The diversity and authenticity that gives reality television its legitimacy is nevertheless constrained by the televisual demands that candidates have the potential to look conventionally attractive after their makeover.

What Not to Wear (US) features very few people of colour, and when it does the hosts often criticize these women's style as 'too hoochie' (Betty C.)[9] as they educate them in the implicitly white, appropriately aged, preppy norms of the show. Viewers' references to race were strikingly few and when they occurred tended to frame this as a technical issue. A few *What Not to Wear* viewers, for instance, recalled some discussion on the show of how to work with black complexions and hair, but women of colour who responded commented on the inadequacy of this advice, coming as it did from white makeup artists and hair stylists.

A few regular *Biggest Loser* viewers observed that this cast was more racially diverse than on other shows, but could not remember any discussion of race on the show. African Americans are generally assumed to be more accepting of being obese (Schwartz and Brownell 2004), although one study found contradictory evidence for this (Davis et al. 2005). A rare mention of race in season two of *The Biggest Loser* reframed this cultural acceptance as a morbid tolerance of obesity in black communities. Andrea, an African American contestant from season one, gave a pep talk to season two contestants during which Shannon, the only black woman remaining, recalled

> being raised in a family that's always telling you that even though you're a Black woman, it's okay to be heavy.
> Andrea: Culturally, it seems that it's more acceptable for us.
> Shannon: It's very acceptable in my family to be this size. My whole family's this size. I got the opportunity to help everyone – my daughter particularly.

Here an acceptance of size among African Americans is described as an unhealthy, even lethal cultural heritage that Shannon must reject in order to save not only herself but her daughter. Audiences, however, could not recall any mention of race on this show, and tended to respond to our question 'Can you remember any discussion of race on *The Biggest Loser?*' by denying any instances of ra*cism*, which the show's implicit multiculturalism works against. Roberts (2007) quotes Paul Gilroy who observes: '"Reality TV has unwittingly done a great deal to transmit the idea that racial and ethnic differences are unremarkable contingencies of social life ..." While [candidates'] cultural otherness is acknowledged, ... it is treated as purely incidental', suggesting that 'we have somehow moved beyond the issue of racial and cultural politics' (239– 40). We might welcome reality television's casual inclusion of people of colour as an overdue alternative to racial difference being a narrative problem to be resolved, but the costs of this include a reinstatement of implicitly white norms of size and appearance.

Interviewees not only talked about whom *The Biggest Loser* and *What Not to Wear* represented, they also discussed *how* they were represented. Many *What Not to Wear* respondents mentioned that however much they might want the $5000 clothes shopping spree given to all candidates, they would not want to be exposed by the hidden camera footage and the 360 degree mirror. One regular *What Not to Wear* viewer remarked that 'when they show the secret footage, a lot of the people look a lot heavier than when they're on the show'. Yet some viewers believed these modes of exposing the fat body were necessary to help candidates to change: 'the candidates say "Wow I look terrible." They're seeing this footage where their butt looks really huge, or their boobs look really saggy, things like that. So that's a big convincer.' For some interviewees, showing the candidate to herself as if through the eyes of another is the linchpin of the transformation.

Biggest Loser viewers expressed greater concern about that show's representational strategies. One regular viewer felt uncomfortable about the way in which the show exposed contestants' bodies during the weekly weigh-ins:

> I always thought it was weird that they put these people on *The Biggest Loser* in what I would consider somewhat skimpy outfits. I wouldn't even feel comfortable wearing those, and I'm a normal-weight person. Like they have the women in these sports bras and little shorts so their

stomachs are hanging out, and they have the men take their shirts off to get weighed. And they're just these little flimsy shirts, so why would they make them take off their shirts? I felt like it was a sensationalism aspect to go, 'Look at how fat these people are.'

Interviewees also complained about the challenges in which contestants 'had to run up and down these stairs. [. . .] I think they want to show the world that fat people can run and they can laugh at them.' As someone who weighed more than 300 pounds (136 kg), this interviewee experienced enough degrading situations 'in real life; we don't need that on TV, letting people make more fun of us'. Some respondents, however, saw the candidates' humiliation as an integral part of motivating them to lose weight: 'I suppose it really helps [in losing weight] to have yourself on camera in those ridiculous little, tight outfits they have them wear when they're weighing in.' In general, however, despite each show's sometimes hostile representational strategies, both regular and comparison group viewers discussed overweight candidates in sympathetic ways.[10]

Treating fat

Even though these audiences were sometimes critical of the representations of obese bodies on *The Biggest Loser* and *What Not to Wear*, they nevertheless frequently found the shows motivating and useful. A typical example of tips picked up from *What Not to Wear* came from a female survey respondent: 'Pointy-toed shoes making the leg look longer, wearing straight cut jeans so as to not create an hourglass from the hip to the ankle.' *Biggest Loser* respondents also mentioned that they picked up tips: 'No eating after 6. Eating mini meals throughout the day to keep your metabolism up. Exercising (even though I don't do it). You can still have your carbs, but good ones.' Regular viewers of both shows nevertheless expressed frustration about the instruction they offered. *What Not to Wear* viewers complained that the show lacks advice for plus-size women, for example:

> They did initially do a diversity of sizes from petite to really tall to kind of big. And now it just seems to be right around the middle. As my mom and I watched the Friday episodes we're like, 'We never can shop in a store,' because we're bigger women who have like five dresses on a rack. It's all these very posh boutiques [on the show], and they just don't make them. We relate to the people that go into the store and are like, 'Yeah I can never find anything in my size, and that's why I dress like this.'

A plus-sized interviewee said that she knew more about how to shop for large women than the *What Not to Wear* hosts: 'I think that it's something that's out of their particular expertise. I mean certainly the rules that they set for these people are helpful, but they all seem to end up at Lane Bryant', a clothing store for plus-size women. Promoting Lane Bryant may of course reflect the show's sponsorship deals as much as it betrays the hosts' lack of knowledge.

Viewers also complained about the lack of specific information on *The Biggest Loser*. The show includes endless footage of contestants working out, doing challenges, and facing temptations, but for many respondents there was 'not enough emphasis on the diet component – the show focuses too much on exercise'. The emphasis on working out over explicit instruction about how to follow a particular diet may have a great deal to do with the televisual demands of the show: It is more gratifying to see contestants' sweat and tears than it is to see a lesson in how to gauge the number of calories in a burger. Interviewees also suspected that the lack of information offered in *The Biggest Loser* was intended to encourage them to seek out other brand products for which they had to pay – books, DVDs, an online weight-loss club, and so on.

Respondents also criticized *The Biggest Loser*'s emphasis on excessive weight loss: many candidates lose more than 10 pounds a week (in contrast to US government guidelines that recommend one or two pound maximum losses).[11] One woman commented:

> I think that because of that [competitive] aspect of it, if you lose fifteen pounds, you're the Biggest Loser that week, so it really champions losing that much at a time. I'd much prefer to see a show that

watches people lose weight in a moderate way, losing a few pounds a week or something like that. I think that would be a much better show to teach people about how to live a healthy life.

Here the demands of television to offer a dramatic 'money shot' (Grindstaff 2002, 19) – the moment of surprise at the weekly weigh-in – clashes with viewers' own knowledge of healthy ways to lose weight and their interest in watching a weight loss show that is more realistic and sustainable. *The Biggest Loser*'s emphasis on the value of losing weight for health reasons is thus contradicted by its televised methods, in which the political and visual economies of television production demand quick and simplistic solutions to complex problems of the self.

Our respondents thus had much to say both about how obese people are represented on *The Biggest Loser* and *What Not to Wear* and the adequacy of the shows' treatments of obesity as a problem. Even if *What Not to Wear* was seen as more benign in its representational modes and treatment, viewers criticized how obese women were represented and counselled there. Yet none of the regular viewers acknowledged that on makeover shows, as elsewhere on television, there can be neither an unapologetic nor an unexplained self-presentation as fat. Even if they distanced themselves from some of the representational and instructional strategies of the shows, regular viewers shared the shows' framing of fat as a problem to be changed or disguised. A couple of the non-viewers in the comparison group did comment on this, however. One woman described *The Biggest Loser* as 'creepy and morally wrong and disturbing', and as exploiting the contestants' self-loathing for the benefit of the advertisers. A male interviewee in the comparison group also criticized *What Not to Wear* for being 'really sex-phobic [and] size-phobic'. The regular viewers, in contrast, endorsed the shows' assumption that fat bodies manifest a crisis of the inner self that the makeover can solve.

Framing the problem of fat

Many regular viewers of both *The Biggest Loser* and *What Not to Wear* framed the candidates' need to lose weight in the terms offered by each show: most explicitly, as a crisis of health impacting the whole family in *The Biggest Loser*, or in terms of professional mobility and self-esteem in *What Not to Wear*. A regular *Biggest Loser* viewer explained:

> I relate more to the people who have actually struggled [with weight] all their life, and those who have children, where they can't be out there playing with them because of their size, they're just tired out, they don't have the physical stamina to be out there playing catch or Frisbee or bike riding.

What Not to Wear viewers repeated this show's assumption that by addressing their image flaws, candidates would be more professionally and socially successful. A regular viewer said that as a result of the show candidates of all sizes 'might get a nice job promotion or be moved to leave a job they're unhappy with, you know, develop that kind of confidence, take a bigger risk at work and saying, "Yeah, I can do that."'

More fundamentally, viewers framed fat as a problem because of what it reveals about the state of the inner self. A regular *What Not to Wear* viewer described a candidate who 'said that she felt like her outer appearance finally matched her inner appearance, that who she was on the inside was now reflected on the outside'. Comparison group viewers also talked in terms of the inner and outer self, suggesting that this discourse is not specific to makeover television but rather is a culturally prevalent belief that is mobilized by the genre. One *Biggest Loser* comparison interviewee, for example, said that 'for most of the people that get overweight, it ain't medical ... It comes from within.'

The perception of the fat body as marking external evidence of inner dysfunction is not new. As early as 1914 a popular magazine declared 'Fat is now regarded as an indiscretion, and almost as a crime' (quoted in Stearns 2002, 22). For both women and men through the twentieth century in the United States, the 'crime' was to indulge in increasingly available bodily and consumer pleasures, the proper response to which was self-discipline evidenced by weight control. This moral focus on controlling bodily appetites was most pronounced in Christian dieting books: Marie Griffith observes that by the twentieth century 'an increasingly moralistic pursuit of extreme slimness would vie with the focus on health as a supreme religious value, a notion aided by the accelerating belief in spirit–body correspondence that steadily advances the body as an expressive language revealing the interior soul' (2004, 47). Only the perfect, i.e. slim, body was an acceptable vessel for Christ. Makeover shows rework this inner/outer relationship, where the moral imperative to be, or look, slim is detached from its expressly religious framework and linked with the demands of neoliberalism for empowered, employable, consuming citizens. Audiences read the crisis of the obese body in *The Biggest Loser* and *What Not to Wear* within two primary frames: in *The Biggest Loser* being fat is both proof of and produces laziness, a lack of willpower; in *What Not to Wear* the badly dressed fat body is both the cause and the effect of a failure of self-esteem.

The Biggest Loser: *Laboring lazy bodies*

Eve Kosofsky Sedgwick (1993) discusses what she calls 'epidemics of the will' emergent in the popular press and self-help literature in the late twentieth century to describe the burgeoning attention to addiction – drug addiction, sexual addiction, food addiction, co-dependency, and so on. She argues that anxieties about addiction are produced by an intensified focus on free will in late capitalism; the increasing emphasis on addiction suggests efforts 'to isolate some new, receding but absolutized space of pure voluntarity' (134). The ideal neoliberal citizen, governed by free will and consumer choice, is constructed in relation to the figure of the addict, unable to cope with the endless freedom on offer. The neoliberal moment that demands self-disciplined, self-directed, *willing* citizens both produces and requires their nemesis: the undisciplined, food-addicted, lazy fatty.

The association between fat, laziness, and the need to develop willpower is constantly repeated throughout *The Biggest Loser*. The opening montage's text challenges, 'Do you have the willpower?' and each episode tests contestants' wills through the show's challenges (competitions of physical endurance) and its temptations (trials of psychological commitment). Much of this emphasis on will and productivity is gendered. With the cast of *The Biggest Loser* equally split between women and men, masculine values of hard work prevail; trainers emphasize the need for contestants to push beyond their perceived limits, and to 'workout like a man', as one trainer tells the all-female team in season two.

This emphasis on work was much of what respondents liked about *The Biggest Loser*. One interviewee told us that the successful candidates 'have to put forth the effort – the show just gives them the vehicle to do it. But they actually have to do the work'. The focus on work and determination was noted by comparison viewers too. One male interviewee said the show's producers 'attempt to drive home that kind of message to the viewer that if you want to make changes in your life you have to work at it and put your mind to it'. Many *Biggest Loser* fans distanced the show from cosmetic surgery shows such as *Extreme Makeover* and *The Swan* by appealing to the value of hard work. One survey respondent, for example, wrote that she avoided *The Swan* and *Extreme Makeover* because 'most of the "fixing" was done externally to them, not like *Biggest Loser* where the contestants have to work to change'. Wilson (2005) found that media portrayals of weight loss surgery characterize this as a lazy option by suggesting that 'fat people are not supposed to have a cheater's way out, damnit! They should be made to suffer for their self-indulgence, laziness, and constant eating!' (253). *The Biggest Loser* reproduces assumptions that the solution to fat should be work, not surgery.

Most respondents repeated the value of hard work to overcome the sloth that weight represents. A couple, however, distanced themselves from this assumption. One interviewee reflected: 'Just because society says that if you're overweight, then you're lazy and stupid, which is totally not the case. But that's just the way we believe about fat people.' In general, however, respondents endorsed the value of *The Biggest Loser*'s emphasis on losing weight through working hard.

Sloth is not only a crisis for the individual but also for the nation. As Kathleen LeBesco writes: 'To be fat is to fail to do one's duty as a productive worker: "Already the US economy loses $100 billion from weight-related sickness … what chance has America in the long run, if [fat acceptance prevails], that it can ever compete with those wiry Filipinos and Koreans?"' (2004, 55, quoting the *American Spectator*). She continues: 'More interesting than the accuracy of this claim is the intensity with which it signals a failure on the part of the fat body to register as a fully productive body in a capitalist economy' (55). *The Biggest Loser* reproduces anxieties about the US economy posed by global outsourcing of labour in late capitalism by positing the unproductive, American fat body as a problem to be solved.

What Not to Wear: *Consumption as self-love*

If Sedgwick's epidemics of the will are produced in part by neoliberalism, so too is the contemporary preoccupation with self-esteem, as Barbara Cruikshank notes (1996). She argues that 'there is nothing personal about self-esteem' (231), but rather, self-esteem is a technology, in a Foucauldian sense: 'It is a specialized knowledge of how to esteem our selves, to estimate, calculate, measure, evaluate, discipline, and judge our selves' (233). Cruikshank argues that contrary to the innocent notion of self-esteem as feeling good about oneself, such positive regard is put to work in the production of a self willing to cooperate with – indeed to joyfully meet – the demands of neoliberalism to self-govern, to look to the self to meet needs, and to consume appropriately. On *What Not to Wear*, especially, being obese is framed as both the cause and the effect of candidates' low self-esteem: their large, badly dressed bodies reveal broken hearts and self-sacrifice. The show's emphasis on self-improvement through 'good' forms of consumption is couched as an obligation for women to care for the self, so no one else has to.

The imperative to have good self-esteem was echoed by many interviewees. One regular viewer observed:

> One of the things that the show has really been really good about is emphasizing fit. They do it because it looks good, but I think also fit does reflect a bit of self-esteem, because so many of the women are hiding under their clothes or using their clothes as a wall or veneer against the world or to protect themselves.

Discourses of the importance of self-esteem were also evident within the comparison group interviewees as well. One male non-viewer saw the purpose of the *What Not to Wear* makeover as to 'give you some confidence and boost your self-esteem. Changing how you perceive yourself.' He was adamant that looking better on the outside had to correspond to another, inner transformation: 'If [candidates] go on there and they just change their wardrobe but nothing else about themselves, then they just kind of have a shell, or something pretty.' Self-esteem has to come from the inside.

Only one interviewee commented on the gendered aspects of self-esteem. A male regular viewer observed that *What Not to Wear* is 'a show that's primarily aimed at women. And if we're talking about appearance and self-esteem, that's traditionally much more a women's issue, although from what I read it's changing and becoming much more of a male issue as well.' The occasional presence of male candidates on *What Not to Wear* and their equal representation on *The Biggest Loser* may not only address the increased pressures on men's self-presentation but may also, in fact, contribute to men's self-analysis and crisis in self-esteem. In general, however, *The Biggest Loser* is somewhat more oriented towards addressing epidemics of will: male as well as female contestants work hard to overcome the effects of laziness and become more productive. On the other hand, *What Not to Wear* is more concerned with addressing self-esteem: mostly female candidates need to care for the self in order to improve their confidence and consume more effectively. Although we do not want to overstate these differences between the shows – after all, losing weight improves self-esteem in *The Biggest Loser*, and improving self-esteem in *What Not to Wear* takes work – their somewhat different emphases reflect the gendered composition of their casts and possibly audiences too.[12]

The body politic

In contrast to critics' concerns that makeover shows offer a chance to laugh at less fortunate people, or that they effectively train citizens in the rules of good behaviour, our study suggests that audiences are able to distance themselves from humiliating representations and to critique the specific instructions provided on these shows. However, most audience members left intact assumptions that the obese body represents the failure of will in a culture in which self-direction and choice are paramount, and a failure of self-esteem where confidence is fundamental to that self-direction and choice. Makeover shows thus join what Rose has called the 'psy disciplines' (1999, viii) in their rationale to

> restore to individuals the capacity to function as autonomous beings in the contractual society of the self. Selves unable to operate the imperative of choice are to be restored through therapy to the status of a choosing individual. Selves who find choice meaningless and their identity constantly fading under inner and outer fragmentation are to be restored, through therapy, to unity and personal purpose. (232)

How these shows restore unity and purpose reflect changing meanings of class, gender, and race in late capitalism. By focusing on being obese as a problem of the inner self, where diet and weight loss are matters of self-discipline and choice, these reality shows efface the broader contexts for weight gain, including the link between obesity and poverty (Davis et al. 2005). Women are increasingly expected to produce themselves as employable professionals as the demands on them to provide for families increase; men find themselves similarly obliged through skilled consumption (as *Queer Eye for the Straight Guy* also attests). Yet the chance of upward mobility that these shows promise necessitates that their lower middle and working-class candidates trade their privacy for the benefits of the televised gym, personal trainers, special diets, or a $5000 credit card they could never otherwise afford. Further, when race is mentioned at all, it is reduced in *What Not to Wear* to technical issues of how to enhance darker skin and curly hair. In *The Biggest Loser*, black communities' assumed acceptance of obesity is framed as a communal lack of will and self-esteem, a heritage that black contestant Shannon must radically dissociate herself from. Here, fat is not only evidence of Shannon's inner dysfunction but also a cultural dysfunction too.

Whereas audiences were able to critique the representations and treatments of obese bodies in *What Not to Wear* and *The Biggest Loser*, the underlying normative thrust of these shows towards self-discipline and self-esteem seems especially difficult to leverage. This is in part because of the congruence between the shows and broader discourses of obesity as an inner and outer problem. Epidemics of will and failures of self-esteem are the stock-in-trade of makeover television in which we must never stop working on ourselves, even if, paradoxically, that work is to value ourselves as we 'really' are.

Notes

1. We use the word 'fat' in accordance with the practice of size acceptance advocates, as exemplified on the website of the National Association for the Advancement of Fat Acceptance (n.d.).

2. The authors thank the rest of the Annenberg School for Communication, University of Pennsylvania, research team: Christopher Finlay, Nicole Rodgers, and Riley Snorton. Also thanks are due to Adrienne Shaw and Alison Perelman for additional research support, and Tania Lewis and two anonymous reviewers for excellent suggestions for the manuscript.

3. The British version of *What Not to Wear* is currently screened in 16 other countries, from Argentina to New Zealand.

4. The number of contestants, location, and specifics of the competition in later seasons differ slightly from this original format.

5. Surveys included questions about viewing habits, likes and dislikes, identifications with hosts and candidates, and picking up and passing on tips learnt from the shows, as well as general questions about reality shows and demographic information. Interview questions investigated these in more depth, including what viewers thought of the instruction offered in the show, whether they imagined participants would experience long-term change, and whether such changes were realistic aims for viewers. For complete survey and interview questions contact ksender@asc.upenn.edu.

6. Original broadcast date: 1 November 2005.

7. Original broadcast date: 15 April 2005.

8. Shows were coded for gender, race, apparent age, and occupation of each participant and host; routines of the makeover; 'problems' and 'solutions'; what is a successful makeover, and so on. Press articles were coded for how candidates, hosts, and audiences were described; critiques and acceptance of the shows' themes; references to other types of shows including cosmetic surgery programmes, etc.

9. Original broadcast date: 19 May 2006.

10. This might reflect in part the research method: because most of our interviewees were regular viewers, and most of this group identified themselves as fans of the shows in question, they were more likely to be sympathetic to the contestants and thus loath to express negative feelings about their bodies. Many respondents identified themselves as obese, meaning that they may be more likely to identify with the heavy candidates. Social norms also tend to preclude negative statements about obesity in such 'polite' speech as an interview, irrespective of the anonymity of pseudonyms – although there was little evidence of *schadenfreude* in the anonymous surveys either.

11. See, for example, US government guidelines on weight loss: http://www.fda.gov/opacom/lowlit/weightls.html.

12. We do not have statistics for the gender makeup of the actual audiences for the two shows, but in the case of our study more men responded to the online survey for *The Biggest Loser* (14%) than for *What Not to Wear* (9%), which may reflect an actual difference in their audiences.

References

Andrejevic, M. 2004. *Reality TV: The work of being watched*. New York: Rowman & Littlefield.

Carlin, P.A. 2004. So, who's a big 'Loser' in watching humiliation derby on TV, hmm? *The Oregonian*, 26 October, C01.

Christenson, P., and M. Ivancin. 2006. *The 'reality' of health: Reality television and the public health*. Washington, DC: Kaiser Family Foundation.

Crow, K. 2003. Fashion expert loves dresing real people. *Pittsburgh Post-Gazette*, 18 October, C12.

Cruikshank, B. 1996. Revolutions within: Self-government and self-esteem. In *Foucault and political reason: Liberalism, neo-liberalism and rationalities of government*, eds. A. Barry, T. Osborne, and N. Rose, 231–51. Chicago: University of Chicago Press.

Davis, E.M., J.M. Clark, J.A. Carrese, T.L. Gary, and L.A. Cooper. 2005. Racial and socioeconomic differences in the weight-loss experiences of obese women. *American Journal of Public Health* 95, no. 9: 1539–43.

Gough, P.J. 2005. News: Television. 13 January. TheHollywoodReporter.com (accessed 4 December 2007 from LexisNexis).

Greenberg, B.S., M. Eastin, L. Hofschire, K. Laclan, and K.D. Brownell. 2003. Portrayals of overweight and obese individuals on commercial television. *American Journal of Public Health* 93, no. 8: 1342–8.

Griffith, R.M. 2004. *Born again bodies: Flesh and spirit in American Christianity.* Berkeley: University of California Press.

Grindstaff, L. 2002. *The money shot: Trash, class, and the making of TV talk shows.* Chicago: University of Chicago Press.

LeBesco, K. 2004. *Revolting bodies? The struggle to redefine fat identity.* Amherst, MA: University of Massachusetts Press.

McRobbie, A. 2004. Notes on 'What Not to Wear' and post-feminist symbolic violence. In *Feminism after Bourdieu,* eds. L. Adkins and B. Skeggs, 99–109. Malden, MA: Blackwell.

Mosher, J. 2001. Setting free the bears: Refiguring fat men on television. In *Bodies out of bounds: Fatness and transgression,* eds. J.E. Braziel and K. LeBesco, 166–93. Berkeley: University of California Press.

Nagler, R. 2007. 'Food devil?' The construction of trans fats as an obesity folk devil. Unpublished Paper, University of Pennsylvania.

National Association for the Advancement of Fat Acceptance. n.d., NAAFA Information Index. http://www.naafa.org/documents/brochures/naafa-info.html#word (accessed 11 December 2006).

Ogden, C.L., M.D. Carroll, L.R. Curtin, M.A. McDowell, C. Tabak, and K.M. Flegal. 2006. Prevalence of overweight and obesity in the United States, 1999–2004. *Journal of the American Medical Association* 295: 1549–55.

Ouellette, L. 2004. Take responsibility for yourself: *Judge Judy* and the neoliberal citizen. In *Reality TV: Remaking television culture,* eds. S. Murray and L. Ouellette, 231–50. New York: New York University Press.

Palmer, G. 2004. 'The new you': Class and transformation in lifestyle television. In *Understanding reality television,* eds. S. Holmes and D. Jermyn, 173–90. New York: Routledge.

Roberts, M. 2007. The fashion police: Governing the self in 'What Not to Wear'. In *Interrogating postfeminism: Gender and the politics of popular culture,* eds. Y. Tasker and D. Negra, 227–48. Durham, NC: Duke University Press.

Rodman, S. 2004. Bring on the 'Losers': New reality show likes 'em pathetic. *Boston Herald,* 15 October, E39.

Rose, N. 1999. *Governing the soul: The shaping of the private self.* 2nd ed. New York: Routledge.

Schwartz, M.B., and K.D. Brownell. 2004. Obesity and body image. *Body Image* 1: 43–56.

Sedgwick, E.K. 1993. *Tendencies.* Durham, NC: Duke University Press.

Stearns, P.N. 2002. *Fat history: Bodies and beauty in the modern West.* New York: New York University Press.

Stein, K. 2007. When overweight and obesity become 'reality'. *Journal of the American Dietetic Association* 107, no. 10: 1706, 1709–10.

Stilson, J. 2003. TLC's fashion police. *Television Week* 22, 27 October.

Wilson, N. 2005. Vilifying former fatties: Media representations of weight loss surgery. *Feminist Media Studies* 5, no. 2: 252–7.

AFTERWORD

The new world makeover

Toby Miller

These were instructions for people who wanted to appear on *Extreme Makeover*, a programme that ran on the US network ABC from 2002 to 2007. The application performed dual tasks. At one level, it was what it said it was – a recruitment device. As such, it was unreliable and rapidly becoming outmoded. In its second, covert, role – surveillance – it was a neatly targeted way of securing data about viewers that could be sold to advertisers. This intelligence was obtained gratis, under the demotic sign of outreach and public participation (via, for instance, plastic surgery for a soldier or fast-food manager who want to advance their job prospects) (Heyes 2007, 25).

That economic subtext runs right through the genre. For makeover television is part of the wider reality-television phenomenon, a strange hybrid of cost-cutting devices, game shows taken into the community, *cinéma-vérité* conceits, scripts written in post-production, and *ethoi* of Social Darwinism, surveillance, and gossip – bizarre blends of reportage, documentary, and fun. Makeover programmes take economically underprivileged people and offer them a style they cannot afford to sustain. The genre speaks to the responsibility of each person to master their drives and harness their energies to get better jobs, homes, looks, and families. It is suffused with deregulatory *nostra* of individual responsibility, avarice, possessive individualism, hyper-competitiveness, and commodification, played out in the domestic sphere rather than the public world.

Tania Lewis has done a fantastic job with this book in bringing together the perspectives we need to understand the makeover phenomenon of the moment. Rather than shilling for the publicity department of corporations, as per all too many works of narcissography (aka fan studies); or buying into the determinism of political economy (aka ownership and control); or favouring the decontextualized, subjective assertions of textual analysis (aka the authority of the critic), she has produced a book that blends the best of these and other traditions in a generously ecumenical form that permits methods to rub up against one another in a productive *frottage*. Whatever your view of makeover television, this is a signal achievement.

The makeover has old origins. The New York satirical magazine *Vanity Fair* (unrelated to its latter-day lounge-lizard/coffee-table/hairdressing salon namesake) ran from 1859 to 1863. Page 215 of the 27 October 1860 edition earned the periodical enduring fame: the first known use of the word 'makeover' appeared there, in a notice headed 'Adornment'. It referred to a fictional figure: 'Miss Angelica Makeover. The men like her and the women wonder why.' Angelica's gift was the ability to transform her 'coarse' hair 'into waves of beauty' through 'miracles of art and patience'. Her eyes were 'by no means handsome, but she ... learned how to use them', utilizing 'art and culture' to pass 'for a fine woman' ('Adornment' 1860lsquo;Adornment' 1860).[1] The word 'makeover' occasionally reappeared in women's magazines of the 1920s. In 1936, *Mademoiselle* magazine offered what has been described as the first formal makeover of an 'average' reader, who had asked for tips on how to 'make the most' of a self that she deemed 'homely as a hedgehog' and 'too skinny' (qtd in Fraser 2007, 177). It turned into a popular regular feature.

The makeover's power to fascinate is achieved through the ultimate consumer desire: self-invention via commodities. As Marx noted, commodities originate 'outside us' (1987, 43). But they are quickly internalized, wooing consumers by appearing attractive in ways that borrow from romantic love, then reverse that relationship. For example, people learn about romance from commodities, which proceed to become part of them through the double-sided nature of advertising and 'the good life' of luxury. Transcendence is articulated to objects, and commodities dominate the human and natural landscape. The corollary is the simultaneous triumph and emptiness of the sign as a source and measure of value. Commodities hide not only the work of their creation but their post-purchase existence as well. Designated with human characteristics (beauty, taste, serenity, and so on) they compensate for the absence of these qualities in the everyday.

Wolfgang Haug's term 'commodity aesthetics' captures this paradox (1986, 17, 19, 35), what Seyla Benhabib calls 'the *promesse du bonheur* that advanced capitalism always holds before [consumers], but never quite delivers' (2002, 3). It is embodied in the difference between those with and those without the class position and capital to define luxury and encourage emulation through identity goods such as fashion items (Berry 2000), even as viewers are interpellated as sovereign consumers who are economically and culturally ready to make informed and powerful decisions about the allocation of their resources. In Alexander Kluge's words, spectators sit 'in front of the television set like a commodity owner: like a miser grasping every detail and collecting surplus on everything' (1981–1982, 210–11).

Commodities appeal because they provide a way to dodge that old Hegelian dilemma: what to do about ethical substance? In the United States, a sense of ethical incompleteness comes courtesy of origins in the underclass of Europe and Asia, the enslaved of Africa, and the dispossessed of the

Americas. D.H. Lawrence identified '*the true myth of America*' as: '*She starts old, old, wrinkled and writhing in an old skin. And there is a gradual sloughing of the old skin, towards a new youth*' (1953, 64). This *ethos* of mobility is about regeneration of bodies as well as professions. Consider Hollywood's promise of the makeover, of turning an off-screen farm girl into a film star, or an on-screen librarian into a siren. It stands at the heart of such projects, and has been advertised as such ever since 1930s fan magazines promoted the emulation of actresses through cosmetics, with stars like Joan Blondell instructing readers that 'the whole secret of beauty is change' (qtd in Berry 2000, 106; see also 107, 27). Or wander through virtually any bookstore across the United States. You will be swamped by the self-help section, edging its way closer and closer to the heart of the shop, as the ancestral roots of an unsure immigrant culture are stimulated anew by today's risky neoliberal one. In the three decades to 2000, the number of self-help books in the United States more than doubled. Between a third and a half of the population participates in a US$2.48 billion-a-year industry of audio recordings, DVDs, videos, books, and 'seminars' on making oneself anew, frequently with 'spiritual' alibis – a whole array of consumables and auto-critique in place of adequate social security. Each item promises fulfilment – but instead delivers a never-ending project of work on the self (McGee 2005, 11–12).

Many cultural critics demonize such tendencies. For example, Christopher Lasch's influential 1970s tract *The Culture of Narcissism* identified a turn for the worse caused by 'bureaucracy, the proliferation of images, therapeutic ideologies, the rationalization of the inner life, the cult of consumption, and in the last analysis ... changes in family life and ... changing patterns of socialization.' Lasch discerned a 'pathological narcissism' of the 'performing self'. People had become 'connoisseurs of their own performance and that of others', with the 'whole man' fragmented. This critique bought into a longstanding obsession, exhibited since the nineteenth century in literature and philosophy, that associated the nation with Adam prior to the Fall – that is to say, a site where new forms of life could be invented that reprised a life before desire (Lasch 1978, 32, 67–8, 93; Stearns 2006, 203; Crawley 2006).

The privileged status of the makeover in the United States can be linked to these complex cultural histories. In addition, makeover television – the focus of this collection – itself has a specifically televisual lineage associated with the crisis in paternalistic television versus populist television, educational television versus entertainment television, 'true' television versus 'pretend' television, costly television versus cheap television. When veteran newsman Edward R. Murrow addressed the Radio-Television News Directors Association in 1958 (re-created in George Clooney's 2005 docudrama *Goodnight and Good Luck*) he used the metaphor that television must 'illuminate' and 'inspire', or it would be 'merely wires and light in a box'. In a speech to the National Association of Broadcasters three years later, John F. Kennedy's chair of the Federal Communication Commission (FCC), Newton Minow, called US television a 'vast wasteland' (Murrow 1958; Minow 1971). Murrow and Minow were urging broadcasters to show enlightened Cold War leadership, to prove the United States was not the mindless consumer world that the Soviets claimed. The networks should live up to their legislative responsibilities and act in the public interest by informing and entertaining, going beyond what Minow later called 'white suburbia's Dick-and-Jane world' (Minow 2001). They responded by doubling the time devoted to news each evening, and quickly became the dominant source of current affairs (Schudson and Tifft 2005, 32). But 20 years later, Ronald Reagan's FCC head, Mark Fowler, celebrated reduction of the 'box' to 'transistors and tubes'. He argued in an interview with *Reason* magazine that 'television is just another appliance – it's a toaster with pictures' and hence in no need of regulation apart from ensuring its safety as an electrical appliance.[2]

Minow's and Fowler's expressions gave their vocalists instant and undimmed celebrity.[3] Minow's phrase 'vast wasteland' has even, irony of ironies, provided raw material for the wasteland's parthenogenesis, as the answer to questions posed on numerous game shows, from

Jeopardy! to *Who Wants to Be a Millionaire?*. The 'toaster with pictures' is less celebrated, but has been efficacious as a slogan for deregulation across successive administrations, and remains in *Reason*'s pantheon of libertarian quotations, alongside those of Reagan and others of his ilk. Where Minow stands for public culture's restraining (and ultimately conserving) function for capitalism, Fowler represents capitalism's brooding arrogance, its neoliberal lust to redefine use value via exchange value. Minow decries Fowler's vision, arguing that television 'is not an ordinary business' because it has 'public responsibilities' (Minow and Cate 2003, 408, 415). But Fowler's phrase has won the day, at least to this point. Minow's lives on as a recalcitrant moral irritant, not a policy slogan.

Fowler has had many fellow-travellers. Both the free-cable, free-video social movements of the 1960s and 1970s and the neoclassical, deregulatory intellectual movements of the 1970s and 1980s imagined a people's technology emerging from the wasteland of broadcast television, as Porta-pak equipment, localism, and unrestrained markets provided alternatives to the numbing nationwide commercialism of the networks. One began with folksy culturalism, the other with technophilic futurism. Each claimed it in the name of diversity, and they even merged in the depoliticized 'Californian ideology' of community media, much of which quickly embraced market forms. Neither formation engaged economic reality. But together, they established the preconditions for unsettling a cosy, patriarchal, and quite competent television system that had combined, as television should, what was good for you and what made you feel good, all on the one set of stations; i.e. a comprehensive service. This was promised by the enabling legislation that birthed and still governs the FCC, supposedly guaranteeing citizens that broadcasters serve 'the public interest, convenience and necessity', a tradition that began when CBS set up a radio network in the 1920s founded on news rather than its rival NBC's predilection for entertainment (Barbrook and Cameron 1996; Scardino 2005). The 1990s saw a shift away from the universalism of the old networks. Where sport, weather, news, lifestyle, and drama programming once had a comfortable and appropriate *frottage*, the new regime saw the emergence of highly centralized but profoundly targeted consumer networks that fetishized lifestyle and consumption *tout court* over a blend of purchase and politics, of fun and foreign policy.

This context, and its localized iterations in other countries, gives the lie to conventional shibboleths of reality programming. Makeover television, fixed upon by cultural critics who either mourn it as representative of a decline in journalistic standards or celebrate it as the sign of a newly feminized public sphere, should frankly be understood as a cost-cutting measure and an instance of niche marketing. Much makeover television originates in an under-unionized sector of the industry, with small numbers of workers required for short periods. This contingent, flexible labour is even textualized in the service-industry world of the genre, which creates 'a parallel universe' for viewers, tightly managed within profoundly restricted norms (Lewis, Inthorn, and Wahl-Jorgensen 2005, 17; Giles 2002). Just as off-screen television labour lacks job security and must remain nimble and skilful, so the madeover subject can never relax for a moment.

What of the claim that these texts empower their viewers? The Kaiser Foundation's 2006 study of US reality television (Christenson and Ivancin 2006) drew on encounters with television producers and health-care critics and professionals to get at the dynamics of how medicine and related topics are represented in the genre. Kaiser found that, for all makeover television's populist alibis, it constructs professional medical expertise as a kind of magic that is beyond the ken of ordinary people – and certainly beyond their engaged critique. Again and again, whether the focus is on plastic surgeons or paediatricians, miraculous feats are achieved by heroic professionals who deliver ignorant and ugly people from the dross of the everyday, transcending what off-screen primary-care physicians have been able to do for them. The Foundation could find nothing in US reality television even remotely critical of this model. Such representations of expertise deem it ungovernable other than by its own caste. This landscape is not about powerful citizen-viewers; it's about deities in scrubs. The use of the commodity form to promise transcendence through the national health-care system, as embodied in patriarchal medicine, is sickening. As with makeovers of housing or personal style, it offers transcendence to the working and lower middle classes – which most such viewers cannot afford to emulate. Helpless, un-aesthetic patient bodies testify to the surgeons' skill – and generate more and more business for medical leeches preying on false needs (Heyes 2007, 19; Theobald et al. 2006). And research indicates that audience views of such procedures are quite wildly at variance with the facts in terms of what is medically advisable and financially manageable (Stevens et al. 2005).

Acknowledgement

Thanks are due to Tania Lewis for her helpful comments.

Notes

1. The author would like to thank Peter Bliss from the University of California, Riverside library system, for bibliographic insight.
2. Not surprisingly, Alfred Hitchcock said it earlier and better: 'Television is like the American toaster, you push the button and the same thing pops up every time' (qtd in Wasko 2005, 10).
3. Minow was named 'top newsmaker' of 1961 in an Associated Press survey, and was on television and radio more than any other Kennedy official.

References

'Adornment'. 1860. *Vanity Fair*, 27 October, 215.

Barbrook, Richard, and Andy Cameron. 1996. The Californian ideology. *Science as Culture* 6: 44–72.

Benhabib, Seyla. 2002. *The claims of culture: Equality and Diversity in the gloab era.* Princeton: Princeton University Press.

Berry, Sarah. 2000. *Screen style: Fashion and femininity in 1930s Hollywood.* Minneapolis: University of Minnesota Press.

Christenson, Peter, and Maria Ivancin. 2006. *The 'reality' of health: Reality television and the public health.* Washington, DC: Henry J. Kaiser Foundation.

Crawley, Melissa. 2006. Making over the new Adam. In *The great American makeover: Television, history, nation*, ed. D. Heller, 51–64. New York: Palgrave Macmillan.

Fraser, Kathryn. 2007. 'Now I am ready to tell how bodies are changed into different bodies ...' – Ovid, *The Metamorphoses*, In *Makeover television: Realities remodelled*, ed. D. Heller, 177–92. London: I.B. Tauris.

Giles, David. 2002. Keeping the public in their place: Audience participation in lifestyle television programming. *Discourse & Society* 13, no. 5: 603–28.

Haug, W.F. 1986. *Critique of commodity aesthetics: Appearance, sexuality and advertising in capitalist society.* Trans. R. Bock, Cambridge: Polity Press.

Heyes, Cressida J. 2007. Cosmetic surgery and the televisual makeover: A Foucauldian feminist reading. *Feminist Media Studies* 7, no. 1: 17–32.

Kluge, Alexander. 1981–1982. On film and the public sphere. Trans. T.Y. Levin and M.B. Hansen. *New German Critique*, no. 24–25: 206–20.

Lasch, Christopher. 1978. *The culture of narcissism: American life in an age of diminishing expectations.* New York: Norton.

Lawrence, D.H. 1953. *Studies in classic American literature.* Garden City, NY: Doubleday.

Lewis, Justin, Sanna Inthorn, and Karin Wahl-Jorgensen. 2005. *Citizens or consumers? What the media tell us about political participation*. Maidenhead: Open University Press.

Marx, Karl. 1987. *Capital: A critique of political economy*. Vol. 1: *The process of capitalist production*, Trans. S. Moore and E. Aveling, ed. Frederick Engels, New York: International Publishers.

McGee, Micki. 2005. *Self-Help, Inc.: Makeover culture in American Life*. New York: Oxford University Press.

Minow, Newton. 1971. The broadcasters are public trustees. In *Radio & television: Readings in the mass media*, ed. A. Kirschener and L. Kirschener, 207–17. New York: Odyssey Press.

———. 2001. Television, more vast than ever, turns toxic. *USA Today*, 9 May, 15A.

Minow, Newton N., and Fred H. Cate. 2003. Revisiting the vast wasteland. *Federal Communications Law Journal* 55, no. 3: 407–34.

Murrow, Edward R. 1958. Speech to the Radio-Television News Directors Association, Chicago, 15 October.

Scardino, Albert. 2005. Sun sets on US broadcast golden age. *Guardian*, 9 March.

Schudson, Michael, and Susan E. Tifft. 2005. American journalism in historical perspective. In *The Press*, ed. G. Overholser and K.H. Jamieson, 17–47. Oxford: Oxford University Press.

Stearns, Peter N. 2006. *American fear: The causes and consequences of high anxiety*. New York: Routledge.

Stevens, W. Grant, Robert Cohen, Steven D. Vath, David A. Stoker, and Elliot M. Hirsch. 2005. Does lipoplasty really add morbidity to abdominoplasty? *Aesthetic Surgery Journal* 25, no. 4: 353–8.

Theobald, A.H., B.K. Wong, A.N. Quick, and W.M. Thomson. 2006. The impact of the popular media on cosmetic dentistry. *New Zealand Journal of Dentistry* 102, no. 3: 58–63.

Wasko, Janet. 2005. Introduction. In *A companion to television*, ed. J. Wasko, 1–12. Malden, MA: Blackwell.

Index